GET FUNDED NOW
Find Out How

GET FUNDED NOW
Find Out How
From Self to Professional Funding

NALIN SINGH

Notion Press

Old No. 38, New No. 6
McNichols Road, Chetpet
Chennai - 600 031

First Published by Notion Press 2017
Copyright © Nalin Singh 2017
All Rights Reserved.

ISBN 978-1-948230-15-5

This book has been published with all reasonable efforts taken to make the material error-free after the consent of the author. No part of this book shall be used, reproduced in any manner whatsoever without written permission from the author, except in the case of brief quotations embodied in critical articles and reviews.

The Author of this book is solely responsible and liable for its content including but not limited to the views, representations, descriptions, statements, information, opinions and references ["Content"]. The Content of this book shall not constitute or be construed or deemed to reflect the opinion or expression of the Publisher or Editor. Neither the Publisher nor Editor endorse or approve the Content of this book or guarantee the reliability, accuracy or completeness of the Content published herein and do not make any representations or warranties of any kind, express or implied, including but not limited to the implied warranties of merchantability, fitness for a particular purpose. The Publisher and Editor shall not be liable whatsoever for any errors, omissions, whether such errors or omissions result from negligence, accident, or any other cause or claims for loss or damages of any kind, including without limitation, indirect or consequential loss or damage arising out of use, inability to use, or about the reliability, accuracy or sufficiency of the information contained in this book.

Dedication

This One Is For My Mentors

Senthil, for showing me the value of money and how everyone of us can create wealth with a lasting positive impact.

Jaiprakash, for guiding me to a path of financial fearlessness.

In you I had the perfect mentors, now I have you as my guardian angels to fulfil what we together visualized.

Contents

Acknowledgements	xi
Authors Note	xiii
Reasons Why an Investor Wont' Invest	xvii

PART I: PERSONAL READINESS

Overview: Setting The Personal Stage	3
Bootstrapping is Underrated	8
Client Funded is Ideal For B2B	10
Personal Readiness	13
The Basic Personality	16
The Traits, Quirks & Characteristics	18
The Young & Restless	23
The Value System	25
Mid Life Readiness	29
The Dark Side	37
Personal Branding & Networking	40
Putting It All Together	45
Conclusion: Personal Readiness	49

PART II: COMPANY READINESS

Overview: Getting The Business Ready	53
Legal Structure: Pick the Right Company Formation	57
Product Readiness: Status of your Product/Service	59
The Team	61
Business Plan: A Simpler Plan for Startups	63
Processes	77

Defining Market Size & Overall Opportunity — 97
Competitive Landscape — 104
Past Financials and Future Projections — 109
Statutory Compliances — 112
Governance — 115
Conclusion: Company Readiness — 122

PART III: INVESTOR READINESS

Overview: Investors' World — 125
Types of Investors — 128
Financial Terms You Must Know — 145
Pitch Materials — 151
What Should Your Pitch Contain — 160
How Much Money Do You Need — 170
Getting the Valuation and Investor Play Right — 178
How to Split Equity Among Founders — 181
Where are the Investors — 191
Conclusion: Investor Readiness — 197

PART IV: INVESTOR ENGAGEMENT

Overview: Engaging with Investors — 201
How to Pitch — 211
What Not to Say When Pitching — 221
Why Investors Delay — 224
Is It Tougher as a First Time Entrepreneur? — 228
What Is the Ideal Time to Approach an Investor — 231
Alternate Investment Strategies — 238
The Soft Side of Approaching Investors — 245
How to Raise Money from Family & Friends — 250

Why Investors Need a Minimum of 10X Scale	255
The Paperwork	260
Exit Strategy	262
Life After Funding Event	270
Closing Thoughts	*283*

Acknowledgements

"Business can fail, relationships should not"

A single genuine friendship fulfils us by filling the cracks that other failed relationships have etched over time. It somehow feels inadequate to say, "thank you" to people who have meaningful impact on your life. Individuals who support you steadfastly without judging you, despite the abundant flaws. But the book would be incomplete without acknowledging the positive and educational impact of the many people who made it possible.

My business partner at Natio Cultus, Dinesh Singh and all the staff who gave me the leeway to pursue writing this book in the face of numerous client deliverables. Jaya Nair who bore the brunt of the drudgery of editing the first version of the book. Numerous entrepreneurs who have and continue to place their faith in me and our company to guide them through unchartered territory. I have learnt as much, if not more from you.

Sachin Gopalan, my business partner and childhood friend based in Indonesia, for opening the world of Indonesian entrepreneurs to me. Sunil Girdhar for his support, encouragement and editing of the book at various stages. All these relationships are precious and make me realise the blessing of having friends who care and nurture each other. It also reminds me of the friendships lost, either due to time, distance or just poor judgement on my part.

My life partner, Aparna whose continued wisdom and deft handling of my misplaced inspirations, are no less important than the strength she provides day after day. My children Animay and Avanti who had to endure my rants about the book for a year and tried their best to add value to an eccentric midlife crazed father.

To all of you, thank you and lets think of the next one.

Authors Note

"Why imagine so much and act so little"

India appears to be in a start-up frenzy and a casual look at the stories in the media of mega valuations and funding deals, would have us believe that, it is raining dollars from the moment you hang up a sign board announcing the start of your business. I am besieged by young MBAs, midlife executives, children of businessmen, housewives and people of all stations of life looking for the mega funding deal because they have an idea! Which, by the way, only proves that they are human and nothing else.

Those who are already entrepreneurs read these media articles with a mixture of awe and cynicism as they have been running around chasing funding options for years and are befuddled as to how and on which planet these deals happen?

Let's cut to the chase and get some bitter truths right, straight up:

- Every IDEA is not a business, let alone a scalable and profitable one
- Ideas are useless on a standalone basis; it is execution that counts
- If you are stepping out to seek funds, when you are already short of funds; you probably will not get funded and you may want to reassess the need to continue. People give money to people who have money and not to those who do not. It also shows that your initial plan on cash flow has failed and either you executed poorly or are poor at managing cash
- Almost 90% of the start-ups fail in the first two years
- More than 95% of the start-ups are funded through personal funds, friends, family or loans
- Angel investors invest in approximately one out of forty curated proposals
- Venture capital funding is normally for the very large, very scalable, well managed and at the early stage or very profitable businesses

- Every overnight funding story you hear has a ten to fifteen-year 'work in progress' story behind it

- Media hype is just that. Hype. Let's take the hype about India having the third or fourth largest number of start-ups in the world currently. What would interest you is that we are still behind Israel, a country smaller than Kerala and a fraction of its population. Further, even if we climbed to number two, the gap between USA, the number one country and India would be ten times!

- Media reports extreme events only. Most of reality and life lies in between and is unreported. Behind the mega paper valuations are realities that you cannot comprehend

- Investors are not fools walking around with suitcases full of cash. They are extremely well-informed individuals who can cut through the nonsense of a typical pitch in a few seconds. Remember they have money because either they spend at a rate slower than they earn it or/ and they are extremely good at finding great ideas at a low value

So is it all gloom and doom? Not really. The facts, economic environment and social conditions are in favour of a start-up boom but you are never going to get funded if you chase the glamour and the money.

There is an art and science to get funded, but it cannot happen in isolation as a binary event. From the time you have an idea to its ultimate execution is just one part of the journey. The bigger journey is nailing down your values, vision and goals that get reflected in what you build. Investors are extremely sharp when it comes to reading entrepreneurs and the wannabes and fakes do not make it and spend a life time wondering why! No investor actually tells them why; invariably it is a handshake with a smile and "we will get back to you." A lot like a promising first date, who never calls back, let alone explain why.

Startups are often seen as a way of making more money than with a degree/ experience. They are seen as your ticket to a better future, assuming you can secure the investment you need. But the reality is that investment is no silver bullet and it will never provide you with a guarantee of success.

It is not uncommon to see startups take a lot of money and throw it right up the wall because they do not know what to do with it. The right team behind a startup with a solid business plan in place will always secure better results.

Investors know this and that is why it is often seen as so difficult to actually get first round financing. Go in prepared and make sure which startup funding tactic is the best option for you.

So stop scurrying around like a restless squirrel and spend time learning deep and wide about what it takes to be a successful entrepreneur and what an investor is really looking for. The trick is in the preparation. Focus and get guided through a step by step easy paced understandable process to achieve the destiny you believe is yours. You may be tempted to go to Part 4 of the book, that has the tips and insights into the investor world. Be warned that tips and insights work only if you have the necessary knowledge to apply them contextually. The base is in the first two parts, the unsexy parts but that is what you have been ignoring all along, in search of the elusive silver bullet.

Reasons Why An Investor Wont' Invest

Over the past month I have been conducting workshops among entrepreneurs and investors. This got me thinking about the hundreds of startup founders who have approached me and some of the things they did that really ticked me off. I have supported hundreds of startups through the funding process so have a good feel of the investors' side.

No matter what stage your startup is in, you are probably going to need some investment dollars. Here are the reasons why I personally would not invest in a startup. We will evaluate and address these points in the book, for smooth sailing when trying to secure funding from an investor like me and others:

Unproven Business Model, Lack of Evidence of Future Success

There is no evidence that there is interest in your startup or that it has some traction. Have you sold anything yet? Have you run a successful Kickstarter campaign? Have you launched a startup before? Passing those tests would prove to me that you have what it takes to get this startup off the ground.

Show me that your business is something worth my putting my hard-earned cash into and that this investment will work for me as your company starts to have success.

Of course, it is generally not enough to just have proof that the market cares about your idea, but you must also show that they are willing to pay you for it. There was a time in the late 90's when entrepreneurs could raise millions of dollars with just a domain name and customer 'eyeballs' but no idea of how to actually make any money. But that was the dot-com bubble and this is now.

Yes, in today's startup-obsessed investment climate you can still find examples of major investments being made without a workable business model in place. But in general, you must deliver some kind of 'business model proof.' How do you plan to make money and do you have proof of that on a small scale? If you cannot answer the question, you will not raise anything.

I Do Not Trust You

I stalk every company that I personally invest in. I typically invest in people. You could walk into my office and pitch me one heck of a product. Yet I'm not sold on you as a person, so forget about my investing in your company. If I cannot trust your character, judgment or leadership skills, then let's not waste each other's time. Look in the mirror, because every investor starts with you. Trust me — you are more important than your idea. Every venture capitalist or angel investor (or bank), I know, takes a hard look at the entrepreneur first. If your character, integrity or leadership is questionable you will not get funded.

Entrepreneurs often struggle to find a balance between ego and honesty. In today's world, overselling is the norm, but make sure you complement your exaggeration with the facts. Do not be afraid to show investors that you are aware of your personal weaknesses and those of your startup. They will appreciate the honesty and you never know, they might be able to help. So look hard and fix whatever is broken in that mirror.

You Have an Inexperienced Team

Members of your team seem to lack the experience needed to operate a startup. Let's say that I like you and your idea but not your team. Do not expect an investment from me. I need to be sure that members of your team have the qualifications and discipline to complete tasks, meet deadlines and follow through on objectives. You are only as strong as your weakest link — right! So your top level team gets the same scrutiny. Share the mirror with them and seriously address any weaknesses. Yes — it is a hard conversation to have. But do it. We have seen plenty of smart entrepreneurs fail to spot issues with their team because they are too trusting, too polite or too focused on themselves. It is your task as a founder to make sure your team is geared for success.

Members of Your Team Do Not Work Well Together

The co-founders or team members of your startup are constantly bickering. So I'm going to become uneasy about your startup. I do not want to risk an investment in a setup if the colleagues cannot get along. Does everyone get along on your team at a basic level?

You Are Keeping Things from Me

You are keeping every piece of information from me. I am not asking you to reveal every little secret regarding your startup. But if I am investing in your company, I have to at least know the basics of what makes your startup tick. Investors want to know everything about your startup. Do not worry: I will not steal your idea. I'm too busy.

You Do Not Have a Plan

You have failed to tell me how and where you expect to take your startup in the next couple of years, though you indicated that there's interest in your product. That is why creating a business plan is such an important piece of the puzzle. If I'm not impressed with your business plan, then I will not invest in your startup.

Evidence That the Startup Will Earn Money Is Scant

There are no pre-orders or not many signups for your product or service. So I will not be interested in your company. If you cannot prove that people are willing to pay for your product, then why should I, as an investor, give you money? Investors with money want to see results. Even if you pass the test as an entrepreneur, and you have a solid team to boot, they still want to see that you can engage customers with your ideas. Because, let us be honest, some ideas just are not worth pursuing regardless of how talented the team behind it is. Do you have proof that your potential customers care about your product? This is your product/market fit and you should not seek funding without it.

I Do Not Believe You Can Build Your Product

A great idea is one thing. Making it a reality is another. You have not convinced me that your product can actually function. I personally need to see some sort of working prototype. I would like to also see a few customers using your product.

Your Company Is Not the First to Enter the Market or Unique

I typically do not invest in a startup that is not trying to create something new or that have not come up with a different business model.

You must have something different or unique beyond what the competition has. Perhaps create a new idea from an old business model.

The Founder or CEO Is Uncoachable

You are not willing to listen to advice or suggestions and become defensive when I criticize an element of your business. Thus I cannot work with you. One time when several founders came to pitch me, I made one suggestion and they became offended. Some even went so far as to blog that I did not know anything. Their company is out of business now. Sounds similar to my first point, but in my opinion this is a hugely important factor for investors that is consistently underrated by entrepreneurs. I have seen investors walk away from potential investments because of it.

Entrepreneurs are expected to be strong, bordering on stubborn. It is good to be passionate about your beliefs and persistent in achieving your goals. But if you are so hard-headed to the point of being unable to listen to input from an experienced and knowledgeable investor then you will not get funded.

Be strong, but humble. Show 'deep domain expertise,' but do not come off as a 'know-it-all.'

Your Startup Costs Too Much

You may think your new company is worth $10 million. But I believe that it is worth only one-tenth of that. Figuring out the value of your startup can be a challenge. The value should be based on past accomplishments and the company's potential. If I feel that a startup is being assessed at a value that is too expensive, I am going to look for another investment opportunity.

You Handle Rejection Poorly

You have come across like those entrepreneurs who gripe and moan about how unfair life is. Sure you'll be rejected by investors. And that is part of the process. But handle that rejection constructively. Identify what went wrong and make proper adjustments. What happens after the pitch and rejection says a lot about an entrepreneur. Investors are watching, even after they have said no.

You Cold-Called Me

You sent your plan to every angel investor or venture capitalist for whom you could find contact information. Your request is just going to be tossed into the trash.

Instead, approach investors through referrals or recommendations from people they trust and who can vouch for you. I only invest in startups when the founders are referred to me or they go above and beyond the call of duty to get my attention. Never cold call an investor. It is as simple as that.

Venture capital firms and angel investors receive hundreds of unsolicited requests for funding from all over the world on a regular basis. Trust us, these business plans remain unopened and will find their way into the trash. Do not let yours be one of them.

I Am Not the Right Investor

Your company is not operating in my area of expertise. Just like a doctor might have a specialty, so do investors. Do some research ahead of time and locate the investors who are involved in your field. Just like you, professional investors (and private crowdfunding investors) have areas of core competency. If an investor has a deep understanding of enterprise software applications and their associated business models, what do you think the chances are of them investing in your pizza delivery service? They might love pizza, but that is beside the point. Do your research and seek out investors who invest in your industry as a consistent philosophy? They will be far more receptive to your idea and will know other investors who might be too.

You Do Not Focus

You are trying to launch every single product idea that you have. Instead stay on track and focus on creating the best product that you can release. You are not going to please every customer. But you do have to please the right customers or the situation will come back to burn you.

You are Way Too Early for My Money

You wanted to develop an idea that could revolutionize your business niche. But your concept is too far out. I am going to stay away until there has been more research, your project has traction with customers or other investors show interest. Investors typically want to stick with proven technology and industries.

Your Company's Technology Is Already Forgotten

Honestly, in the past six months I have received pitches concerning CD's and DVD's. Business trends, especially in the technology, move extremely fast.

Why should I risk my money supporting a startup that makes CD's and DVD's more efficient.

You Are Too Slow to Launch a Product

Your company is moving too slowly. Whether it is because you lack confidence or are a perfectionist, the longer it takes to launch your product, the longer it takes for me to see a return. Remember, there's nothing wrong with releasing a version 1.0 and making the appropriate adjustments as time goes on.

You Lack a Marketing Strategy

Your startup is poised to begin selling a product but lacks a plan for how to boost sales and gain a competitive advantage. I, along with thousands of other investors, can tear your startup apart in seconds. Have you set marketing goals? How will you promote your product? These are crucial marketing questions that need to be addressed before you come knocking on my door.

What Problem Were You Trying to Solve Again?

When you founded your startup, you did it with the intention of solving a problem. But you, the entrepreneur, have shifted your focus from contemplating an idea to running an actual business, you have lost sight of the original problem. I need to confirm that you are still addressing a problem that exists and your solution is feasible.

You Do Not Understand the Industry and Lack the Domain Knowledge

As an entrepreneur, you do not seem to be familiar with the business sector involved so I'm not interested in investing in your startup. If you had experience in a related area, that would at least inform me that you have some knowledge relevant to potential customers or an inkling about how to enhance the industry.

Break down the actual numbers that concern your particular niche of the industry and know them solid. If you do not have those figures, I will assume the worst or even more awful, I will come up with my own calculations.

Speaking of deep domain expertise, you'd better have it. Entrepreneurs who think they will raise money for their idea in an area or industry (or with a customer) they know virtually nothing about are in for a brutal reality check.

Those who raise serious money know what they are talking about. They are deeply embedded in their niche or area of expertise. They know the industry. They know the players. Most importantly, they know where the market is heading and they know how to get ahead. If you feel as if you lack this knowledge or would not be able to reproduce it when asked by an investor, I would consider switching industries or devoting more time to market research.

Failure to Understand the Word "Lean"

You are spending money on things like branded hats, key chains or coffee mugs. Why would I want to invest in your startup? An investment is supposed to go a long way toward getting a product ready for launch. That means not spending a ton of money on swag. A couple of T-shirts for promotional purposes is fine, but do not go on a spending spree.

Not sure what is meant by a lean startup business model? Imagine this scenario. An entrepreneur walks up to an investor and asks for a million dollars in order to "raise awareness" about their business through some form of marketing campaign. This entrepreneur has shown no understanding of how to operate a lean startup.

Investors want their money back. That is why they invest – to earn money. Every entrepreneur should at least understand the concept of running a lean startup – using funds wisely and in a targeted manner to ensure maximum efficiency – even if they do not actually do it. Investors want to know that they are not investing in a bottomless pit of money. They want to imagine their money being used to maximum effect and ultimately that means generating revenue.

Also, do not be paying yourself a big fat salary just because you are the boss. A study by Compass indicated that 66 percent of Silicon Valley startup founders using its benchmarking tool gave themselves salaries lower than $75,000. The range around the world is $32,000 to $72,000, according to Compass. How much are you paying yourself?

You are Not Concerned about Tomorrow

Your startup seems to be based only on a current trend. You cannot expect a startup to have longevity this way. I know that we cannot predict the future, but I want to invest in startups whose owners are thinking about the future, not just contemporary trends.

There Are not Any Other Investors

I do not see evidence that others have invested in your business, even a couple of thousand dollars. Unless I am a fervent believer in your startup, I need to see interest from other investors. The presence of other investments gives me an indication that someone else sees potential in your startup and that other people are supporting your vision. Having a couple of investors is good as they will help promote your business.

You are Oblivious: Inability to Stop and THINK

Many of the above issues apply to you and you have not realized it. That is a serious problem. I cannot stand dealing with people who cannot see flaws and are clueless about trying to overcome them. Remember, no one is perfect. Accept your weaknesses and work on correcting them. I saved the most frustrating pitfall for last. There are entrepreneurs out there who have passed from confidence into arrogance and are blind to all of the issues above, believing none of it applies to them. Good news! The fact that you've read this far suggests you are not one of them.

Startup financing is seen by many investors as similar to gambling because the chances of success are always dwindling. While every entrepreneur is sure they will succeed, it is the job of the investor to look beyond that all-consuming self-belief and see whether they are truly willing to gamble on you and your startup.

Your startup may well be the next Uber, but at some point you will need funding from an investor. For many entrepreneurs that is when reality kicks in – hard. To prevent this, you need to know what will make a prospective investor splash the cash or run in the opposite direction.

It does not matter whether you look to a bank, friends and family, angel investor, venture capitalist or crowdfunding platform. Start taking steps to avoid these pitfalls now and do not get caught out by when the time comes for funding.

Self-doubt can be healthy if you use it for self-improvement. Always ask yourself "why?" every day. Why am I doing this? Why am I doing it this way? Take a few minutes out of your workflow on a regular basis to assess your priorities, where you are going and how you are getting there. Does it all still make sense?

I have personally met with entrepreneurs who, suffering from one or more of the issues above, seemed to be going nowhere with their capital raise. But then, presumably after some deep soul-searching, they altered their team or switched their business plan and eventually got the investment they needed. Investors want to see that you are flexible, willing to adapt and ready to give up on a lost cause.

PART I
Personal Readiness

"The more you cling on to who you think you are, lesser the chance of you becoming who you think you should be"

Overview: Setting The Personal Stage

As a business and life coach I am often asked to assess whether a business has the potential to make it big? Often an euphemism for getting funded big. Another simple question I get from aspiring entrepreneurs, and ironically one of the hardest, is "How do I start?" I want to tell them to just start anywhere, but I realize that most have no idea where "anywhere" is. They just are not prepared for the life they want and are asking me how to learn to be an entrepreneur. It takes more than passion and a course on business basics.

We all come from the era where our society and education prepared us for the labour market, meaning working for someone else as an information professional, factory worker or retail associate. Now change is driving an opportunity driven society, where the next step is undefined and entrepreneurs are in the forefront of the wave of people whose best skill is learning how to learn. I ask them just as I am asking you, think about it from various perspectives to calibrate your expectations at a very personal and individual level.

- When was the last time that you did something for the first time and hit it out of the park? Did it so spectacularly well that you were the hero? Think Think! We all do things for the first time, like walking, swimming, writing an exam, dating, attending an interview, giving a speech, etc. Ok, how often have you won a lottery or even a cake raffle in your apartment or street fair? So, not lucky and definitely not the first time, what makes you think you will be wildly successful the first time you attempt entrepreneurship?

- You have probably undergone 15–18 years of education as preparation to get to where you are. If you have worked for a few years, you have those years in addition as preparation. If you are a successful executive, you probably run one of the departments in a large company with relatively better performance than similarly educated peers. How does this prepare you for the job of running a company end to end apart from competing with highly driven individuals where there are no limits, rules, referees and umpires.

- I know you are passionate about your idea but so are you about cricket or movies or your car. You do not expect to be paid every time you live your passion by playing a game or driving your favourite car. Why do you expect others to pay for you to pursue your passion?

- I can see how protective you are of your idea; like it is your baby. I keep hearing you say that. From when have people started to expect others to pay for their babies? Why have one if you cannot afford to bring it up till it can stand on its own? And for god's sake people do not sell their babies for economic benefit, do they? At least not normal parents.

- You had your parents to guide you through your early years, teachers to guide you through education, bosses and company guidelines to help you grow through the years at your job; who is guiding you through entrepreneurship? Even Roger Federer, Tiger Woods, Virat Kohli, Narendra Modi and almost all corporate, business, sports or political leaders have acknowledged coaches and continue to have them throughout their careers. Who is yours?

- Experience of taking a loan for buying a house or car is pretty frustrating for most of us. Bankers always ask for dozens of documents and hundreds of signatures, not to speak of guarantors and physical checks of your home and work place. Of course, they almost always ask for a piece of paper that you do not have as well. All this for lending you 80–90% of the amount you need against a fully saleable asset. What checks do you think an investor will conduct for giving you money against almost no collateral in a sector where they know you have a 90% chance of failure in the first two years?

- Except falling in love, which is what most entrepreneurships are about, at least at the start; what goals can you drive to, without the lubricant of money? Actually, even love once transitioned to marriage requires the continuous lubricant of money. For almost everything from registering the company to ultimately requiring clients to pay, requires a continuous and ever increasing pool of money. Unless born to a rich and philanthropic family, in which case this book is not as useful to you; you need money other than your own to back your dreams. Much like you needed money from your parents for education and living to launch you into life, for economic independence.

So how are you planning to succeed? Doing things for the first time, having just about normal luck, little or no entrepreneurship education, no coaches or mentors to guide you, let alone a rudimentary knowledge of the brutal world of funding. These are just a few of the so many other personal readiness and awareness points that are pertinent and will have a deciding role in the degree of your success. Are you banking on fluke, chance, karma, destiny or waiting for a white knight on a white horse to angelically propel you to your imagined heights?

And why should anyone, let alone someone who is a stranger; fund your passion, your baby, your goals taking as much risk as is obvious to one and all; for no guarantee of returns. What we all intuitively know is that, the earlier one seeks funding in the business cycle of your ideas implementation and fruition, the more equity you have to part with. What you need to REALIZE is that the earlier someone funds you in the same business cycle the more likely they are funding YOU vis a vis funding the idea or business. So how prepared are you? How do you need to prepare?

The Founders' Giveaways

The first, is the most important question that everyone around you wants to know. The one question that an investor starts looking for answers to, from the moment they know about you:. "WHY are you doing this?" If it is for money and/or fame; there are many other ways to get there. If it is for a sense of ownership; you could get that by buying shares of a listed company in the same sector, for far less risk and pain. If it is to escape a boring career, a bad boss, a stagnant career, to be your own boss or you feel it is glamorous to be an entrepreneur or any other such escapist thrill-seeking reason; then you are not likely to last the tough course of entrepreneurship.

The only reasons you should be an entrepreneur is similar to the reason you proposed to your spouse or vice versa i.e. : if you do not do this you will remain unfulfilled as a person. Only this sense of obsessive commitment will reflect in your wanting to contribute something that the world needs or will make customers happy or lead to unending learning opportunities and ultimately to the investor backing a person who has the best chance to succeed and get his investments the multiple times return that his initial risk deserves.

The second, after the WHY you are doing this is answered in the investor's mind, is HOW are you attitudinally setup to achieve the stated goals? Here there are many stereotypes of a typical entrepreneur, often reinforced through popular culture in movies and television. Of the long haired, maverick entrepreneur frenetically multi-tasking during the day, playing drums at a local pub in the evening and going for bike rides on the weekend. Nothing could be further than the truth. Look around you at the promoters of all the Unicorn startups (i.e.: those with a valuation of > USD 1 Billion); do you see anyone that fits that stereotype? Yes, sure there is that rare exception but those are statistical outliers that are evident in any scenario for any data set.

It is essential that one goes through the complete 'reality check' and 'reflection' phase prior to jumping into entrepreneurship. However difficult your current corporate job and however big an executive you have become, it still is only a small part role in an organization supported by many other individuals with established rules and expectations. Entrepreneurship, on the other hand, demands an almost impossible array of skills and an incredible level of humility and maturity. Often our bloated corporatized egos are unable to cope. Hence, it is important to introspect on 'why' you want to be an entrepreneur. Equally important are your expectations. For example, your current corporate success is the result of years of education, decades of hard work and mastery over a field that has led to your lifestyle, respect, etc. Entrepreneurship will likely take a lot of this away and will take years of similar hard work to get back to where you are now. Albeit the learning curve can be shortened but there is no guarantee of success, at least not immediately.

Is It a Young Person's Club?

Entrepreneurship does not have to be a young person's game. No one is really rooting for the over-50 entrepreneur. Our role models are not obvious. Entrepreneurship has the reputation of being an edgy, youthful business and is often measured by the tales of Mark Zuckerberg, Steve Jobs and Bill Gates who dropped out of college to make their fortunes.

What about the rest of us? Not all of us dropped out of college or had a blinding insight at age 20. Entrepreneurship need not and should not belong only to the young. Indeed, the hesitations, stereotypes, and ageism that can sometimes inhibit late-career entrepreneurs can be a detriment to the economy as a whole.

There are a few practical things that IT-boomers should think about before stepping off into the unknown. Do you have the time? What about resources to carry you over the start-up period? Have you formulated a detailed business plan? The most important question: "Do you have a clear business idea?" However, if you are someone who...

- likes to call the shots and live life on your own terms
- has a strong desire for autonomy and independence
- takes action on your convictions
- knows how to evaluate and take calculated risks
- is highly self-motivated

...then entrepreneurship could be right for you.

In fact, if you look carefully at all the role models mentioned earlier, you will notice that even if they started out a bit "wild" almost all of them ascribe their success to having become calmer. If it is one quality that you will see running common through most successful people, it is their inner calmness. This in turn comes from a sense of deep self-awareness. It is not to be mistaken for faked or cultured cool behaviour or self-control alone. It is a quality any astute investor is looking for; it shines through and inspires confidence that their money will be in safe hands with someone who can weather the pitfalls of entrepreneurship and guide the venture as a risk manager with steady hands.

Bootstrapping is Underrated

You may find it paradoxical that I am speaking of self funding in a book that is supposed to guide you on professional funding. But you need to give it a serious thought before plunging into the swirling waters of the world of investors. Agreed, maybe you need the money. Maybe that is what your business plan says. But seriously: Do you really want to have investors involved in your dream startup?

I have said it often to entrepreneurs, bootstrapping is underrated. I get frequent emails from people asking how they can get investment for their new startup and my first reaction is to ask them to bootstrap or spend their time getting clients. Here are ten reasons to consider not to seek investors for your startup.

- It is almost impossible to get investment for your very first startup. If you do not have startup experience, get somebody on your team who does. If neither you nor a leadership team member has started a company, it makes it very hard.

- You are selling ownership and often control. Investors write checks to own a serious portion of your business. I admit that is patently obvious, but you should see how many entrepreneurs think of investors as if they were some sort of charitable public agency. Once you get investment, you do not own your entire company.

- Investors are bosses. You are not your own person when you have investors; you are part of a team. You cannot decide everything by yourself. Politics matter. Investor relations matter. If you screw up, you do it in front of other people and it hurts those people.

- Valuation is critical to them and you. Simply put, valuation means the price. If you want to give only 10 percent of your company to investors who pay $100,000, you are saying your company is worth $1 million. And so on. Simple math, but wow, not so simple negotiation.

- Investors do not make money until there's a liquidity event. That is why we always talk about exit strategies. You can be the world's happiest, healthiest, most cash-independent company, but your investors will not be happy until you get them their cash back. The win is getting money back out of the company. Some big company stock buyers like dividends. Startup investors do not.

- If it is not 10 X scalable, forget it. The real growth opportunities are scalable. It used to be products only, but now there are some scalable services, like web services and aggregated services for example. But if doubling your sales means doubling your headcount (that is called a body shop).

- If it is not defensible, it is tough going at best. Not that I trust patents as a defence, but trade secrets, momentum, a combination of trade secrets and patents, plus a good intellectual property defence budget… if anybody can do it, then investors are not interested.

- Investors are not pure financial people. Some become collaborative partners and even mentors, some are nagging insensitive critics. Some are trojan horses. Some help, some do not. Better choose carefully which investors you approach.

- Just getting financed does not mean anything. You have not won the race when you get that cheque? The difficult part is after the funding.

- Investors sometimes take your company from you. Not just physically (that happens too) but in terms of vision, culture, client focus versus financial goals.

So if you can, then bootstrap as far as possible. Try spending the time and energy chasing clients instead of investors. While the process of preparation for funding has benefits for the organization, regardless of whether you take funds ultimately and is worth going through just for that.

Client Funded is Ideal For B2B

Early stage startups seem obsessed with getting investment and are worrying how to scale even before they find product-market fit. News about huge investment rounds on unicorns helps fuel the notion that the measure of startup success is investment and that once you are invested you graduate into the "real startup big boys club." I would argue that in most cases the real and only measure of success is having clients using your product, paying for it and coming back for more.

So if you are an early stage startup please stop focusing on your existential need for investment and put your effort on building your product by co-developing it alongside a good client. To be clear, a "good client" is one that knows your product is not perfect yet but holds potential and believes that you will be able to deliver. A "good client" gives you real feedback and has his interests clearly aligned with yours.

Here are some reasons why a good client is better than investment if you are an early stage B2B startup:

1. Keep a bigger part of the equity

From the onset your startup is most likely not just yours. Your co-founders probably have a considerable part of the equity and your early hires another bit. If you delay investment as much as possible, you will not only increase your startup's value, you will also need to sell a smaller stake to keep afloat until the next investment round.

2. Seed money is expensive

Seed investment deals are calculated by the amount of risk involved in your startup and when you do not have a respectable client to prove you are on to something, you are a very risky investment! This means that seed money is really expensive for you and you will be selling a large chunk of your startup cheap.

3. Get much better usage feedback

Investors can be "smart money" and help you access new clients, help guide you with their experience but ultimately, if you do not have a paying customer they will be guessing whether there is a need in the market. Sure they may have developed better intuition but nothing compares to real customer feedback from usage patterns. Nothing.

4. It is on you not your investor

While it is true that investors may be a good sounding board on some topics and decisions, many of them do not know how to play their role as investors and stop thinking about how you will be able to multiply what he put in. This naturally is to be expected and not reproachable per se as getting a return is what investment should be about. Now, many startups get sucked into potentially conflicting needs and end up blaming the investor for not letting them do as they choose and pivot beyond recognition. So, without an investor, you are, without question, the only one making the decisions and it is all on you. If it fails or if it succeeds, it is you.

5. Have the right kind of pressure and focus

When you bring investors on board they will be more involved in your business and you will have to keep them happy. Note, however, that those you should focus on keeping happy are your clients and your team. So, the time and energy you will spend on taking into consideration investor worries and the self-censorship you will impose on yourself will likely drain some of the short resources you have. With a good client your drive is to make the product work and provide clear value to your client. This is what your startup needs.

6. Build your product's reputation

A good client gives you the best sales tool you can wish for: a real life use case you can show future clients and mitigate their "fear of being first." There's nothing more powerful than dropping some big names when selling to new clients. This, in fact, is a very predictable behaviour and you can bypass the "nobody gets fired for hiring IBM" syndrome.

7. Do not waste precious resources managing investors

Unlike the hyped Silicon Valley stories where startups easily raise millions on whim, Asian investors tend to have a more cautious approach to investing their money. This means that you'll need to dedicate considerable amount of time and energy (and frustration) on preparing your pitch deck, establishing relationships, taking part in investor pitching events and negotiating lengthily. Your time would be better spent rolling out your product on a single strategic client that not only will provide you some cash to survive, he will help you improve your product.

So here's the skinny: if you are an early stage B2B startup looking to grow, start by working alongside a good client. Develop even a single strategic relationship with a client that will help you improve your product and give you the credibility to attract your next ones. Furthermore, avoid diluting your equity and increase your valuation by focusing your team on what is really important: your product, making that big first sale and keeping them coming back for more.

Personal Readiness

For every stage of your life you have spent time preparing for it. Be it physically, emotionally, socially, financially or spiritually. It is imperative that you treat your foray into entrepreneurship and the world of investors with the same seriousness and preparation.

Before you start, you need to define what success means to you. It may include financial gain, but more likely the lasting satisfaction and happiness will result from your legacy of change in technology or your impact on the social ecology of the world. If you cannot tell me where you want to go, I cannot really tell you how to start.

There are fairy tale stories that get reported in the media about the glorious life of an entrepreneur. The details are generally missing as it would be impossible to document the ups and downs of an entrepreneur throughout his or her journey. That would drive the reader insane for sure. The journey in simple terms is akin to a "wild" roller coaster ride in the dark.

Assuming that you are entering entrepreneurship for the right reasons, you are probably aware that it will be demanding physically and mentally. Most tend to brush these off in the initial exuberance of the startup and get a deadly hangover later. It is best to approach it, like you approached your selection for colleges. Speak to entrepreneurs who have experienced both the highs and lows of a startup. Even better, go and work for one for some time, preferably in a similar industry. Or consult with a startup for your area of expertise and you will learn a whole lot about the limitations of looking at complex business issues uni dimensionally. You will get an idea of the time, energy, determination, skills and mental fortitude you require to meet the challenge successfully. It is a hugely invigorating and electrifying experience if you go into it prepared and for the right reasons, else it turns into an unmitigated nightmare.

It is best to take some basic steps to ensure you are getting into this phase of life in the best possible shape.:

- ♦ Get your finances in order and try to enter this phase without EMIs or rentals plaguing you. Any successful entrepreneur will tell you that if you are worried about your startup paying the bills you might end up making bad decisions because you will be too focused on the short-term, thinking, "I cannot pay for marketing because I have to pay for my family's food."

- It is best (if married) that your spouse has a stable job as a security net and to keep basic expenses going
- Get into good physical shape and medically ready
- Ensure you are emotionally in a reasonable shape and not bouncing off a divorce or death of a near one or some similar traumatic experience
- Speak to people, especially people who were in charge of judging your performance and skills, like ex-bosses spouse, parents and people who generally gave you feedback that you did not like. This gives you very good perspective
- Prepare your family by explaining the time commitment at the start and the changes that are required financially and socially
- Unclutter your life in terms of daily tasks. Either get someone to do it or find a way to get rid of it. Be it paying bills, driving people around, managing other mundane but necessary activities
- Get major time consuming activities out of the way. For example, do not enter this phase of life if you are busy building your house or marrying off your children or completing your Phd

Having a college degree and some work experience is highly desirable for most entrepreneurs. There are exceptions that the media glorifies but this is not the general rule. Even if you have successfully worked before, you need to remind yourself that running a small department in a big company with a relatively better performance than similarly educated colleagues, does not qualify you to run a complete business.

You would have noticed how the greatest coaches, athletes and role models speak about couple of things ad nauseam. We hear them but probably do not listen, let alone follow. The first thing you will hear is that they follow a process or regimen and they expect the results to follow. The second is that, at the very top what differentiates the winners is to do with their mental makeup and not their education, skill, passion, hard work etc., because those are a given and not differentiators. What is your winning regimen and how do you prepare mentally?

The personal readiness is often the most neglected and overlooked part of an entrepreneurs' journey. I consider this to be the foundation of the mega monument of your dreams. Time spent in understanding yourself and adapting your approach, creating your founder team and business model to this reality will go a long way in ensuring success for the business in general and not just for funding. So, let's take a deep and varied look at the aspects that need to be considered by you.

The Basic Personality

Let us discuss a few traits you need to think of before you take the plunge, in order to prepare yourself because investors are looking for these signs in you.

Here are five quick personality assessments to evaluate before taking the entrepreneurial plunge:

Are You Santa or an Elf?

Entrepreneurship requires managing a wide variety of tasks as part of the business, from marketing and accounting to training, customer service and more. Can you wear multiple hats, as Santa does at Christmas, or do you prefer to be the elf that loves to execute specific tasks? Do you take initiative or do you want clear instructions? Santas make better entrepreneurs than elves do.

What's Your Relationship with Money?

Starting a business requires money to start, to operate and for you to live on while it scales. If you are a big spender and are not great at managing money, those bad habits are likely to follow you into a business. And if you are usually unable to make worthwhile investments in the future of your business for fear of ending up living in a cardboard box, if things go wrong then you may end up penny wise and pound foolish, as they say. Having a solid, non-emotional money relationship will help you make wise business decisions.

Are You Comfortable Flying Blind?

The only thing that is certain in business is that nothing is certain. Are you comfortable with being uncomfortable? Can you handle taking educated risks and surviving the constant ups and downs of owning a business? If you are looking for certainty or a drama-free zone, you may find yourself terrified of the entrepreneurial rollercoaster.

Are You Ready to Commit?

Running a successful business is not just about having great ideas. It is more about strong execution. So, if you have a hard time staying focused, you are lousy with commitments and you are averse to the idea of working day in and day out on the same thing, then entrepreneurship may just be a passing fancy for you.

Were You Born for Business?

Were you interested in business as a child? Did you seek out entrepreneurial roles in school, in social organizations or even in your previous job? A natural inclination of past interest in entrepreneurship seems to be a good potential indicator of future success.

The Traits, Quirks & Characteristics

There are a variety of ways to assess yourself. Here is another way to think about it and calibrate yourself.

Pressed to describe the stereotypical entrepreneur, which words would you use? Passionate? Dedicated? Optimistic? Sure, those apply. But insecure and troublemaker are more accurate, according to entrepreneurs who know a success when they see one. Do the following traits, characteristics and quirks describe you? Well then, you might be an entrepreneur (at heart, if not yet in practice).

1. You take action

Barbara Corcoran, founder of The Corcoran Group, co-star of TV's 'Shark Tank' and author of 'Shark Tales: How I Turned $1,000 into a Billion Dollar Business,' says people who have a concept but not necessarily a detailed strategy are more likely to have that entrepreneurial je ne sais quoi.

"Invent as you go," rather than spending time writing a plan at your desk. In fact, she believes that people with life experience have an active problem-solving ability and think-on-your-feet resourcefulness that can be more valuable than book smarts alone. Those who study business may be prone to over-analysing situations rather than taking action.

2. You are insecure

Many entrepreneurs judged as ambitious are really insecure underneath," Corcoran says. When evaluating potential investments, investors say they want someone "who is scared to death." Those who are nervous about failing can become hyper-focused and willing to do whatever it takes to succeed. If you feel insecure, use that emotion to drive you to achieve your business goals.

3. You are crafty

"One of my favourite TV shows growing up was 'MacGyver,'" confides Tony Hsieh, CEO of Las Vegas-based Zappos, "because he never had exactly the resources he needed but would somehow figure out how to make everything work out."

A lifelong entrepreneur, Hsieh has done everything from starting a worm farm to making buttons and selling pizzas, so he admires MacGyver's "combination of creativity, optimism and street smarts. Ultimately, I think that is what being an entrepreneur is all about – playing MacGyver, but for business." It is not about having enough resources, he explains, but being resourceful with what you do have.

4. You are obsessed with cash flow

Before founding Brainshark, a Waltham, – based developer of technology for business presentations, Joe Gustafson bootstrapped a venture called Relational Courseware. "All I ever thought about was cash flow and liquidity," he says, admitting, "there were seven times in the company's eight-year history when I was days or hours away from payroll and did not have enough cash to make it."

How did he respond? "In the early days, you could step up and put expenses on your personal credit card, but that can only go so far," he says. "You need cash – even if you have the best company and the best receivables in the world – to fight the battle one more day." Other strategies he recommends include working with a partner who can provide cash advances on projects and maintaining close communication with suppliers.

5. You get into hot water

Stephane Bourque, founder and CEO of Vancouver, British Columbia-based Incognito Software, says true entrepreneurial types are more likely to ask for forgiveness than permission, forging ahead to address the opportunities or issues they recognize, even without approval from higher-ups.

"Entrepreneurs are never satisfied with the status quo," says Bourque, who discovered he was not destined for the corporate world when he kept coming up with new and better ways of doing things – ideas that were not necessarily appreciated by his bosses and often were interpreted as unwanted criticism. Now, he says, "I wish my employees would get into more trouble," because it shows they are on the lookout for opportunities to improve themselves or company operations.

6. You are fearless

"Where most avoid risk, entrepreneurs see potential," says Robert Irvine, chef and host of Food Network's 'Restaurant: Impossible.' True 'treps are not afraid to leverage their houses and run up their credit card balances in order to amass the funds they need to create a new venture. In some ways, he says, they are the ultimate optimists, because they operate under the belief that their investments of time and money will eventually pay off.

7. You cannot sit still

Entrepreneurs have unbridled energy that fuels them long past the time when their employees have gone home. They are eager, excited and energized about business in a way that makes them stand out. Irvine would know: He owns a restaurant in South Carolina, is opening another in the Pentagon and has a line of food and clothing products, on top of hosting his TV show.

8. You are malleable

"If you have only one acceptable outcome in mind, your chances of making it are slim," cautions Rosemary Camposano, president and CEO of Silicon Valley chain Halo Blow Dry Bars. If you are willing to listen, your clients will show you which of your products or services provide the most value.

Her original vision for Halo was part blow-dry bar, part gift shop, "to help busy women multitask," she explains. But she quickly learned that the gift shop was causing confusion about the nature of her business, so she took it out, replaced it with an extra blow-dry chair and things took off. Smart entrepreneurs constantly evolve, tweaking their business concepts in response to market feedback.

9. You enjoy navel gazing

"Without direct supervisors, entrepreneurs need to be comfortable with the process of evaluating their own performance," says Laura Novak Meyer, owner of Pennsylvania's Little Nest Portraits. That requires "a willingness to solicit feedback from those around you to self-improve," she says, as well as paying close attention to feedback you may not have asked for, such as customer complaints or being outpaced by competitors. Little Nest surveys every client to ask for opportunities for improvement and Meyer has worked closely with a business coach for the past five years to identify personal areas where she needs to improve.

10. You are motivated by challenges

When confronted by problems, many employees try to pass the buck or otherwise wash their hands off the situation. Entrepreneurs, on the other hand, rise to the occasion. "Challenges motivate them to work harder," says Jeff Platt, CEO of the Sky Zone Indoor Trampoline Park franchise. "An entrepreneur does not think anything is insurmountable... He looks adversity in the eye and keeps going."

Candace Nelson, founder of Sprinkles Cupcakes, agrees. Despite naysayers who questioned her idea for a bakery in the midst of the carb-fearing early-2000s, she persevered and now has locations in eight states. In fact, she was one of the first entrepreneurs in a business that became an ongoing craze, sparking numerous copycats.

11. You consider yourself an outsider

"Entrepreneurs are not always accepted," says Vincent Petryk, founder of J.P. Licks, a Boston chain of ice-cream shops. They may be seen as opinionated, quirky and demanding – but that is not necessarily a bad thing. "They are often rejected for being different in some way, and that just makes them work harder,," Petryk says. When his former boss did not approve of his off-duty research into ice-cream quality, he went out on his own to develop a made-from-scratch dessert in bold flavours. Rather than copying what most other ice-cream shops were doing, including buying from the same well-known suppliers, Petryk forged his own path. His early competitors? All but one are no longer in business.

12. You recover quickly

It is a popular notion that successful entrepreneurs fail fast and fail often. For Corcoran, the trick is in the speed of recovery: If you fail, resist the urge to mope or feel sorry for yourself. Do not wallow; move on to the next big thing immediately.

13. You fulfil needs

"Many people recognize marketplace holes, but it is the true entrepreneur who takes them from cocktail napkin to reality," says Jennifer Dawn, partner in New York City-based Savor the Success, a business network for women. "Entrepreneurs think of a way to fix it and take steps to fix it. They are innovators.." So when Savor's network of women began asking for advice and input from co-founder Angela Jia Kim, she and Dawn created a new product: Savor Circles. These mastermind groups connect four members who give each other tailored inputs and expertise; even better, they provide Savor the Success with a new revenue stream.

14. You surround yourself with advisors

Actress Jessica Alba, co-founder and president of Santa Monica, California-based The Honest Company, which sells baby, home and personal-care products, notes, "It is important to surround yourself with people smarter than you and to listen to ideas that are not yours. I'm open to ideas that are not mine and people that know what I do not, because I think success takes communication, collaboration and sometimes, failure.."

In other words: True 'treps do not hire yes men; they talk to those with experience and conduct thorough research, gathering as much information as they can to make informed decisions rather than taking a shot in the dark.

15. You work and play hard

"Entrepreneurs fall down and pick themselves up until they get it right," says Micha Kaufman, who snowboards and sails in addition to running Fiverr, the fast-growth online freelance marketplace he co-founded.

"Like in sports, the key to success in business is staying super-focused," the CEO notes. During Fiverr's launch, instead of trying to deal with 'an endless number of potential challenges,' Kaufman and his team focused on "the single biggest challenge every marketplace has: building liquidity.

Without liquidity, there is no marketplace. "It is like worrying about the skills needed for frontside -360 jumps before getting on a snowboard and learning the basics."

The Young & Restless

The very young need to understand readiness in a whole new way. I have adapted the key recommendations here for aspiring young entrepreneurs who are launching startups into cutting edge and rapidly changing new technology areas or socially impacting businesses.

1. **Business gamification and simulation.** Learning does not have to be all work. We know now that people learn from a younger age and keep coming back for more, from sources that are entertaining and educational (*edutainment*). With new tools like Thrive15 and GamEffective, people of any age can learn to start or take their business to the next level.

2. **Adaptive business advising and learning.** Every business and every entrepreneur is at a different stage, so it is time to seek out learning tools that can adapt to you, rather than the other way around. Universities and the marketplace are spawning tools like OpenStudy, which is a learning network enabling massively multi-player study groups.

3. **Help entrepreneurs with constant learning.** The wealth of online education offerings is a great start, but is not enough. Business advisors need to be ready to help at every stage and I see it beginning to happen. Yet many new entrepreneurs are hesitant, perhaps out of fear or ego or both. If you are not constantly learning, you are falling behind.

4. **Mix business learning with doing.** Entrepreneurs do not need to know everything about business before they start. They do need the first few steps and where to find the next steps. There is no standard course for this, but the answers are accessible online, if you know how to search, follow blogs and interact with the relevant social media groups.

5. **Business financial aid alternatives.** Crowdfunding is just the latest alternative for assistance to entrepreneurs who need help, supplementing the existing alternatives of loans, grants, angel investors, venture capitalists and many others. These days, if you cannot find

money, you have not tried hard enough or maybe your idea is not a good one.

6. **Utilize business content curators and coaches.** Potential resources available to entrepreneurs are enormous, but often under-utilized. The challenge is to find these just-in-time, including community and university startup incubators, accelerators and advisors. Entrepreneurs should be monitoring online curator platforms and blogs.

In this new opportunity society, the personal traits for success have also changed from the industrial age and the information age. The days of long-term loyalty to an employer and methodically following direction are gone. Now the premium is on creativity, willingness to take a risk and ability to keep up with change. Persistence and problem solving are sought-after virtues.

Nurturing these traits and practicing incremental and continuous learning, are the best ways to start the life you want as an entrepreneur.

The Value System

1. Learn to keep promises to yourself

Forget for a second about the promises that you make to others – you need to learn to keep the promises that you make to yourself. When you are an entrepreneur, you will make lots of promises to yourself (sometimes nobody will be listening to you – so you cannot make promises to others) and the only way you can get through to the next stage is by keeping those promises that you make to yourself.

2. Learn to be likable

Being likable is harder than you think. The immediate temptation is to think about pleasing others as the easiest path to be likable. Being smart, you know that it will not work and most probably it will backfire anyway. To keep this short, here are a few quick tips:

- If you want to be likable, genuinely care for others. Care as if their problems are your own. If you are genuine, it shows. If you are not genuine, it shows even more.
- Be an energizer. Do you leave other people energized or do you suck the energy out of them? If you are doing the former, it would be impossible to be likable.
- Do not take yourself seriously. If you do, you will be worried more about you than caring for others.

Why should you be likable? Simple answer: It is easier to get things done if you are than when you are not. As an entrepreneur, you will have to get more things done with less resources as compared to someone who is having a job. Investors are always asking themselves if they can work with you for the next decade.

3. Learn to build lasting relationships

If you are thinking about someone only when you need something from them, you have got it all wrong completely. A lasting relationship at the core is about enrichment. Are you both mutually being enriched as a result of the relationship? If not, the relationship may last only as long as it is convenient to keep it alive.

As an entrepreneur, relationships are your currency and treat them as such. If you have learned to build such relationships and already have built lots of them before you jump on the entrepreneurship bandwagon, life will be a bit simpler compared to the alternative.

4. Build a personal brand

Whether you want or not, your personal brand will add weightage to your message. There is a fine line between telling your story and showing off. Choose the former and you will pay the price of diluting your personal brand rather than enhancing it.

A note of caution: Because "personal branding" is such a cliched term, you may be tempted to build a brand on social media channels as there are gurus out there who are telling you how to use all the social networks to amplify your brand. The keyword to watch here is – "amplify." If you do not have valuable accomplishments, there is nothing to amplify. Personal brands are first built on valuable accomplishments and then amplified through variety of channels that are available. The order is important.

5. Lead a volunteer effort where you are accountable for the results

The best way to test your influencing skills is to lead a volunteer effort where:
- You need to sign up for some measurable results (e.g.: raise $XX funds)
- Recruit volunteers
- Plan and execute the campaign to meet or exceed the results

If you can recruit and lead a team of volunteers and keep them motivated until the results are achieved, you would have learned a host of things that will serve you well in your entrepreneurship journey.

6. Make powerful requests

In short, a powerful request does not come across as a request at all – it appears like an opportunity for the other party. Your ability to transform a request and convert that into an opportunity on the fly will serve you well later during your entrepreneurship journey. Remember that people are flooded with requests but are starved on opportunities. You are a minority in their life if you are bringing them thoughtful opportunities. That is the fastest way to get people on your side.

7. Learn to reframe your questions

Reframe as the name indicates is to look at something from a different angle. Here are a few questions and the reframed versions of the same:

- Get vs Become

    What am I getting?

    Who am I becoming?

- Victimization vs Accountability

    Why is this happening to me?

    How am I contributing to this?

    or

    What am I learning from this?

- Ecosystems and Choreography

    How can I get this done?

    What is the right combination of (available) resources to execute this in the most optimal fashion?

- Identity

    Do I matter?

    How do I matter?

8. Learn the fundamentals of storytelling

This is a MUST whether you want to be an entrepreneur or not but if you WANT to be an entrepreneur, mastering this art will give you a huge competitive advantage. Storytelling skills are not required just when you are on the stage or when you are giving an elevator pitch to someone. It is required whenever you want to talk about your startup – even during a casual conversation with ANYONE. We as human beings operate on stories – the ones that we tell, ones that we tell ourselves and the ones that we hear from others.

9. Make meaningful and measurable contributions to other startups

A startup looks very different from outside but it is another world once you are in it. If you have never been part of one and try to start one, you will be in for a big surprise. One way to be "less" surprised is to avoid the sandbox and actually get involved in startups (for free) and make meaningful and measurable contributions to their growth. You will be trading time for the experience – it will be the best investment you would have made in preparation to your own entrepreneurship journey.

The side benefit of this approach is that you are also building "good karma" along the way and one day it will pay back in ways that you cannot imagine

Mid Life Readiness

Entrepreneurship is one midlife bug against which there should be a law. While men have a fixation for opening restaurants, women have one for opening play schools. As people reach midlife and achieve their financial goals, hit midlife career stagnation and get generally restless with the way things are in their life, they hit an AHA! moment and decide they will have their own business. Many an individual has been ruined in chasing this elusive dream or attempting to 'try and fail rather than not try at all.' Full of themselves, with a puffed up ego and delusions about their own knowledge and capabilities, they set out to light the business world on fire only to realize the difficulties, their skill limitations, their lack of energy for hard work, the fickleness of markets and investors, etc. They get the pasting of their lives financially, emotionally and socially before they either try something new or like most, scale back their ambitions and go back to jobs where the knowledge they acquired over the first 15–20 years of their career is relevant. A miniscule few do make it, which are the stories that media and society highlight, thereby fuelling a frenzy of hundreds of others who are destined to ruin themselves trying.

Visions of grandeur as an entrepreneur characterize this phase. This is a classic and financially dangerous symptom that afflicts mid and senior management professionals, depending on where they have reached in midlife. Starting with casual conversations with colleagues and friends, where every known success of professionals who ventured out on their own and succeeded is glorified and looked upon with respect and awe, it quickly moves to a near obsession on setting out as an entrepreneur, either alone or in the company of like-minded friends. This often leads to a quick exit from the job and comes as a surprise to the spouse and family.

At 22, you might wake up and say: "I'm quitting my job today to start a business." But it is a different story when you are a first-time entrepreneur in midlife, in a down economy, with kids, aging parents or just the screaming awareness that you will be facing little or no income for the foreseeable future.

For many people launching businesses in their 40s, 50s and 60s, the process more closely resembles that long trip up the ladder to the high dive, where you linger, staring at the water, until one day, you jump.

Midlife career changes were not something that the mentors and role models taught me growing up. Yet, in my 25 years in corporate life most recently as a senior consultant, I have changed my focus more than a few times.

Most recently, I went out on my own and began exploring both the life of the independent consultant and that of an inspirational writer. And believe me, the life of the entrepreneur is a different world. It is equally scary and exciting.

JP, a successful business strategy consultant confesses: "I'm one of you. Like many of you, I looked around and asked myself, 'What's next?' I published books; I dabbled in consulting. A few years ago, I began to wonder how I could expand my platform."

Using Midlife Career Changes to Explore Who You Are

What I have learned is that midlife career changes are not really about the job. It is really about something inside you that has changed. It is about who you are today, and what's important to you now.

A short aside: I'm a writer and consultant and I'm also someone who's been knocked around in corporate life (layoffs, re-orgs, demanding clients, companies going bankrupt). Sometimes, it was painful.

Yet, I look back and recognize that every bump in the road conspired to lead me to where I am today. Living a life of Freedom, away from the 9 to 5, serving amazing clients and writing about what's most important to me.

So whether you are changing careers in midlife yourself or you've been (ahem) 'compelled' by your organization to seek new opportunities, use this time to explore yourself more deeply. You, the entrepreneur, will need to be quite different than you, the employee. And no matter what your area of expertise is, your business will end up being an intimate reflection of your heart.

Ask: what do I really love to do? What's my passion? Why did I create midlife career changes now, what's the meaning of all this? And – how could I transform the challenge of changing careers in midlife, into a remarkable opportunity?

Why Is It Important?

Here are 10 Practical Reasons for Becoming a Midlife Entrepreneur:

1. You are healthy with many years ahead of you.
2. You want to stay involved and engaged.
3. You enjoy generating extra income.
4. You get to build a business around something you enjoy and are passionate about.
5. You have an extensive network of contacts and 20–30 years of experience to back you.
6. You want the independence and flexibility that comes from working for yourself.
7. You have confidence and experience and know what you are good at.
8. You may already have a pool of money saved to help finance your business.
9. You can do business from home, using the Internet as your storefront.
10. As an entrepreneur, you are not discriminated against because of your age.

Being Gentle with Yourself, as You Adjust

When in the midst of midlife career changes, make sure to be gentle with yourself. Your world has changed and your body and heart may need time to catch up. If you are actively seeking ideas, allow your imagination to expand, helping you tap into your intuition and easily recognize the new career that suits you.

It is possible that you may consider entrepreneurship and then decide to return to the career or profession that is familiar to you – or you may choose to completely reinvent yourself, become an entrepreneur, start a business from home or something in between.

Early in your transition, hold everything lightly and welcome the best outcome for you. Stay open to opportunities in every form.

To help you with the uncertainty that midlife career changes bring, I suggest that you surround yourself with positive people and ideas. Entrepreneurship may be the most exciting thing you've ever done: but it is not for the faint of heart.

Releasing the Security Myth

When I was part of the corporate culture, it was really easy to feel secure. I knew when the pay cheque was coming and when I'd have time off. When I went out on my own, I faced a different reality. I'd have weeks where my income was way higher than in corporate life. Then I'd have weeks and (ugh) even months without being paid. In order to adapt, I had to dig deep in my heart and redefine what I meant by security.

The truth is, we all have a tendency to 'want it now' and if you are looking at turning your midlife career changes into entrepreneurship, you will be faced with your own views on security. And, they may surprise you.

For you, is security a nine to five job? Or is security the peace in your heart you get from doing something you passionately love, knowing that all will be well?

The former is built on an illusion. The latter, you control and no one can ever take it away from you. When you get there, the feeling is unlike anything else.

Some Ideas to Cope

Here are some practical ideas for you to consider as you begin:

Flowing with the unexpected

One thing you should know. Your midlife career changes will go through a transition period where for a while, you may not be sure of your new direction. Or if you are sure, they may change or not feel as if your plans have 'legs,' solidly moving you forward.

Example: Though it ended up in exactly the right spot, the path was not a straight one…

Planning is no longer what it was

Are you a planner? Me too. But to get to the next stage of my midlife career changes and embrace my own business, I had to give some of that part of me up.

Sure, create some goals for next year if you are immersed in midlife career changes. But hold all of it lightly. For the transition period is both a creative and unsettling time, which may last many weeks or months before your new venture unfolds profitably.

Here Are Generic Tips for You

- Use midlife career changes as an excuse to do some research into areas that you find interesting. Expand your imagination. Notice those things that you've always found impractical yet loved. Notice when your heart expands and soars. Notice where you feel scared. It is all good.

- Consider meditation, or other stress-relieving techniques to maintain your energy. Meditation is also a way of increasing your intuition and recognizing opportunities as they come along (you'll need to be able to do this).

- Explore more about yourself (It is not just about midlife career changes: it is about your heart). You are changing. Who are you now? Re-take the Myers Briggs. Read 'What Colour is your Parachute?' Read 'Callings' by Gregg Levoy. Take a reflective retreat.

- Create a support group. If you have friends going through midlife career changes as well, meet for coffee once a week. Warning! If your friends are complainers – skip this step and fire your friends. Really.

- Read books you find inspirational. 'The Magic of Thinking Big' is quite good. Or read biographies of people that you admire (I really liked 'Steve Jobs: a biography'). Understand that your soul and intuition is tapped in directly now and that ideas will come in unexpected forms.

- Get connected online and put it out there that you are going through some midlife career changes and seeking the next opportunity. If you only pick one network, I'd recommend LinkedIn.

Recognizing Opportunities in Unexpected Packages

Sometimes during midlife career changes, we get stuck in how we 'think' things should look. The title, the job, the salary, the industry, the business model, how quickly our new clients should recognize our value and make us millionaires.

As you explore midlife career changes and the possibility of creating your own business, I encourage you to stay open to ideas and opportunities. Why? Because they may come in a package you did not expect. And – they could offer more than you could have imagined.

Stay open to the unexpected during midlife career change. Be prepared… to be surprised by serendipity. As unexpected opportunities make themselves known, check them out. Then, once you know your direction, take big, clear action. Revisit, re-assess often, while continuing to take action as new information comes in.

Lessons for Midlife Entrepreneurs

Assuming that you have a clear business goal and a solid plan, you will still face many challenges. And the pragmatic entrepreneur can overcome these hurdles by keeping a few points at the top of mind:

1. "It is never too late to be who you might have been"

These words of wisdom are from the English novelist George Eliot. I think Colonel Sanders would have agreed. At the age of 65, Sanders' business ventures had failed. His only assets were a $105 social security check, a Cadillac and a recipe for fried chicken. Rather than grab the beach chair, Sanders hit the road and sold his recipe to various greasy-spoon establishments. After years of washing up in rest areas and sleeping in his car, Sanders sold his franchise for millions. The lesson is obvious: it is never too late to start a new career.

2. Remember that you have the advantage

Older entrepreneurs often have deeper ideas based on experience and can better appreciate subtlety, nuance and opportunity. Their ideas often emerge not necessarily from their ability to re-imagine the world but from being able to see specifics. That is, older entrepreneurs can better find unfilled niches in their markets and have a better understanding of why certain processes are not efficient. The baby-boomer entrepreneur will often find that his or her ideas do not emerge whole cloth, but rather are a result of incremental experiments more commonly called 'experience.'

Do not forget that in your leadership toolbox you have years of experience, strong networks and a number of important skills. You know how to do certain tasks quicker and better than younger people.

3. Partner with young people

While IT-boomers may have good ideas with real value, they may often feel that the channels open to them to introduce, support and disseminate their ideas are blocked. They become trapped by inertia simply because they do not know how to get their ideas out there. They have the hard business skills, but they may not have a firm handle on emerging technologies and social media trends. Using Facebook, twitter and the like to drive your social life is one thing – using social media to drive your business is another entirely.

IT-boomer entrepreneurs should consider partnering with younger people who are knowledgeable about online branding, writing, advertising and design. Consider reaching out to local colleges for interns or even family members for help. While younger interns and employees can teach you technological skills, you can mentor them by sharing your experience.

4. Use the internet to test, assess and experiment

The pragmatic baby-boomer can easily start an online business these days without too many overheads. Even if you are selling physical products, there is no need to start a business with an actual brick and mortar location right away. You can experiment with your products or services before you commit to a lease or to a large marketing or advertising budget.

It is never too late to be an entrepreneur. As Colonel Sanders proved, the entrepreneurial game is not just for young college kids. It is for anyone that is patient enough to withstand adversity and fight for a good idea. As Sanders said, "Work is the basis for living. I'll never retire. A man will rust out quicker than he'll ever wear out. And I'll be darned if I'll ever rust out."

5. Getting a boost from a board

In 2013, Ravi knew he had the experience and connections to launch his Bangalore-based business, which offers a comprehensive single platform customer engagement and digital marketing tool. But after years working in one of the Top 5 global consulting companies, many of them in senior client-facing roles, he had to overcome the fear of prospecting for clients for a company no one had heard of.

"It was like, if you do not have a Dell behind you, who are you?" said Ravi. Prospects would say, "Who else is doing this?" and he could not give them examples.

But Ravi knew enough from his decades of experience to create a board of advisers, since they could help make connections that he could not. After pulling together a founder board, the business began to fly.

The Dark Side

Being the founder of a business is tough and lonely. The challenges it poses whether successful or not, are varied and take a steady toll on the person's emotional, social and overall mental well-being. Recent studies have shown an alarming rise in the levels of depression among entrepreneurs. While preparation and readiness discussed earlier prepares one for the life ahead, reality can be stark and a different ball game altogether. A lot like practicing your golf swing in the practice range versus the pressure of a real matchup on the club's premium green.

Investors and to a lesser degree, employees and clients are acutely aware of this and watch out for signs that could lead to a business impact or investment impact. Here are some of the things to watch out for and ways to deal with them:

The Cold, Hard Facts

No matter what you have heard from your friends with supernatural success stories, the odds of any venture succeeding in the marketplace are bleak.

About 25 percent of even funded startups fail during their first year and that percentage increases each year in the business's lifespan until by the tenth year, 71 percent of startups will have failed.

Success is highly dependant on both the type of industry and founder's experience level. The tech industry is the toughest to breakthrough, in fact, 90 percent of tech startups fail. But more than half of startups in other industries like finance, health, education, agriculture, services, wholesale and mining do not make it either.

Unfortunately, the reason most startups fail boils down to incompetence including lack of planning and no knowledge of financing. Unbalanced or lack of managerial experience remains the second most common reason for failure.

As an aspiring entrepreneur, you should be prepared for the worst. The way to deal with this is to train yourself to see failure as an opportunity in disguise.

You might experience failure, but it is how you respond that will have the final say in what comes of your endeavours. In many cases, failure can serve as a redirection, leading you to a new pursuit you would not have thought of otherwise.

Do not get caught in a trap of negativity. If you fail, get up and keep going.

Your Social Life Will Suffer

Entrepreneurs often site having relationship problems. While on the journey to growing a venture many report not having the room or mental capacity to be fully involved in the lives of others. Long hours are spent at the office, in fact, the office may even be home, so an entrepreneur never truly leaves work. Phone calls will demand to be answered around the clock.

Friends and family might not understand. You'll find yourself apologizing for being unable to breakaway. It will be a continuous tug-o-war between your personal life and career endeavours.

But, you might have a personality that can handle it.

Interesting research from the University of Stockholm and the University at Jena found, as children, entrepreneurs exhibited certain behavioural tendencies. These children had a higher tendency to break rules, disobey their parents, cheat at school and even use drugs. This suggests that those who have a little rebellion in their hearts might be more cut out for the entrepreneurial world than the rest. The way to deal with this is to surround yourself with supportive people.

Your all-encompassing career endeavours might take a toll on your relationships, but with the right people in your life, your relationships will be strong enough to withstand even the most disastrous days.

Choose supportive people to invest what little time you have in. You'll know they are supportive when they show compassion and understanding when your plans change quickly. Dark times may tempt you to isolate yourself, but do not. Those are the times when you need to reach out to your friends and family most. If they truly belong in your life, they will be there to break your fall.

Neglecting Your Health

It is no secret that stress has hard effects on your health. Stress is even causing 43 percent of Americans to lie awake at night – leading to lack of sleep, according to a survey – which causes even more stress, 45 percent say. Thirty-nine percent of respondents said they have skipped exercise because they felt stressed. Though, 32 percent say they feel less stressed after exercising.

The health of a startup founder can go downhill fast. Lack of time due to long hours means less healthy eating choices, too. A study from the American Journal of Epidemiology shows that combinations of poor diets, stress and high blood pressure due to long work hours may be the cause of many workers' health problems. This can be managed by taking frequent breaks.

Counterintuitive as it may seem, taking breaks actually helps improve productivity. It is easy to want to breathe every last breath of your life to help your business venture take off. But, before anything else, you and your health need to come first. Otherwise, you might burn out and be incapable of taking care of the business long-term.

Every couple of hours, step away. Take a walk, go out for lunch, see a movie or meet up with a friend and for an hour talk about anything other than work. You'll slowly begin to feel more balanced.

The Most Important Thing: Do not Define Yourself by Your Business

I have seen several business owners lose their identity in their business and just like anything in this world you can place your identity in, it failed them. Their career was their whole life, their whole world. Do not let anything as fickle as the economic market define your life.

You, just yourself, have an intelligent mind with an abundance of ideas. You have access to networks and communities of people who can help you pursue any endeavour you wish and you can help them too. Us forward-thinking, passionate, entrepreneurial-minded folks are creators, but we are not defined by what we create.

Personal Branding & Networking

Investors ultimately back the person and bet on the team to execute. With that fact it is imperative that your personal brand be built and protected at all costs. This coupled with careful networking will pay more dividends in finding matched investors and save you months of wandering.

Power of Networking

This is one of the most essential personal skills for business people, but it is extremely important for entrepreneurs. Communication and strong presence in the entrepreneurial ecosystem are productive approaches which will help you along your way to building strong relationships with other entrepreneurs from different age groups, nationality and fields of interest.

Business networking events organized around the world bring together extraordinary groups of highly-skilled and talented entrepreneurs who are united around the idea of communication, sharing, creating and developing ideas and last but not the least, meeting with potential investors. These events attract people from different experience levels and backgrounds. All these people are looking for connection, inspiration, advice, opportunities and mentors.

Networking is powerful in many different ways. Not only entrepreneurs will feel inspired and motivated after attending specific events or meet ups, but also many exceptional opportunities can occur if they impress potential investors or business partners. Do not forget to be yourself and present your company the way you want other people to see it in order to create honest fundamentals for one potential business relationship.

Approach the networking as any other part of your business. Create a plan with specific goals that you need to follow. Know when, where and why you are going to an event, what your goals are and what do you want to achieve with your attendance to this particular meet up. As an entrepreneur your time is very important and you must have clear vision of what you are going to spend it on. Cautiously select your options and choose the one that will bring the most advantages to your business. It is widely known that connections come as a result of other connections and as usual the hardest part of the whole network-building process is the start.

In order to impersonate your business and yourself it is not enough just to be present, you need to be active, memorable, to provide value to others with your presence and to make them want to stay in touch with you. Be ready to impress, to be remembered and desirable for future business relations.

Once you meet the people you wanted to establish relationship with, keep this connection going after the event. Stay in touch and manage to continue the actual communication which will be foundation for your strong relationship and network.

Do not underestimate the power of local networking and attend networking events and meet ups around you. Knowing the local community has great advantage and you never know where the next big chance or inspiration will come from.

In the era of communication, it is unnatural to limit yourself by staying solely local, even if your business is devoted to the local community. Attending international meetings and reaching out to people from around the world will expand your vision and improve your business approach. Meeting other entrepreneurs, angel investors, bloggers and all other business enthusiasts will inspire you to reach for your personal improvement.

It does not matter which part of the world you come from, if you share the spirit of entrepreneurship you are most likely to be very welcome to attend different network events. Knowing your business and goals you have various opportunities to attend different events, by choosing from casual groups to highly professional associations. Never forget that successful, strong connections are built when your tools meet your right interlocutor. Pick your approaches according to the type of event you are attending. Choosing a casual behaviour can be just fine for local network events, but joining and being part of specific association is a difficult task and you need to put more effort to it.

Online networking for business is a great way to use the power of the internet. While you need to list your attendance to different events far ahead in the upcoming schedules, you have the opportunity to stay connected and build strong network online. Your business is unique, so be sure that you are able to present your uniqueness online as good as offline.

Leveraging Personal Branding

An essential part of developing a personal brand is mustering the boldness to discover and express authentically who you are and own it.

Listed below are a few of my favourite examples of people who have created impeccable personal brands:

Virgin CEO Richard Branson said, "Branding demands commitment; commitment to continual re-invention; striking chords with people to stir their emotions and commitment to imagination. It is easy to be cynical about such things, much harder to be successful."

The type of boldness we are referring to is born out of courage, hard work, blood, sweat and tears, and a complete acceptance of who you are, what you stand for and what you are willing to do about it. Your brand will be comprised of mistakes and successes that are publicly known and privately kept.

Are you open to the concept that your personal brand could be great?

Not pompous, egocentric or arrogant, but truly great at what you believe in and do each day. An individual who personified this ideal was Dr. Stephen R. Covey.

People who had the opportunity to work with him up close and personal say how just like all of us, he experienced days in his life when nothing seemed to go right. People judged unnecessarily, threw stones in the form of gossip and insults and he simply rose above it. Part of his personal brand was an extraordinary ability to offer unconditional kindness because it was truly in the marrow of his bones. Stephen was approachable, open, humble, grateful, giving, forgiving and so much more.

As individuals develop, not every day will be a walk in the park. When I have a challenging day, I simply rise above it. I have not nailed it yet, but it is a piece of my personal brand and that is the best part about your personal brand. You get to choose!

Decide today who you want to become and then start creating your personal brand.

Why Does Developing Your Personal Brand Matter?

Social media has rewritten the rules of work and blurred the lines between personal and professional brands. An authentic exercise in defining, developing and communicating your personal brand will likely make you uncomfortable. Recognize this is as a good sign.

Ten years ago we were taught to be masters at cultivating the professional aspect of business, following the rules and creating linear businesses. Anything personal was strongly discouraged. You did not show emotion at work. You were strongly encouraged to leave your personal brand at the door prior to entering.

The game of work has evolved, yet one thing that did not change, is we can all go back to the basics, which are: define, develop, communicate and be open to input.

We can learn from feedback. We do not need to accept or incorporate it all into who we are becoming. I have always felt that those who care for me the most will be my toughest critics and they deliver their feedback in a way that I want to receive through their true kindness and desire to help me become the man I want to be known as.

Define

We live in a world that requires us to grow in ways not required of our predecessors. Your personal brand is your personal best and worst. We define who we are.

"Your brand is what people say about you when you are not in the room," said Amazon founder Jeff Bezos. You can learn a lot about people's personal brands when they are talking about other people in the room. This is an interesting paradox.

Your personal brand is like the wake behind a boat. It comes as the natural result of you moving forward. The best place to begin developing your personal brand is to figure out what you are not.

Bezos is a master at this. I was surprised to discover that the original name for Amazon was "Cadabra" and that Bezos changed the name because it sounded too similar to "cadaver."

Bezos searched through words starting with the letter A in the dictionary (so his company would show up at the top of the list) and selected "Amazon." The Amazon River is the biggest river in the world, which suited Bezos's idea for his company perfectly. By figuring out what he was not, his unique and extraordinary personal brand was born.

Develop

Defining your personal brand involves revealing to the world who you are and what you stand for. It is liberating. The liberation comes because it is what you have chosen to become, not what your environment has dictated. As you grow and evolve, expect your personal brand to develop, too.

Communicate

Joe Woodard, CEO and founder of Woodard Consulting, is an example of an entrepreneur who effectively communicates his brand.

He helps people feel uplifted, energized and inspired. He created the highly successful Scaling New Heights conference. It is how his personal brand shows up in the world.

Our personal brand is revealed every day in our work and life. Joe's personal brand closely matches who he is in real life. He is personable, friendly, a guru on his subject matter (accounting and QuickBooks) and a born teacher. He is regularly listed as one of the top 100 most influential accountants in America and his Scaling New Heights conference has grown to include nearly 1,000 consultants.

You can be great at this one thing: Be true to yourself. I am just beginning to understand what this means to me and NOT what it means from others. Once mastered, perhaps it becomes a bit easier to honour the truth in others. Your brand will follow.

Putting It All Together

Preparing to be a founder of a business is as difficult and requires as much preparation as preparing to be a first time parent, if not more. The key question is, what can you do in six to eight weeks to be more "ready" to start a startup? So you have completed an assessment of yourself objectively and dispassionately, with the help of feedback from others and the occasional psychometric tool. So, what do you do with this mass of data and how do you internalize it. Here is how you can approach it in a short six to eight weeks.

Mindsets Trump Skills

It is very hard to materially improve your hard skills in eight weeks. But that does not matter. Marginal improvements in skill are totally eclipsed by marginal improvements in *mindset*. Mindset appears to be almost totally dominant in determining outcomes.

This is good news for aspiring founders because you can develop new mindsets more quickly than you can develop (high levels of) new skills. I think there are five mindsets in particular that entrepreneurs need to develop: long-termism, growth mindset, competitiveness, personal exceptionalism and honey badger-ness.

Long-termism

It is taking longer and longer for startups to exit. If it takes 10 years to IPO (or equivalent), you need to ask what you can do for that length of time and stay excited — or atleast sane.

Realistically, that means you need to be driven by a mission. This idea—"you need to be a missionary, not a mercenary"—is perhaps a cliche in Silicon Valley, but not repeated anything like often enough in Asia. Almost all the breakout companies have missionary founders.

So, what could you spend a decade on? I do not think you can answer that in terms of product (too much will change), but you can in terms of a problem you want to solve; perhaps a technology you want to bring to the world or a group of customers you want to serve.

It amazes me how many founders do not spend a long time thinking about this or at least do not commit to their answers, before they start a company. This is an area where you cannot be willing to compromise.

A client of mine, who has been most willing to commit to the long run has been among the most successful. In his words: "I mean, I figure I'll just build a $1 million dollar company first. That way, it'll be easier to build the $100 million company I have been thinking about."

Growth Mindset

It is undoubtedly one of the most important mindsets for founders. In the words of its most prominent proponent, growth mindset is that "people believe that their most basic abilities can be developed through dedication and hard work—brains and talent are just the starting point" (Its opposite, fixed mindset, believes that ability is largely set and cannot be changed through effort).

There are two reasons why this matters so much for entrepreneurs. First, a growth mindset allows founders to take more risk. If you have a fixed mindset, you end up interpreting failure (or even wobbles along the journey) as an indictment of your abilities and so your sense of self-worth. This makes it hard to take risk: the costs of failure are so much psychologically higher than if you see working harder as the appropriate response to failure, which is what a growth mindset suggests. Second, founders with a growth mindset learn faster — not least because they value learning more. If you know that you will not only know more, but actually become better when you iterate, you are likely to iterate faster.

Competitiveness

Great founders are highly competitive—and they have to be. Startups are a battle for survival from day one; none has a right to exist. Some founders would be more successful if they realised just what a fight they were in: they would work harder, they would be more relentless, they would be more creative. The problem is that most of the competition you face is *unseen*.

By that I do not just mean the classic, "we have no competitors" line. There probably *is* someone, somewhere trying to do what you do.. But that is not the bad news. The *real* competition that you are in is a race against time — to prove that you are creating something valuable before you run out of money or willpower.

The trouble is, seen competition is really easy to respond to — and it fires founders up — but unseen competition is far more dangerous. If you do not behave as though you had a well-funded competitor sitting right next to you, you'll find it difficult to struggle hard enough. You have to work as determinedly and relentlessly as though they were based in the very next office and you caught sight of them every day, looking smug, in the local cafe. That is the reality that you are in and believing it is a mindset you need to develop.

Personal Exceptionalism

I love Michael Dearing's notes on The Five Cognitive Distortions of People Who Get Things Done. It is not a scientific study (and does not claim to be), but it is an excellent qualitative summary of the mindsets of successful people. First among them is "personal exceptionalism." A good definition is the mindset where you know the odds of success are extraordinarily low, but you believe that they do not apply to you. Or, rather, you believe that conditional on being you, the odds are much better.

Working closely with over 200 founders over the last five years, I have reached the conclusion that you'll never be surprised if you believe you cannot do it. Never. (Unfortunately, you might be surprised if you think you *can*, which is what makes it hard). That does not mean that you will not or should not experience self-doubt. Personal exceptionalism is not insanity or even arrogance. It is a deep belief that you will find a way.

Even more, it is a mindset that allows you to process the inevitable negative feedback you will get as a founder. Throughout the entrepreneurial journey, you will have meetings with people who think you are crazy and that you are wasting your time (and possibly other people's money). It is normal to walk out of those meetings and worry that they are right. What a mindset of personal exceptionalism allows you to do is take the feedback and iterate, again and again, without losing faith that you are going to succeed.

Honey Badger-ness

The honey badger is an interesting animal. Honey badgers are the most tenacious, fearless and relentless animals. They are impossible to cage; they kill lions by running under them and biting their testicles off; and—yes—they eat cobras.

Entrepreneurs have to be honey badgers. Honey badgers are the opposite of excuse makers. If you find yourself reaching for an excuse, you are doomed to fail. If you tell yourself that something is impossible because "the key guy is on holiday until next week," "I could not get hold of anyone," "no one replied to my email," etc., well—you need to be more of a honey badger. When people say, "it is impossible," investors now usually think, "Yes, it probably is impossible for you."

It is striking to me how much "honey badger"-ness explains the difference in outcomes among EF companies. In practice, this means that you have to find a way to expand your comfort zone. Small comfort zones are fatal for founders. If you've never made a cold call; if you have never tried to get someone to do something they were not inclined to do; if you have never tried to sell anything, now is the time. If you have tried all those things, what makes you uncomfortable? That is what you should be working on.

When people take this to heart, the results can be extraordinary. One favourite example is a startup whose founders hung around outside their (enterprise) customer's offices until they figured out which pub the key decision maker went to after work and then cold approached him in the pub, bought him a drink and convinced him to trial the product. It was a breakthrough for them. Without it, they would have been months and months behind. Another startup with better product, better tech or a better story would have lost out to them, simply because they were great honey badgers.

As a founder, you have more control over your mindsets than you do over almost any other variable that will have a big impact on your outcome. Time spent in developing the right ones is the best investment you can make as you prepare to get started. Time to get started.

Conclusion: Personal Readiness

Successful entrepreneurs continuously iterate & adapt to the external business environment, ones who are not internally ready, are like pilots learning to fly a plane in mid-air.

There is no point getting on to the stage as an actor without preparation for the role. The audience (aka investors, employees and clients) will see right through it within days. An honest and objective self-assessment is the key to readiness for this phase of life. It is obvious that there are certain skills that you must possess as an entrepreneur or at the very least have it in your founders group. These are widely recognized as the ability to sell, to manage cash and to solve problems. On the mental side the ability to soak pressure, deal with variability and continuously evolve is paramount. So here are the takeaways from this section:

- Declutter your life, make time and get physically and emotionally ready for this phase
- Conduct a self-assessment on various aspects of your personality, skills and mental make up
- Use external help in terms of psychometric tools and feedback from others
- Give yourself time for the assessment and actions that will lead to modifications in your behaviour and thought process
- Prepare your friends and family for this phase
- Speak to as many entrepreneurs and investors as possible
- Try and work or consult for a startup
- Take up meditation or anything else that allows you to purge and cleanse emotionally
- Pay close attention to your personal brand and build it assiduously
- Network like crazy

Patience is a virtue. Be patient. Raising outside capital almost always takes longer than the entrepreneur wishes. The typical equity fundraising process usually lasts up to about six months, but can take much longer, particularly if your company is still in the start-up stage and lacks a track-record of meeting its financial goals.

You must be mentally prepared for a long and winding negotiating road paved with rejection. There will be countless economic, legal, and emotional hurdles that you will have to overcome to get the best deal for your business.

Remember that you have chosen this path for a purpose and that requires changes on your part. You have chosen to step forward and create an identity for yourself and that means you will always be held to a higher standard. The ability to successfully cope for the life you have dreamed of, can only be honed by creating a foundation of readiness for that desired life. Later, will be too late.

PART II
Company Readiness

"The most difficult problems lead to the greatest insights; but often in hindsight"

Overview: Getting The Business Ready

There is an iconic scene in a Govinda (Indian Leading Actor) movie called Hero No. 1. In this scene Govinda is late for work and in an attempt to make it on time, he is using the car as a washroom and walk in closet, to get ready. I cannot help but relate it, to the way most startups prepare for funding. Last minute, rush job with patchwork showing all over, reflecting poorly on the state of the business and the founders' business acumen in general. Most companies and ideas deserve better.

More businesses are prioritising growth – 62 per cent of mid-sized firms viewed it as a high priority in 2015–16, up from 46 per cent the previous year. External investment is often key to that growth.

External investment supports expansion plans, helps grow extra workforce capacity and helps businesses develop and market new products, enter new markets or move to larger premises. Whatever that extra finance is used for, businesses that continue to flourish need further funds for the likes of an acquisition or the creation of a complementary company.

More prosaically, businesses need access to external investment to ensure cash flow. A mistake that has proved fatal for many businesses is having insufficient operating funds. Business owners may underestimate how much money is needed or may have an unrealistic expectation of revenues from sales. Access to the right types of finance is vital to a business' success, according to the Confederation of British Industry (CBI). Yet difficulty in accessing trade finance can and is holding businesses back.

The CBI claimed access to trade finance is becoming increasingly difficult for some markets. In a survey of global trade finance providers, it was found that found 69 per cent of respondents cited anti-money laundering and 'know your customer' requirements as a highly significant impediment to trade finance. Some 59 per cent cited issuing banks' low credit ratings as a highly significant impediment to trade finance.

Entrepreneurs find it incredibly difficult and emotionally draining to accept, that they need to continuously prepare and market themselves for the next phase of growth. With a ninety percent failure rate in early stage startups in the first few years, it is important to understand the reasons behind the failures. A laundry list of reasons and research into them broadly leads to two conclusions. Startups fail because of the founders' incompetence and/or inability to get funded on time. Seeking funding is a full-time job and most founders fail to accept this. This lack of acceptance leads to the poor preparation and groundwork that is so essential before putting the company in front of potential investors.

Think of the time when you were buying a new car and were selling your old car or motorcycle. Did you not prepare the vehicle for sale to get an optimal price? Yet was there not a gap between what you thought you should receive (Emotional perceived pricing) and what the buyer thought it was worth (risk assessed reality)? This is similar to getting your business funded, only amplified multiple times as there is often no hard asset or collateral.

With the first step of getting ready as an individual, taken care of. Now is the time to get your company ready. Whether you are a startup, a SME or a large sized running enterprise; the process and principle remains the same. The scale and extent of preparation may differ slightly based on how much money you are seeking or/and from whom you are seeking it. For example, if you are raising money from family and friends, the level of scrutiny may be less intense as there is a base level of trust and familiarity. However, if you are raising money from strangers or a very large amount, then the scrutiny is like to be intense. Much like what you would exercise if you went to purchase a toy house for your kid versus a real one for yourself.

Another way to look at this is to think of the days you were dating or used a matrimonial site to get married. How did you prepare before you put yourself out there? Why should your company require any less preparation? If anything, it needs more. The ten aspects that you need to look at objectively and prepare for are:

- Legal structure of your company
- Status of your product/service
- Team
- Business plan
- Processes

- Market size & overview of the opportunity
- Competitive landscape
- Past financials and future projections
- Statutory compliances
- Governance

Here are a few pointers to keep in mind for the preparation process:

- Treat the opportunity to prepare for an investor as a reset mechanism for the way you look at your business and an opportunity for improvement, in general. Do it for yourself, not just the investor. It is like spring cleaning of your house for an important house guest. Long after the house guest is gone, the family feels good, reaps the benefits and often it leads to longer term behavioural changes, for the better.

- Even if your business does not seem to require external investment right now, it is good practice to prepare for that eventuality. Businesses that have done the leg work necessary to approach investors and win additional finance are far more resilient in the face of unexpected market changes. With a solid portfolio of options for sourcing finance, businesses may be more flexible, innovative and responsive to opportunities for growth and success.

- A key question we ask our clients is "What does success mean to you?" The answer can change over time as personal and business circumstances change, so it is important to ask this question on a regular basis. However, most business owners plan on exiting their business one day, hoping to achieve the maximum possible valuation when that day comes. If you are starting to think about exiting your business, it is usually best to start the planning and preparation at the earliest possible time.

- Small enterprises face perennial challenges in attracting funding. They not only suffer from credibility issues when trying to attract outside capital, but also endure endless internal issues. You have been running a business for a while, but you now need to get external capital into the business. This money can be in the form of loans or you now are contemplating bringing new shareholders into your business.

- How can you as an entrepreneur position your business to attract these potential financial backers? Why is it important to consider bringing in new funds and how can this be done?

- There will likely come a point in time when your company undergoes changes at an exponential rate and you consider additional resources to continue building your business. Adequately scaling your business and enduring hyper-growth are not obstacles all entrepreneurs may encounter, of course, but if there is potential for momentum to be gained, you do not want to miss out on the opportunity.

- It is important to note that while opening up your business to outside investors, increases the level of oversight over its financial affairs and can improve accountability and performance, however, most small business owners are not comfortable to have somebody else scrutinise their business affairs. There is a loss of control as a principal founder. This is despite the fact that experience shows that such businesses tend to be better-run because of the additional accountability.

- The decision to bring outside investors into your company will be one of the most important decisions of your life. Raising money through angel investors, private equity or venture capital can put you on a path to great expansion and market share. Against that, you must weigh the loss of control you will incur and the increase in oversight you will most certainly experience. Still, for many companies—particularly those with serious growth ambitions—outside funding is a necessary precondition for success. So how can you prepare your business so that it will be attractive to potential investors?

While there is nothing called the "perfect company" and investors know that as well, it is all about the trade off between risk, opportunity and the investor play available, at a particular point in time. Anticipate the due diligence that investors will expect to undertake and get prepared, so that you are credible to a potential investor. Let us look at each aspect (in no particular order). In Part 3 we will look at the relative order of importance from an investor's perspective.

Legal Structure: Pick the Right Company Formation

Companies can form many types of business entities. From simplified sole proprietorships, to complicated corporations, your options run the gamut when starting up. But for those companies looking to bring in equity funding, only a few types of business entities work best.

In cases where you are funding your own business or taking in capital from a close group of investors, structuring your business as a limited liability company (LLC in the US, Private Limited in India, PTE in Singapore or PT in Indonesia) is a good option. LLCs enjoy the liability protection of corporations while avoiding the double-taxation associated with C corporations in the US and akin to Public Limited Companies elsewhere, wherein shareholders pay taxes on both annual earnings and dividends. Taxation rules in individual countries will differ.

However, if you are raising capital from outside investors, you should probably structure your company as a Corporation/Public Limited. This enables companies to have multiple classes of stock (i.e. preferred and common), allow incentivized option plans and are the industry standard from a corporate-law perspective. Sophisticated investors and their legal teams rely on the predictability of public limited companies, which have a much longer history of case law than LLCs or other types of companies. This is what makes them the ideal organizations for equity investors.

A legal structure is the framework and basis on which the company operates in a particular geography. It is very difficult to get funded in a proprietorship or a pure partnership. Professional investors (non-family & friends) look for at least a Limited Liability Partnership (where applicable) and ideally an incorporated Private Limited Company. If you do not have this, then more than likely they will ask you to convert your company to one that suits them. Depending on the tax residency and other considerations, of the investor, you may be asked to open an entity in another country and make your company a subsidiary of the new foreign country. Investors use this method for tax efficiency and/or for better legal recourse in their home country.

Simply filing articles of incorporation with your local authority does not make your company a duly-formed corporation. Your company must take additional steps, depending on the laws of incorporation for your particular country and state. These can include appointing a board of directors, adopting corporate bylaws, issuing stock to shareholders and obtaining an Employer Identification Number, a tax account number and so on. Without these steps, your company may not be a duly incorporated Corporation.

Product Readiness: Status of your Product/Service

How ready is your product or service (In this section read product to mean product and/or service)? Depending on the stage it is at you will have to think of some or all of the following:

- If it is at an idea stage then be sure to document the idea and articulate the vision for the product. More specifically what it solves, which will compel consumers to pay for it. You should also be able to articulate a plan to build the product with the skills, tools and technology required. Any patent/trademark or copyright opportunities should be identified.

- If your product is at a proto type stage then apart from the above, you will need to be able to demonstrate the working parts and simulate real time transactions/processes. Any learning from the development stage should be captured and be available in a documented form. Field trials, sample testing, client user experiences should be captured and be readily available. If there is a patent/copyright or trademark opportunity, it should be in sight and paper work being worked upon.

- If the product is already released in the market, then apart from the two points above, you should be able to prove market traction. It could be in a limited scaling unit (pilot) of geography, gender, industry, demography etc. The metrics related to customer acquisition cost, lifetime value of a customer, time to acquire customers, customer retention rate, customer feedback, customer growth rate, product fail rates etc. should be documented and available.

- If there is a patent/copyright or trademark opportunity, it should be applied for. All test reports and documentation of the product specifications, user manuals, product architecture, product build methodology etc. should be available.

- The vision for the product in the form of a product road map should be available. This should outline the future developments and features to be added.

- Do You Own Your IP? You might think this is an easy question to answer – of course you own your IP, right? Maybe, maybe not. If, like many startups, you've worked with independent contractors who have done programming work or similar types of creative work, those workers might have a claim to ownership over the products they've created if there was no invention assignment agreement in place. In addition, if you moonlighted for your startup while working at another employer with which you do have an invention assignment agreement, your employer may also have a claim to ownership of your IP. Any potential investor might discover this in due diligence and demand that these issues be addressed, or worse, may simply pass over your company. It is better to avoid such questions and concerns at the outset and make sure that these kinds of issues are thought through and dealt with.

The Team

Hire the right people. Building the right team is crucial for the growth and success of your business as the people you hire can either help or hinder the development of your company. Factor in the amount of time it takes to train someone, their ambition levels, background, etc. Keep in mind that while experience is important, are they ready to roll with the punches that come with a business gaining traction at rapid speed? All successful businesses have a common element: people who are 110% dedicated and committed to seeing the company prosper. It is particularly vital to have dependable team members for support during hyper-growth.

This is often more important when you are seeking investment (as opposed to an acquisition). Investors feel more confident working with someone who has a proven track record. If this is your first investment round and/or your business is relatively new, having a strong background and pedigree is particularly important (even if that background is in a different industry). The pedigree and skillset of the owner is sometimes the key determining factor for an investor.

Have qualified leadership in your business. Company leadership is one of the greatest concerns of most financiers. Bankers and buyers of equity in your business will worry about the quality of management in your business.

If you are selling out completely and are not going to be part of the future of the business, any new investor or lenders would want to have confidence in those who are going to remain behind managing the business.

The ideal scenario is that your business should be able to grow and flourish even without you being there. Take care to ensure the following:

- Key positions have appropriate leadership. For example:, not having a CTO in a technology company or a Marketing Head in a B 2 C company is an obvious no no. Other positions that are critical are those of a CFO & HR Head, of course, depending on the type of business and affordability. While the critical positions must be filled, the supporting ones should be identified and planned for.

- Ensure there are signed employment contracts for all employees including the founders. These should be backed with personal files containing backup forms and data, including that for the founders.
- If there are family members in the team, identify them and articulate their future roles. Often family members come into the business initially and then ease out as professionals come in to take specialized roles.
- While everyone pretty much does everything at an early stage startup, it makes sense to have an organization chart with roles and responsibilities.

Business Plan: A Simpler Plan for Startups

A business plan is a draft of your business goals, reasons they are attainable, and plans for reaching them. Preparing a business plan is one of the first things that you should do as a founder. An accurate, easy-to-read, and well-organized business plan conveys professionalism and credibility. Although it takes a while to do all your due diligence to craft the perfect formal business plan, it is essential that you go through the process for your own clarity than just for an investor.

For a startup business, creating a business plan is like creating a game plan in sports. You need to scout out all the information to create a winning strategy for the game. While business plans for existing companies may have a special focus, such as setting overall goals, reviewing specific operations, evaluating new products, assessing new technology in the industry, or some other specific purpose. The business plan for a startup company is the blueprint for its formation, its operation, and its success. A business plan exposes a new company's strengths and weaknesses. It reveals ways to capitalize on the strengths and minimize the weaknesses, uncovers every facet of the business that can be developed, and points to the best method for development. It provides a structure for the company's pursuit of the winner's trophy.

Even though creating a business plan takes time, thought and effort, and may seem like an impediment to getting on with opening or growing your new business, it is imperative in today's competitive business climate for you to have all relative information available and evaluated before opening your doors. With a thoughtfully prepared business plan you will enter the business world prepared, ready to run your business and ready to compete.

Although researching and writing your business plan may seem like a monumental task, with preparation it can be quite painless. As you go through the process, you will develop your knowledge and understanding of your business, improve your chances of success, and diminish your risks of failure as a startup owner.

Prior to writing your business plan, there are several issues you must resolve. A basic checklist is provided, so you can explore some of the subjects more thoroughly. As an entrepreneur of a startup company:

- Business advisors, experienced entrepreneurs, bankers, and investors generally agree that you should develop a business plan before you start a business. A plan can help you move forward, make decisions, and make your business successful. However, not all business plans are the same, not every business needs the same level of detail. One could argue that some businesses at a very early stage do not need a plan at all. Definitely one that goes beyond a few months.

- It is important to understand that a business plan is not cast in stone and neither is there an expectation for you to come good like an astrologer. It is a document that helps you and the leadership (foremost) to provide clarity on the strategy, chosen path and other possible variables. For an investor (secondary) it provides an insight into your thinking, planning, understanding of the business environment and ability to foresee/plan for risks.

How Mature a Plan Do You Need?

You might develop a fairly simple business plan first as you start a small business, and that might be enough for you. You can also start simple and then elaborate as you prepare to approach bankers or investors.

For a simple business plan example, imagine a woman making sweaters at home and selling it at a local flea market on the weekend. A business plan could give her a chance to step back from the normal flow and look at ways to develop and improve the business.

The planning process should help her understand her business. It should help her define what she wants from the business, understand what her customers want, and decide how to optimize her business on her own terms. She might benefit from developing a simple sales and expense forecast, maybe even a profit and loss, so she can plan how to use and develop her resources. She might not need to create detailed cash flow, balance sheet, and business ratios. A simple business plan may be just what she needs to get going. One that takes into account how she will service clients, time she will need to get goods to the market, in short a basic strategy.

This first stage of a plan, focuses only on a few starter elements. The mission statement, problem you are solving for your customers, your solution, and market analysis, give you a critical head start toward understanding your business.

However, not all startups are that simple. Many of them need product development, packaging, retail fittings and signage, office equipment, websites, and sometimes months or even years of payroll before the sales start. Unless you are wealthy enough to finance these expenditures on your own, then you will need to deal with bank loans or investors or both; and for that you will need a more extensive business plan. Startup company or not, the plan has to meet expectations.

What Kind of Plan Do You Need?

One suggestion for getting started is to develop your plan in stages that meet your real business needs. A few key topics might be enough to discuss the plan with potential partners and team members, as a first phase. You may well want to add a basic sales and expense forecast, leading to profit and loss, as the next phase. Adding business numbers helps you predict business flow and match spending to income.

Ultimately, the choice of plan is not based as much on the stage of business as it is on the type of business, financing requirements, and business objective. Here are some important indicators of the level of plan you will need, even as a startup:

- Some of the simpler businesses keep a plan in the head of the owner, but every business has a plan. Even a one-person business can benefit from creating a plan document with ideas written down, because the process of producing a plan is useful and valuable.
- As soon as a second person is involved, the need for planning multiplies. The plan is critical for communicating values, goals, strategies, and detailed implementation.
- As soon as anybody outside the company is involved, then you have to provide more information. When a plan is for internal use only, you may not need to describe company history and product features, for example. Stick to the topics that add value, that make you think, that help support decisions. When you involve people outside the

company, then you need to provide more background information as part of the plan.

- For discussion purposes, text is enough to get a plan started. Try describing your mission, objective, keys to success, target market, competitive advantage, and basic strategies. How well does this cover your business idea?

- Can you live without a sales and expense forecast? Sometimes the one-person business keeps numbers in the owner's head. However, it is much easier to use some tools that can put the numbers in front of you, and add and subtract them automatically. That is where a plan helps.

- Do you really know your market? A good market analysis can help you see opportunities that might not otherwise be obvious. Understand why people buy from you. What are the needs being served? How many people are out there, as potential customers?

- Do you manage significant amounts of inventory? That makes your cash management more complicated, and usually requires a more sophisticated plan. You need to buy inventory before you sell it.

- Do you sell on credit? If you are a business selling to businesses, then you probably do have to sell on credit, and that normally means you have to manage money owed to you by your customers, called accounts receivable. Making the sale is no longer the same thing as getting the money. That usually requires a more sophisticated plan.

- Do you do your taxes on a cash basis, or accrual basis? If you do not know, and you are a very small (one person, maybe 2–3 people) business, then you are likely to be on a cash basis. That makes your planning easier. However, most businesses big enough to work with a CPA and have separate tax statements use accrual accounting because they want to deduct expenses as they are incurred, even if they are not fully paid for. By the time you are using accrual accounting, you will probably need more sophisticated cash flow tools, and a more extensive business plan.

- As you approach banks and other lending institutions, expect to provide more detail on personal net worth, collateral, and your business' financial position. Some banks will accept a very superficial business plan as long as the collateral looks good. Others will demand to see detailed monthly projections. No investor can lend money on a business plan alone; that would be against banking law. A good bank wants to see a good plan.

- If you are looking for venture investment, take a good look at your plan. Professional investors will expect your plan to provide proof, not just promises. They will want to see market data, competitive advantage, and management track records. They will want to see robust and comprehensive financial projections. True, you will hear stories about investors backing new companies without a plan, but those are the exceptions, not the rule.

So, however you cut it, your business plan is very important, even at the early startup stage and even if you can keep it in your head. Before you purchase business stationery, telephones or rent a location, you should have a business plan

Purpose

While preparing your business plan, it is very important to understand three things:

1. **What**: What problem does your startup solve or what market needs does it cater to?
2. **Why**: Why should people pay for this product/service?
3. **How**: How does this business make money or plan to make money?

It is critical that as a founder you take time to identify and articulate their business's core values and purpose, which will serve as your startup's compass for decision making at all levels.

Vision

The success of any startup is determined by the clarity of their vision about what you want to achieve in the long run. While it is difficult and not always possible for a startup to have long-term vision at a very early stage, it is imperative to understand where you are headed and evolve as your company evolves. While drafting your business plan, you have to develop strategies on how you are going to realize this vision.

Business Model

A good business plan always includes financial projections for the next few years. But before you can figure out facts and figures, you will need to work through potential scenarios to make sure your business model is going to work. You need to include details of hiring, pricing, sales, cost of acquisition, expenses, growth, etc.

Analysis of Feasibility

You will need to come up with a few hypotheses and test out different monetization avenues. Udyamita Samachar, is the perfect example to understand this concept. Udyamita Samachar provides curated entrepreneurship content to the vernacular audience. According to their research, the way the vernacular population consumes business information on the Internet is vastly different from the rest of the world. Most of the quality content is in English; it is technical and not specifically targeted for the local audience. Udyamita Samachar bridges the gap by developing quality content specifically targeted towards the vernacular audience, helping them understand their options and make better decisions about their careers and business. They studied what mainstream content-driven websites that provided content in English were doing. Then, they tested the feasibility of their business by talking to people at the ground level, in startup events and with investors and understanding how they engage. Although it is good to have spent hours in front of the computer, at some point you should go out and talk to industry experts, potential customers and other entrepreneurs to determine the feasibility of your business idea.

Here is a road map of what your business plan should look like.

- Executive Summary: Summarize the elements of your business.
- Describe your Startup: Introduce the reader to your company and your business concept.
- Industry Analysis: Provide a picture of your industry and how your business is positioned within this framework.
- Market and Competition: Evaluate what you are getting into. Know how your customers are segmented and who the target market is. Understand how you can offer more value than the competition. An analysis of both of these together will help in explaining your market share.

- Strategies and Goals: Analyze the market and your competition in order to determine how and where your company or product/service fits.
- Product/Service: Describe your products or services and how they match your findings of your strategies and goals.
- Marketing and Sales: How will you market your products or services with the best positioning and to forecast your sales based on the findings of the previous points.
- Management and Organization: Present the management and personnel who will run the business.
- Operations: Present the detailed explanation of how the business is or will be run.
- Financial Requirement: Present the type and amount of financing needed, based on the previous points, to accomplish the entire business plan and ultimately your vision.

Writing a business plan and approaching big venture capitalists can be intimidating, but think of it as simply as writing about your business as attractively as possible to get investors intrigued. Making a fair assessment of your needs and planning accordingly will ensure that your plan is stable enough to get you off the ground. Understanding the nature of your business, its purpose, what you are selling, who your audience is and how you make money, is the key to producing a great business plan.

Very Early Stage or Concept Products

For certain products that are too early or do not have a defined target market or there is just too much uncertainty or lack of data; it may make sense to take a different approach. Although I would caution you that such instances fall in the rarest of rare categories. You may not be able to:

1. Write a business plans; instead build prototypes & test them with customers.
2. Create five-year revenue projections; create 12-month expense projections.
3. Create detailed marketing plans, but focus on unit economics and metrics/analytics of:

a) Predict what customers cost to acquire,
b) Forecast what products cost to build/deliver,
c) Foresee how much customers generate in revenue and when
4. Test and iterate on your assumptions – instead turn your business plan into a business metrics dashboard of KPIs and continue to measure and improve every week.
5. Maintain sufficient cash flow. Check your monthly burn rate, cash in the bank; figure out your remaining runway and try not to get below six months of cash.

Pointers for a Typical Business Plan

Here's a list of pointers that will help you craft the right business plan for your organization. Keep in mind: All businesses are unique and have their own specific challenges that must be met. But, if you stick with these characteristics, you will already be miles ahead from where you started.

1. Keep it brief

Many people consider a business plan to be the novelization of their ideal path to creating a company, jamming all hopes, dreams and projected profits into a pages-long document that, frankly, no one is interested in reading. A business plan does not have to be filled with everything you have ever wanted in your business — it just needs to be straightforward.

"People think that a business plan needs to be a multi-page document that is poetic in nature, and that is not the case," says Barbara Findlay Schenck, author of Business Plans Kit For Dummies. "What you need to have is a piece of paper that details the main things that will keep your business on course."

Schenck says the myth of the business plan as a lengthy document does not match reality. In fact, just writing down the basics of your business is enough to think about your company's pathway clearly and how exactly you or your team will move forward.

2. But, still be thorough

Simple does not mean sparse — the best business plan will be diligent in outlining the characteristics of the company that are most important.

Hammering down the basics of your business, everything from a personnel onboarding plan to securing the proper name rights and trademarks, will ensure no important detail is left unchecked.

These tentpole concepts may seem obvious to some, but I am surprised at how often these characteristics are missing from business plans of all kinds.

Even though it is trite, the "roadmap" analogy is the most accurate way to approach the development of a business plan. By outlining all of the major points and remaining stringent about your details, you can have a solid pathway without the need for unnecessary details — and perhaps learn more about your own business in the process.

You always should have a business plan just so that you guide your own steps. The reality is that it has a certain value — it is not just plotting out Step A to Step B to Step C. Once you start putting details on paper, you see stuff you would not have seen otherwise.

3. Uniqueness speaks volumes

No two businesses are alike, so business plans are not one-size-fits-all. Although it may be tempting to rip off a boilerplate business plan or to copy the plan from a successful business, that denies you the ability to address the unique challenges of your particular company. Worse, an untailored business plan is an easy way to set yourself up for failure.

The business plan needs to mirror the proposed business endeavour. So, what goes into it is everything that is necessary to depict that particular proposition, whether it is a candy store or some high-tech venture.

When writing a business plan, it is important to write to your particular audience. If the business plan is a strictly internal document meant to keep the performance and growth of your company on track, then it should emphasize internal information that will help that (such as hiring order or important partnerships). If the business plan is an external document, then it is all about writing about your business as attractively as possible to get investors intrigued.

Even seasoned people do not necessarily get that you need to think about who is reading your document. Your audience is different and your audience can only be judged in relationship to yourself. If you are Ram or Leo and nobody knows your background, you need to write differently and make a different pitch for venture firms.

Understanding the nature of the business is key to producing a great business plan. It is important for founders to think about the purpose of the business, what they are selling, who their audience is and how it will make money. Those are questions that need to be answered right on paper, although many businesses cannot answer them right away.

These questions can be answered on the back of a napkin for all I care, but when you have answered them, you are in business. Those questions answer what you are doing, who you are doing it for, how you are doing it and how you are going to make money doing it.

Remember, your business is unique and deserves special care when crafting a plan for success. Making a fair assessment of your needs and planning accordingly will ensure that your plan is stable enough to get you off the ground.

The Nuts & Bolts of a Winning Startup Business Plan

Do not be concerned if you are not familiar with all of these concepts. Writing a business plan for your new business is a straightforward process that you can move through step by step to completion. The whole process can be accomplished in two to four weeks, depending on your business.

A professional presentation

In surveying many successful business plans, you will find that no one format fits them all. Depending upon the nature of the business, certain topics take precedence over others. Often the owners write their business plans, since they know the most about their business operation and management and they have learned what elements to include to make the best impression.

A complete business plan for a startup company is best organized according to the logical development of the business and is comprised of at least 12 basic components.

1. Executive Summary: By definition, to summarize the elements of your business
2. Company Description: For identification, to introduce your readers to your company and your business concept
3. Industry analysis: To provide a picture of your industry and of the position of your business within the larger framework

4. Market and Competition: To evaluate what you are getting into. While some business plan proponents separate market and competition, it takes an examination of both, together, to come to one very important final conclusion: your market share. Consequently, it is best to examine and present them together.

5. Strategies and Goals: To analyze the market and your competition in order to determine how and where your company, products or services fit and to maximize your position with your target market

6. Products or Services: To describe your products or services and how they match your findings of your strategies and goals

7. Marketing and Sales: To market your products or services with the best positioning and to forecast your sales based on the findings of categories four, five and six, in that order

8. Management and Organization: To present the management and personnel who will run the show. This section can be separated into two sections for more complex companies.

9. Operations: To explain how the business is run

10. Financial Proformas: To forecast successful financial performance for all activities

11. Financial Requirement: To present the type and amount of financing needed, based on the previous sections, to accomplish the whole plan

12. Exhibits: By definition, to close the plan and separate any supporting materials that would otherwise interrupt the flow of the story

A professionally written startup business plan has all 12 of these basic sections presented in the order of the outline. Most of the segments listed will also be reflected in the same order of presentation, although there may be slight variances depending on your type of business. When your business plan is written to obtain financing, the financial requirement section may be tailored either as a loan request or as an investment offering proposal and then titled accordingly.

A winning first impression

The saying, "There's no second chance to make a good first impression," is highly appropriate when it comes to the opening sections of your business plan and its overall appearance. With current desktop publishing, business plans are looking more professional – prospects are competing for neatness and an impressive presentation that sets them apart.

- Format: As to format, the norm is to bind your business plan in booklet form with high-quality materials. Better ones have quality report covers in dark or rich colours and are labelled in front. The title page serves better than a label if laminated or positioned behind a windowed cover or behind a full clear cover. Some businesses go the extra step to have printed covers or printed binding strips. Three-ring binders have been used for years and are still acceptable, but you improve your odds for making that favourable first impression by using the latest and most professional-looking, high-tech materials available.

- Page layout: Make sure the layout of each page is balanced and artistically pleasing, with a lot of open space – paragraphs, lines and characters should not be too closely spaced. With desktop publishing, many types of fonts are available. The text is generally easier to read if you use a font with serifs, such as New Times Roman, Charter or Garamond and the margins are justified. For a professional quality, use a sans-serif font, such as Arial, Modern or Verdana, for titles, sideheads, tables and outlines. Choose one of each and stay consistent throughout the presentation.

  Using the latest software printing design tools, such as boxes, borders, shadow lines, and enlarged and bold characters, can add a professional look if correctly done without drawing attention to their use and stealing the show from the material itself. Colour printing, judiciously placed, is being used more all the time.

- Tabs and titles: Each subject, with titled heading, should have its own section and be separated with indexed partitions keyed to the table of contents. Tabbed index partitions make it easier to locate information, especially during a personal presentation. Another feature is to use coloured partitions, preferably muted or soft colours that coordinate with the colour of the cover and with the colours of any charts or graphs inside. Instead of custom tabs, some plans are assembled with printed tab indices with miniature plastic covers, but if you have access to pre-printed laminated tabs, they are preferable.

- Within each section, set off subsections or segments with crossheads usually set bold in a sans-serif font. When these are justified to the right or left margin, they are referred to as sideheads.

- Colour and charts: Charts, graphs and illustrations are commonly acceptable if appropriate to the text. Colour is often better than black and white; however, choose reds and blues, not yellow-oranges or some other unusual colour. In fact, if you are going to use extensive coloured charts and graphs, choose a theme of three or four rich colours and use them consistently throughout the work. Reserve photographic prints for the exhibits. Even then, they should be presented in protective sheets or converted to colour copies and labelled or captioned in font styles consistent with the rest of the business plan. If needed in the main body of the business plan, pictures look more professional when scanned and merged into the layout.

- Printing: Use laser or ink-jet printers to print on paper of stationery quality. Paper should be the brightest white you can find, laser quality or one of muted colour stocks in soft grey or ivory. Staying consistent by using the same type of paper for text, graphs, charts, and illustrations yields a quality professional look. Using bits and pieces of different paper gives the impression the plan was thrown together.

- Proofreading and copyediting: Have your figures checked by an accountant and the text proofread by an editor or proof reader. An accurate, easy-to-read and well-organized text will convey professionalism and credibility. Too often this important step is avoided or forgotten: despite all the work that has gone into creating an impressive presentation, typos, missing words, poor sentence construction and figures that do not add up become a significant part of that first impression made on a reader.

Important Points to Remember

- An accurate, easy-to-read and well-organized business plan conveys professionalism and credibility.
- You improve your odds for making a favourable first impression by using the latest and most professional-looking, high-tech materials available.

- Do not necessarily try to balance the material from section to section. Place your emphasis in the proper perspective and accent the features that are most important for your business.

- Always include a cover letter (separate for print and email versions) with your business plan, because it may get passed on to other staff members who will not know about your venture. This should include a detailed analysis of your market and where you see opportunities and threats. Strategic partnerships, if any, should be highlighted. There are plenty of great software tools and templates that can help you through this tactical process.

Processes

Many of the entrepreneurs I work with dislike the pain associated with "Process". Some refuse to institute any type of process in their startup. That is usually their undoing.

My first business partner prided himself on being an "idea" guy. He would say, "Do not bother me with the details." One of my partners in a more recent venture loved to say, "The only thing we are dogmatic about is not being dogmatic about anything." Neither one of those ventures turned out very well.

The devil is in the details and a certain amount of dogma is necessary in any business – especially in a startup. While process is not exactly dogma, it is a close cousin and is also akin to culture. In fact, I would argue that the most successful entrepreneurs are dogmatic about both process and culture. A startup that does not have a fervent (almost religious) belief system and a culture that embraces good processes, will never scale or mature into a highly profitable business.

Setting aside the nuances between process, dogma and culture, allow me to define what I mean by good process.

Whether they are found in a garage or inside an established enterprise, startups struggle with decisions about process and infrastructure. The speed at which a startup can learn is its competitive advantage and the defining factor in its success. But startups cannot rely on the processes and infrastructure that their established competitors use, because those "best practices" tend to kill disruptive innovation.

Even when your startup is a one-man show, you will soon find that you are "out of control," unless you start organizing and writing down how and when key things need to get done. Like it or not, you are now entering the dreaded realm of "formal business processes." The right question is "What is the minimum that I need?"

Still, startups develop some kind of processes — whether it is disciplined, haphazard, bureaucratic or empowering — because building a great product depends on it.

They just need to balance process with innovation. Companies that insist on building a world-class infrastructure before shipping a product are doomed to "achieve failure," because they are starved of feedback for too long. I learned this lesson first hand in a previous company (read the sad story here). On the other hand, companies that take a "just do it" attitude without any process at all are also taking a major gamble. High-profile startup Friendster had first-mover advantage in the social networking space, but created openings for competitors when it could not scale to meet the demand.

Finding the right balance requires an understanding of the fundamental feedback loop that powers all startups. It begins with an idea, which is translated into a product via the "build stage." When customers interact with that product, they create data, which startups harvest in the "measure stage." And, with any luck, that data will inform the company in the "learn stage" and that learning will influence the next set of ideas. This three-stage feedback loop sounds simple, but it is powerful nonetheless. It gives rise to this heuristic for evaluating any process or infrastructure change in the context of a startup.

Always choose the option that minimizes the total time through the feedback loop.

In other words, any change that accelerates learning is a win and everything else is waste. This is very different from the trade-offs that need to be made in situations where the goal is to optimize for profit, margin or growth.

The lean movement has been preaching waste reduction for many years and anyone familiar with those ideas will understand how it applies here. The only difference here is that instead of measuring the creation of value by our ability to produce tangible high-quality artifacts, startups measure value by validated learning about customers.

This approach clashes with classic software product management and product development. The detailed specification documents that PMs demand go stale too quickly to keep up with a fast-learning team. Massive data warehousing reports used in product development do what warehouses do well, store data. They do not promote learning, because people learn best when presented with a small number of actionable metrics. And engineers who build heavyweight architectures may design a technical triumph, but lack the agility to adapt when the goal of the system changes radically.

Every process a startup uses operates at one stage of the feedback loop. But lean startup practices have the effect of optimizing the total time through the loop. Practices that are harmful are the ones that optimize our ability to do just one of the three stages well. For example, you can build much faster if you do not "waste time" measuring. That is like suggesting you can drive faster if you close your eyes and hit the accelerator. It is true, but dangerous. The same is true for departmental structures that work like silos. They may work in large companies, but in startups they are dangerous because they encourage people to improve at their specialized job rather than maximizing learning.

Using just the right amount of process can help startups accelerate. But, for the entrepreneur starting from scratch, investments in process and infrastructure are expensive and take time and energy away from work that directly benefits customers. Even worse, process investments can quickly become obsolete as a company grows and management challenges evolve. Adapting a process to this ever-changing reality requires a commitment to continuous improvement and incremental investment, which you can never take your eyes off as an entrepreneur.

How to Go about Setting up Processes

The simple answer is that you need to implement one process at a time, starting with those things that are most critical to your business, until you feel a relief that things are starting to happen naturally and consistently, without the attendant stress and continual recovery mode. If you feel that the process itself is a burden, you have likely gone too far.

What are systems? A system is a set of processes that can run without you. As your business grows, you will need to build systems and processes that can be automated as much as possible. You will need to build distribution systems, inventory systems, marketing systems, customer support systems, research and development systems, accounting and hiring systems and many others.

Systems are rules, policies and procedures that trained individuals can repeat as your company grows and run independent of you.

First of all, process for the sake of process is bad process. Bad process is often why talented professionals become disillusioned with corporate life and decide to strike out as entrepreneurs. Thus, their inherent dislike of process. Bad process is also how bureaucracy creeps into an organization. Bad process is about unnecessary controls and irrelevant rules. They are often designed to benefit the few at the top of the organization at the expense of everyone else in the organization.

Conversely, a good process is:

Simple. It is fool-proof and can be quickly learned and applied by new hires and temps.

Efficient. It works flawlessly and it measures the right things – including when to change the process.

Understood. It is crystal clear about the end it is designed to achieve.

Practiced. It is religiously observed by every single person in the company.

Self-reinforcing. The more people practice it, the easier their jobs become.

Self-evident. Its value is not debated or questioned. When it is not practiced, it is missed.

Consistent and Predictable. No one has to guess if or when to practice it.

A good process is documented and enables transparent decision-making. It does not depend upon interpretation, tribal knowledge or secrets. This is not to say good process is inflexible. It is just not so flexible to cause wide deviations in how or when it is practiced by different people in the company. Most importantly, everyone knows how it is used by management to improve the company's performance.

Over the course of my career it has often fallen to me to create and institutionalize a startup's company-wide processes. The first thing I learned NOT to do was to try and transfer processes used at an old company into the new company. This is a common mistake of first time entrepreneurs. They leave their job at a big tech company and try to institute the processes they used there at the startup – often with disastrous results. Every startup is unique. Its processes should be considered, debated, created, tested and instituted with a fresh perspective.

Teams support what they help create. Conversely, they tend to be indifferent, if not downright apathetic, about things that are forced upon them. For this reason, it is a good idea to ask the team who will be bound by the process to help create it or to at least provide input. As new team members are hired who did not help create the process, ask them how well the process works for them and what adjustments they would like to see to improve it, after they have been using it for a while.

The very first step is to consider and debate whether a process is actually necessary. Lots of startups operate just fine on tribal knowledge and informal ways of doing business, especially if they have an open and vibrant culture. If you think a formal process might be necessary, it is a good idea to assemble everyone in front of a white board and write these questions:

- What do we need a process for?
- Or, if you already have one in mind...
- Do we need a process for [blank]? Where [blank] might be...

Let everyone debate the question and reach a consensus on whether a formal process is needed or whether the informal and undocumented process currently in place, if any, is sufficient for the time being. In my experience, the team will clamour for a defined process, especially if the company is growing. It is wise for the founder or department head not to be the first to express an opinion. If the team thinks the leader wants it or does not want it, they are likely to express that same opinion.

If the consensus is that a process is needed, the second step is to solicit everyone's input on the broad strokes. It is usually best to ask a series of pointed questions to spur thinking and discussion. For example:

- How should the process be structured to make you more productive and the company (or dept.) operate better?
- What are the business drivers that the process should support?
- In what ways were a similar process implemented at your last company and what was good or bad about it?
- What are your expectations for why, what, who, when, where and how this process should work?

This step is essential for implementation and adherence. Employees take a certain pride in helping to create the processes that everyone will use and that will contribute to the success of the venture. They will make darn sure that new hires practice them, which is an essential part of building a strong company culture.

The third step is to consider adaptability, compatibility and extensibility with other systems or processes and with the company's culture. This step also involves defining the criteria by which the effectiveness of the process will be measured. These things should be considered in the light of the company's growth projections. This step can often be completed by a small committee or the department head, but again, by welcoming input from everyone who wants to give it.

The fourth step is to ascertain the budget and implementation requirements. In my experience, this is easier than it sounds. Most processes can be implemented quickly for little or no money, especially those that will get the job done for the foreseeable future. Given the company is a startup, the costs and implementation requirements should be as light weight as possible. The worst mistake is to expend precious cash and human resources to implement a process that might not work as expected or worse, be completely rejected by those who are supposed to use it.

The fifth step is to look at industry best practices and off-the-shelf solutions that will get the job done. There is a tendency among some tech startups to want to create certain systems from scratch, especially if they involve writing software. Nothing creates job security for IT guys as much as a system (process) they developed and only they can maintain. As a startup, always try to source and adapt existing tools to implement a new process.

The sixth step is to deploy and test the new process in a limited environment. Do not open it up to everyone all at once. Take it for a test drive, work out the kinks. If you find a fatal flaw or the results are subpar, look for another option. When you are satisfied that it works flawlessly and meets the requirements of a good process, then formally institute it as a new process, document it and insist that everyone practice it religiously.

Finally, do not hesitate to seek expert advice and assistance when instituting processes that are mission-critical and for which no one at your company has much experience. In my last venture, we needed to create a series of processes for investing in startups and assisting them to grow. All of the partners had experience as angel investors, but none of us had experience as venture capitalists. We hired a consultant who had such experience to guide us through the process of creating our processes. In the absence of this guidance we would have floundered around, making it up as we went — which is how bad processes take root.

Finally, after deploying the process, measure its effectiveness by the criteria you established in step 3, and continue to tweak it or upgrade it as needed. If it is a good process, it will become ingrained in the company's culture and everyone will wonder how the company could have ever done without it.

What Processes Do You Need?

In the entrepreneurial phase, try to be light on formal systems (aka bureaucracy). You just need to have the minimal necessary amount of efficient systems that run smoothly. As you grow, you can put in place more complex processes.

You will need to build systems for performance reviews. You will need systems for simple things like getting food during the day to feed your employees if needed. You need systems to train your new people; to notify customers when your product is not working; to review the operations of your business; to gain and collect feedback on your product; to do expense planning and financial planning and pay for purchases; to pay salaries through payroll; to determine how happy your customers are; to handle vacation requests for your employees; to test your marketing using the scientific methodology that we talked about earlier; to manage requests for proposals (RFPs); and so on. You will need systems for setting up your hardware; for providing tax documentation, legal contracts, and full 360 feedback to your employees; for communicating internally and externally. These are just a few examples of the hundreds or thousands of systems that will be running in complex, large organizations.

During your first year in business, your success is really about what you personally do and the product you build. After the first year in business, your success is determined more by the people you hire than by you. After the first year or even the first few months, stop trying to do everything. Hire smart people and help them put systems in place so that things happen even when you are not there. Let us look at a few key systems that you should think about creating in the early stages of your business, generally prioritized by criticality. Think about the implications of each to your own business and the potential impact of getting them done incorrectly, or forgetting to do them entirely.

- Manage your financials and physical assets

    I'm continually amazed at the number of entrepreneurs who go for months into a new business without really keeping a formal record of money spent or assets acquired.

    Use a simple accounting tool like QuickBooks, get away from co-mingled funds and you have the first business process you need. Make sure you hire a bookkeeper to keep track of and categorize your revenues and expenses (and if you cannot afford one, learn how to do it yourself). Have them send you a monthly income statement, balance sheet and cash flow statement. Learn how to read a financial statement if you do not know how. It is up to you if you want to see you statements in a cash basis or accrual basis.

While you are at it, define the processes for financial transactions that routinely take place. These could be simple travel reimbursements to complex vendor payments.

- Develop your business plan

    Write down the key elements of your business plan very early and keep it current as things evolve. This will include the first version of many critical processes that can be split out later, including market opportunity, requirements, product definition, business model, sales process and organization. We have covered this in the earlier section, so by now you get what this is about.

- Product development process

    Even if you are doing the work yourself, you need to document requirements, features, metrics and milestones. If you are contracting or outsourcing, this is even more important. Otherwise you will find yourself, a year later, being no closer to a product than you were yesterday, with no idea why.

Product management is the process of defining what you are building in advance of building it and then assembling the team and building that product. Product management is a profession that employs many people. You might see hundreds of product managers in a company like Google or Microsoft, maybe even thousands.

From my experience, I've learned that there are two extremes in product development.

There is the controller, the maniacal dictator who says, "This is my vision and nothing else will be taken into consideration as I build this product." Then there is the "design by committee" approach where there is no strong leader at all and all the decisions are made in a 10 or 15 or 20-person committee. At that stage, you often get very little innovation as you end up aligning with the lowest common denominator, with no real inspired thinking.

The goal of a great product manager is to be at the right place in the spectrum between those two extremes—between the maniacal, singular, controlled vision and the input from multiple stakeholders. As a product manager, a product developer, you want to be in what I call the green zone where you have strong, focused leadership and strong, focused vision, but you also take the time to incorporate feedback from the right people.

Who are the right people? The right people are the particular examples of customers who may be using your future product and the select people within your organization who can really contribute to your ability to create a great product. But it is important to keep those numbers few and keep your leadership and vision strong in order to end up with a truly innovative product.

With product design, you want to be slightly right of centre — a little bit closer to the maniacal side. It is better to have a strong vision and be slightly over-controlling than be completely unsure about the product you are trying to build and the change you wish to create with it in the world. But you also want to have a little balance.

A great product owner must be absolutely passionate. Great product development only happens when the person who is owning that product and seeing it through to reality is absolutely passionate about the change they wish to manifest in the world.

When passion is lacking in products, a company's sales will go flat. When a CEO, a leader, is no longer passionate (or perhaps was never passionate) about the company's mission and purpose, the sales results and that company's profitability and stock price is going to go flat or go down.

It is important to define and understand the external personas that you will listen to as you build your product. What is a persona? A persona is an example person that you are modelling your product development after.

For example, if you are building an email marketing product, you would define four or five key personas who might use it. We would often give them names. One of ours was a small business owner who had maybe five or six employees and often tried to do the marketing himself or herself. When you create your personas, you need to understand the demographic and psychographic factors and give them human identities. As you develop your products, you can ask yourself, what would the average customer think about this?

Systems for Building Software

Let us talk about building great software. I have a lot to learn still about building great software, I found that from my experience, great software is built using various methodology, the most popular today is, Agile Development, in which you are able to be responsive and reflexive to the customer's needs and the demands of the marketplace and you are able to release updates at least every two months, if not every month or even every two weeks. In some companies, they release every day.

This is a departure from the prior methodology of product development known as waterfall, where you would write a very long product requirement document and then take six, nine or twelve months to come out with a new iteration of the product.

Agile development is also made possible by the Internet, where you can deploy software overnight in just a few minutes instead of having to ship a bunch of CDs.

You also want to make sure that your code is test-driven and has quality assurance built in and automated throughout it. You want to do your programming in something called object-oriented where you create templates and you are able to make those templates talk to each other rather than creating long scripts that are very complicated to understand or bring new developers and engineers into.

You also want a development team that under-commits and over-delivers and factors in the time it is going to take for bug tracking, bug fixing, quality assurance, scalability, and security.

Finally, you want to make sure you have clear code that is easy to understand for new developers that you bring into a project and standards that any engineer can understand.

Funding process

Unless you are bootstrapping everything, you need to have a clear plan on what networking and documents are required to get to friends and family, angel investors and institutional investors. Measure yourself against a researched plan or your "out of cash" brick wall will be looming before you know it.

Manage human resources

At this stage, you should start recruiting, hiring, paying, and training others to help you run your business. In addition to effectiveness and consistency, you now have a myriad of legal and tax considerations to get right. Do not try this without a formal process. Unless you are purposely masochistic, there is just no reason to attempt to do your payroll yourself. Hire a firm like Paychex, ADP or Intuit Online Payroll to do it for you (there are numerous smaller providers in every country). They will take care of all the tax withholdings, calculations and government compliance. If in the US, ADP and Paychex can also set up a 401(k) program for your company.

Putting in Place an Employee Handbook

Creating a single digital or printed manual that employees can refer to when they have questions about things like stock option plans, paid time off policies and health benefits can be really helpful and save you and your fledgling HR department a lot of time. Try to document all the key policies and procedures you have and publish them annually in an Employee Handbook.

Creating a Performance Review Process

As your organization grows, you will eventually hire a full-time Director of HR and install what is called a Human Resources Information Systems (also known as a Human Resources Management System) that manages all aspects of HR including:

- Payroll
- Talent Management
- Recruiting
- Performance Reviews
- Total Rewards/Compensation

Services that perform these tasks range from outsourced payroll providers like Paychex and ADP to web-based tools like SuccessFactors and Taleo. SAP, Oracle, Workday and PeopleSoft also have HRIS solutions for larger companies.

Eventually, you should implement a 360-degree performance review form. This form can be used for managers to get feedback from their peers and their staff members.

For now, you just need a basic performance review process in place. This can start with an Excel Spreadsheet or Microsoft Word document.

Setting Up a Medical Insurance and Health Care Plan

As you get past a handful of team members and your sales volume can support additional investments in your team, consider setting up a 401(k) retirement program and beginning to provide health coverage to your employees. You can often use your payroll provider to set up a 401(k) program. To encourage employees to save, when you can afford to, you may wish to match a percentage of employee contributions.

To set up a health care plan, go online and find a couple health care providers in your state. As you consider which plan and provider to select for your company, take into consideration the major components of each plan outside of cost:

Creating an Incentive Compensation System

There are many reasons why people are motivated to work—for money, to be part of a team on a common mission, to feel challenged, to make a positive difference and to have their talents appreciated. Getting your non-monetary compensation system right is just as important as getting your monetary compensation system right.

Compensation has a few different components to it, including base salary, incentive compensation (also known as bonus compensation), the ability to participate in the upside of a company via stock options or restricted stock units and your benefits package.

For the first few employees, you will likely have to use every ounce of your persuasive abilities to convince great people to work for you for free or next to nothing. In the beginning, you pay what you can in cash or deferred salary and the rest in an ownership stake in your business.

Once you get to a multi-layered company in which everyone no longer reports to you (this tends to happen around the 5–8 employees mark), it becomes important to define in writing how your employees will be compensated.

The base salary component is generally established at the time of hiring and adjusted annually or at the time of promotions.

Incentive compensation is known by various names, including incentive comp, performance-based pay, variable pay and bonus.

You can either create an employee profit-sharing pool or have a bonus for each employee as a percentage of their pay that is paid out quarterly, twice per year or annually. This allows the management to tie compensation directly to quantitative company, team and individual performance.

How much of someone's total compensation should be in the form of performance-based pay? It depends on their role in the organization.

Sales executives usually have the most amount of their compensation in the form of variable pay, as they are the individuals who are most driven by monetary incentives and want their compensation to be representative of their performance.

For SVPs and VPs outside of sales, 30% is a normal percentage for variable pay, going down the scale to 10% at the staff-level, who often want the large majority of their pay to be guaranteed.

The measures that the incentive compensation are based on can be set quarterly, semi-annually or annually. I prefer to set the company and departmental KPIs to which the incentive compensation system is tied twice per year. Every quarter is too often and once per year does not provide enough flexibility to adjust incentives as the business changes.

The employee should be able to overperform on their incentive compensation if they and the company do really well.

The incentive compensation component should be based on both how the company performs and how the individual performs. I have found that having 50% of someone's incentive compensation based on company performance and 50% based on individual performance aligns incentives well.

Setting Up an Options Plan

Once you have your incentive compensation plan for each team member, it is time to set up your options plan. Your Board of Directors should approve a pool of shares in your company that you can use for your key team members.

The right size option pool for your company will depend on how much you want to use stock options as part of your compensation mix as well as how much you can pay in cash. If you can pay a market salary, then there is no need to use stock options widely. If you cannot, they can be of significant use.

Let us assume you are a normal high-growth start up and you can only pay salaries that are 50% of what is normal. In this case, here are some guidelines for options in the first four years. This system is designed for employees, not founders. The ranges are in place based on the amount of experience the individual brings to the table.

It is standard for stock options to vest over four years, meaning that if someone leaves after a year they will only receive 25% of the total amount.

When you provide stock options to employees you usually provide incentive stock options (ISOs) which have certain tax benefits to non-qualified stock options that can be used for contractors and service providers. One downside to ISOs you should know about is that an employee must usually exercise their incentive stock options within 90 days after they are terminated from employment at your firm or lose them.

Even if the options you grant early are at a low price, a cashless tax bill problem can occur when employees later exercise their options as, at least under current law in most countries, a person must pay taxes in the year they exercise stock options on the difference between the current fair market value and the original option strike price. This is a really bad tax rule, as it causes people to have to pay taxes on stock that usually cannot yet be sold (due to the company being private) – often forcing the employee to not be able to exercise the option at all. Possible solutions include granting Restricted Stock Units (RSUs) instead of options (and pay the taxes on the compensation that year) or to set up a profit-sharing plan instead of an options plan. RSUs vs. ISOs vs. profit sharing may be too much detail for now, but are important questions to discuss with your corporate attorney when you create your options plan.

Leverage information technology

Find an IT person you can trust and plan how you will acquire, implement and utilize computer technology to run your business. How do you access the Internet, what servers do you need, applications required, databases designed and backups scheduled? It all has to be written down and maintained.

Billing and revenue collection

Whether you provide an online subscription service or sell products in a store, you need to consistently and economically sell your product and collect revenue to survive. Here you will likely need to train others to help you, so more detail may be required in this process.

Customer service and support

Here is another often overlooked area of process that kills many startups, both in cost and time. Do not assume that you can fix every problem yourself or that there will not be any problems to fix. Even if your business is online, people want a contact, real expertise and quick response.

By the time you get to six employees, it is time to install a basic tool for keeping track of your customers and contacts. There are innumerable tools from the mature Salesforce.com to Nimble, Zoho CRM, Highrise, SugarCRM, and Batchbook. You can also use your email marketing tool as a basic CRM system.

Regardless of what you use, your customer list and prospect list is gold. Make sure you are collecting information on who your customers are—whether they purchase through the web, by catalogue or at a store. To grow your business, you need to be able to get in touch with your existing customers and find out how to convince them to spend money with your business.

Putting in Place Real Time Dashboards

One of the most valuable things you can do is to create dashboards for key metrics. At the very least, you should have a dashboard that is displayed on a flat screen TV somewhere in your office that shows basic information like how many customers you have, your monthly sales and how many new customers you added that month. If you do not know how many customers you have and how many customers you added per month to date, you should start tracking this most basic data. Even in a brick-and-mortar business like a florist shop or a restaurant, you should know how many new and repeat customers you get in a month.

I've found there to be a correlation between companies that have real-time or near real-time visible metrics displayed in their office and companies that are wildly successful and reach lists like INC 500 and can raise outside investment capital.

While your company is small, set up your system of dashboards now so that you can manage the business effectively as you grow.

Creating an efficient meeting rhythm

Too often, people put systems in place that end up causing far too much time to be spent in meetings. One thing I would encourage you to do as an entrepreneur is to adopt what's called a "maker schedule."

A manager schedule is one that goes from meeting to meeting to meeting (maybe six, seven, eight or nine meetings per day). You may have experienced that yourself. A maker schedule, however, is generally better for someone who is designing or developing things. For someone who is an engineer or designer, a creative person or someone working on hard problems, often the minimum amount of time the brain needs to be able to truly focus on solving a difficult problem is a block of about four hours. So, if you cannot provide an uninterrupted block of four hours to your employees during their day, they might get very little done.

Have one meeting that lasts about 25 minutes in the middle of the day, where everyone goes around and shares their accomplishments from the prior day and what they will be working on the next day. Before that meeting, you will have about a 3.5–4.5 hour work block and after that meeting, you will have another 3.5–4.5 hour work block. It ends up being a very productive day that has two "maker blocks" within it.

I find that to be much more effective than having 6–8 meetings a day where you are constantly pulling the most creative innovators in your organization out of their focus zone — out of their state of "flow,"

One of the things you could implement with your executive team is to have a very specifically timed meeting, like 9:46 every morning, which is a very specific time so everyone would be on time every day, have a daily standup meeting where you take 10 minutes and went around your executive team and just shared what you will be doing that day.

Once a week, you could review the company's weekly results (sales, trials, conversions), track progress against each of your quarterly priorities, and review the status of each of your company-wide projects. This will help you eventually come up with Key Performance Indicators and quantitative measures of success and start marking each KPI as red, yellow, green or supergreen based on how you are performing. Be as objective as possible about results and do your best to leave subjectivity out of the assessments. By making it clear in advance which metrics individuals are responsible for and would be compensated on, you will have an easier time assessing performance later.

As you feel the need, you could hold a company-wide offsite every six months at which you can talk about strategy and the future of the business.

As you grow beyond the 200 employee size, you will require a more complex meeting rhythm.

At different companies, you will need to innovate and have different meeting systems and processes within the organization. The key is to think about things consciously—things like meetings, processes, and accounting—

so that you end up creating systems that are effective, efficient, and enable you to build a business that eventually operates even without you.

Benefits

Aside from providing comfort to investors, defined processes accrue innumerable benefits to the leadership team and company. Reinforcing the point that preparation for potential investors is a great way to improve the way things are done within the company. Some of these are:

1. Increasing inbound sales conversion rate

Do you map out your marketing and sales processes? You may often find that your company is failing to convert inbound traffic, despite the best efforts of your marketing team to drive visitors to your website. This is because the handshake between marketing and sales has not been agreed with measurable targets. In many organisations, sales and marketing engage in a tempestuous relationship, despite the importance of the two working together.

2. Increasing team productivity

Uncertainty kills productivity. When people are uncertain about the tasks they need to do each day, they tend to rely on their email inbox to prioritize their work. Once you map the major processes for each role, your employees will now have a daily/weekly rhythm of work, meaning you can accelerate the acquisition of your first 100–1,000 customers.

3. Onboarding new hires quickly

Processes are a great way of training in new hires quickly. Startups tend to comprise of smaller teams, hence critical resources are split between training new hires and delivering on critical tasks. You might find yourself saying the same thing over and over again. However, if you train the new hire through the critical process for their role and how role interacts with other members of staff, they will get to grips with things more quickly.

4. Releasing products faster

In a startup, it is critical to map the bug fixing and product release schedule. Failure to map these processes will mean that bugs are not always fixed based on criticality to customer acquisition or revenue. Often, new features are based on a wish list by the sales and management team. But imagine a process that has the decision making criteria defined and a scoring mechanism for prioritizing bugs and feature releases!

5. Improving revenue collection

Have you agreed on the billing cycle? Is it adhoc, daily, weekly or monthly? Do you need to get a purchase order from your customer? I'm always amazed by the number of enterprise companies that forget to issue this. It results in a cancellation of the old invoice, and having to issue a new one. Have you agreed on the credit and collection terms? Is it payment up-front or 30 days+?

6. Improving staff happiness

Have you agreed on how and when your team should submit expenses and holidays for approval? This can be an unnecessary pain point, especially as you grow. You will need to agree a time in the month, what format and to whom the expense form is sent. Here is an example of an expense request process. You need to agree the threshold that requires manager vs CEO approval.

7. Improving customer onboarding

Usually in a startup, the sales team provides all of the onboarding support in the early months. However, as the business grows, you are likely to hire an Account Manager or Customer Service person. I recommend documenting the customer onboarding process and explain the tasks that the sales team must complete to finish a sale and also the point at which a customer service/account management takes over. This will help to improve the onboarding of new customers, increase customer satisfaction and reduce churn. Whilst documenting the onboarding process, you are likely to find tasks that can be automated and thereby shorting the onboarding cycle.

8. Improving visibility and customer satisfaction rating

How is customer feedback captured? How are the top questions analyzed? What is the speed of response? Is your first resolution rate high? When in a startup, you are likely to be managing customer service via your inbox. Consider documenting this process and agree on key KPIs. There are some very good tools available to automate and improve visibility of your customer service process.

9. Improving partnership engagement

Do you have strategic partners that are critical to your revenue and your market share goals? If the answer is yes, do you know which partners by market will drive most of your success? Do you have an onboarding process by which you review and weigh up each partner? Do you have a legal process map to review partnership agreements and IP assignment? Have you agreed on revenue share with the partners? Are you both aligned on legal definitions, calculation methods and when revenue should be paid? There are a lot of tasks associated with partnerships that, if not properly documented and managed, can leave money on the table that will drive up costs and in the worst case scenario, end up in court.

10. Scaling your organisation for growth

Large organizations invest heavily in process management. Process management is used to create agile organizations that save both costs, drive revenue, increase customer satisfaction and allowed organizations to scale for growth. I have personally used IBM BlueWorks due to the simplicity and ease of use, but there are many other equally good tools to use.

Key Points to Remember

If you are a great startup, you will not just copy the processes of your competitors, even in these basic elements. Innovation is the key, to keep each process small, but make it more effective than competitors and big-company processes.

But having no process does not make you more competitive. In my experience, no process sounds more like a hobby than a business. Hobbies can be a lot of fun, but they usually cost money rather than make money. What is your business objective?

Standardize your processes. Regardless of company size, having the proper procedures in place from the get-go will make scalability that much easier. Having the right systems, tools and processes is a surefire way to manage workflow. When business owners disregard process standardization, they struggle to keep up with the ever-changing business environment. In the early stages it might be easy to get by without systems in place, but as time goes on it can have a detrimental effect on your company. If you see your most productive employees struggling to stay afloat under the current processes (or lack thereof), it might be time to step it up.

Process management requires time and effort, but it is incredibly worthwhile. When I started in process management, I was skeptical. This quickly changed as I started to see how processes helped my team and my colleagues. Our product development teams were able to build quality services and products that both delighted and excited our customers.

Is it difficult? No. Just write down a list of tasks in order of priority, and state who should complete which ones. Now draw a line between each task and you have a process. The next step is to enter these into one of the tools mentioned above. When you have the funds available, consider hiring a process person.

Defining Market Size & Overall Opportunity

Besides developing an exceptional product or hiring the right talent, doing some much-needed market research is the most critical step for any startup. A part of this research should involve market size. Without knowing your market size, you may be conducting business in a market so small, it is next to impossible to make any money.

When you start a business, you may have a sense that there is a market for the products or services you have in mind, but you need hard facts. You have to know the numbers of potential customers in the marketplace, so that your business plan will be realistic. If you use arbitrary figures based on wishful thinking, no one will take your business plan seriously. You can estimate the size of the market if you use reliable sources and a reliable method.

Understanding market size helps you distinguish between two categories: the addressable market, which is the total revenue opportunity for your product or service; and the available market, which is the portion of the addressable market for which you can realistically compete. By outlining the difference between these two, you can develop a product offering to tackle that consumer sweet spot.

Without a solid grasp on your market size, you endanger your business' success in not only the early stages, but also throughout its entire life cycle.

Market sizing gives you a sense of market trends. It can clue you in on the necessary drivers of demand, as market movements often continue in one direction or another for a period of time. What's more, those trends often indicate whether a substitute for your product is on the horizon that could potentially affect market size.

Take Kodak, for example. Prior to the late '90s, almost every picture in the U.S. was developed on Kodak film. Its name was synonymous with photography. But then digital broke big, and the number of digital cameras went from 4.5 million units in 2000 to 28.3 million units in 2007. Instead of doubling down on digital photography, Kodak steadied its course, neglecting to look at what digital meant to both the addressable and available markets. As the addressable market dwindled, so did the available market and the company's complacency led to the downfall of its brand.

Brand new markets are very tough to estimate in size. Your best estimate can be wildly off on both the downside or the upside. Startups routinely overestimate their markets. Even the CEO of IBM once said the worldwide market opportunity for computers was only 5 machines. In evaluating the new market opportunity, you look for genuine pull from customers and you watch out for false demand from unsustainable marketing practices.

Ways of Estimating Market Size

For most businesses, the concept of market sizing is readily understood but not easily accomplished. Many get stuck on establishing boundaries or defining the market before they even get to the data analysis and implications of their research. Determining market size can answer strategic questions about levels of investments in the business and profitable growth targets. Market sizing can also serve as a quick understanding of the potential for a B2B market opportunity in terms of volume or value and is therefore pertinent to business strategy and decision making.

- Defining the Market: Get estimates for the potential market. The potential market is the total number of people or businesses that may be interested in your product or service. You can find these estimates through the Small Business Associations, the federal/central government and industry associations. You will find very large numbers. For example, if you want to sell a cleaning product for cars, you will find that there are 243,023,485 registered passenger vehicles in the United States, according to USA.org. Knowing the level of detail necessary to approach your strategic questions is the key to properly scoping your market sizing approach.

    Defining your target market should always be the first step in estimating market size and it is critical that you do not stray from your determined market definition through the data collection process. Market size can be viewed in terms of Total Available Market (TAM), Served Available Market (SAM), and Share of Market (SOM). Total Available Market refers to the combined revenue or unit volume in a specified market. Often a company or investor will require the market size or Total Available Market for a particular geographic area. If we take the example of food packaging, the Total Available Market can be calculated by adding sales of food packaging producers in a particular geographic region or market segment. The Served Available Market refers to the percentage or size of TAM that a company can reasonably serve based on product, technology and geographic constraints. SAM typically will be less than TAM. Using the same example of food packaging, if the TAM for food packaging is $200 BN, then the Served Available Market for companies making flexible packaging would be only a percentage of TAM.

Lastly, Share of Market or SOM refers to the percentage of SAM that a particular company currently serves or plans to serve. Again, SOM should be less than SAM except in the case of a monopoly. In your market sizing process, start by determining what products or services should be included as part of your TAM. Then narrow down by geographic scope — US, North America, Europe, etc. Another factor to consider is the timeframe. Are you looking for historic market sizing or future projections? By defining what should be included in your market sizing estimation, your company can more accurately determine the market potential and the estimated available share of the market.

- Determining Your Approach: There are two basic methodologies for determining market size: top-down and bottom-up. Your selected approach may be based on what market information is available. However, the best approach is to develop market sizing estimations using both methodologies in order to gain a higher confidence in your estimation. The top-down methodology uses a broad market size figure and determines the percentage that the target market represents. For example, to determine the TAM for food packaging, you might start with retail sales of packaged food and multiply by an assumed packaging cost (e.g. 10% of the total retail food value is packaging cost).

In general, a top-down approach is typically a quicker, more time efficient approach. It is great for validation or a quick assessment of market size but seldom will provide the detail necessary for a true opportunity analysis. The bottom-up methodology builds the TAM by totalling the main variables of the target market. Using the same example of food packaging, a researcher might total the food packaging sales of packaging producers – all food packaging or by package type or by geography. This method is generally considered to be more accurate and takes considerably more time to complete. As a result, the bottom-up method is a more valid estimate because it is less likely to include non-addressable revenue or units.

A key metric can be anything related to your industry. Determine what statistic or piece of information investors would be most interested in knowing about your industry. Keep in mind that information needs to be relevant.

- Data Structuring: To further develop your understanding of the market, it is important to gather trend information, which is typically in the form of qualitative data. This information can come through secondary research or comments from primary research. If we look at food packaging, it may be of interest to evaluate trends for specific food segments, such as dairy/meats/poultry/fish/beverages. For example, look for trends in beef packaging that differ from chicken or pork. It may also be valuable to look for trends in packaging type (cans, cartons, trays, etc.) or fill technology (hot fill, aseptic, ESL, etc.). Once the trends information has been collected, you can start structuring data by group or theme. Typology is the strategy for qualitative data analysis to group findings into distinct categories in order to identify data themes. This process allows the researcher to quickly consider the value of information by comparing with other information in the same "cluster" or "line." Typology is also useful for creating a story line as the project moves into analysis stage and the development of conclusions.

- Data Analysis: It is important to use relevant statistics when talking about your market size. Often times I hear entrepreneurs make the statement, "If I do not show a huge market size, investors will not be interested." This statement is valid, but only to a certain extent. Ideally, investors would like to see you in an industry with a lot of potential but they are also able to see right through any B.S.

Let's take a look at an example, if you are selling wiper blades for vehicles, stating that the U.S. auto sales market was $570 billion in 2015 is a bit too broad. Instead try saying the U.S. aftermarket parts are a $62 billion industry. Finding a statistic about how much Americans spent on windshield wipers would be even better.

- Relevance: Finding the relevant statistics you need about your industry is going to take some time and effort, but finding the right statistics can make a world of difference to investors. As mentioned above, it is often necessary to develop multiple estimates using different approaches or sources. This is called triangulation. When multiple sources or estimations triangulate, the confidence in a market estimate increases. If the approaches widely differ, additional research is required to reduce risk and is recommended to narrow the range of market sizing estimates. Common pitfalls or mistakes often start early on by not properly defining the market or gathering data from non-reputable sources. The market definition should remain consistent throughout the data collection process and methodology should be based on market knowledge — not just demographics. Where possible, attempt to verify each significant finding through multiple published source materials or primary research. By confirming findings, you are able to leverage the value of various information sources and thus increase confidence in the final results.

How fast is your industry growing? Try comparing it to the growth rate of a similar industry to provide prospective. For example, the market for the energy drink industry is growing at 6% a year vs. the entire carbonated soft drink category is only growing at 3% per year. On its own a 6% growth does not sound too impressive, but when you can show that it is growing twice as fast as a similar industry that growth seems more substantial.

- Estimate your market share. Do some research on companies that sell your type of product or service and find out what their annual sales are. Remembering that you are a startup, calculate how much of that market you could capture. Many successful businesses make a living by appealing to 10 percent to 20 percent of the market. Do not choose such a number arbitrarily. Conduct a survey of people who buy products or services such as yours to find out how many would be open to considering a new product. Assume that half of those would actually buy, because interest is not the same as taking action. Though your figure remains an estimate, at least you have a rational basis for your market-share figure.

Points To Remember

Once you understand its importance, how exactly should you go about determining your market size?

1. Define your sub segment of the market

Not even the largest, most established company has a 100 percent share of the market. In the case of Airbnb, its first big grab came from the shortage of hotel rooms during the 2007 Democratic National Convention. Zero in on your initial pool of customers and make sure you have a handle on this group before you expand.

2. Conduct top-down market sizing

Look at the total market for your product or service, and then establish a realistic estimate for your market share. Take, for example, the hospitality industry. U.S. travellers spent $23 billion on vacation rentals in 2012 – if Marriott International accounted for $13.8 billion of that spend, it would probably be a stretch to count the remaining $9.2 billion as yours for the taking.

3. Follow with bottom-up analysis

Determine where you will sell your products, how many locations will stock them and how many comparable products typically sell. Try to be as objective as possible – it will help you figure out where realistic growth could take you in five years. Then, compare your numbers with the overall addressable market. If it is 1 to 5 percent of the pie, you have a realistic plan.

4. Look at the competition

How crowded is your industry and what types of companies are at the forefront? If, for instance, you were the only steel producer for a specific type of product, it would be reasonable for you to get to a 50 percent market share. As a new airline in the travel industry, on the other hand, the likelihood of getting even a 10 percent market share is slim.

5. Assess the static market size

Doing business in a static market comes with fierce competition. You and your competitors vie for the same pool of customers every year. Looking at hospitality again, a new hotel company must determine if the budget segment is growing faster than the luxury segment. This will inform how the long-term total addressable market size will likely change, which can help you respond to trends.

Being realistic about your projections is really the most important aspect of determining market size. That means staying objective and impartial about not just your product or service, but also about consumer need and want. Otherwise, you could find yourself doing business in a market too small to stay afloat.

Competitive Landscape

If your business can easily be copied or ripped off by a competitor or new entrant, it is a risky and unattractive investment. Legendary investor Warren Buffett talks about businesses having a "moat," which essentially means they are difficult to copy. This 'moat' could be Intellectual Property or a certain patented product for example – but to ensure the maximum valuation, it is essential you have one. A couple of good questions to ask are: "What makes this business different?" and "Why would someone invest in/buy my business instead of one of my competitors' businesses?"

Every business has competition. Understanding the strengths and weaknesses of your competition – or potential competition – is critical to making sure your business survives and grows. While you do not need to hire a private detective, you do need to thoroughly assess your competition on a regular basis even if you only plan to run a small business.

In fact, small businesses can be especially vulnerable to competition, especially when new companies enter a marketplace.

Competitive analysis can be incredibly complicated and time-consuming… but it does not have to be. Here is a simple process you can follow to identify, analyse, and determine the strengths and weaknesses of your competition.

- Profile Current Competitors

    First develop a basic profile of each of your current competitors. For example, if you plan to open an office supply store you may have three competing stores in your market.

    Online retailers will also provide competition, but thoroughly analysing those companies will be less valuable unless you also decide you want to sell office supplies online. (Although it is also possible that they– or, say, Amazon – are your real competition. Only you can determine that.)

    To make the process easier, stick to analysing companies you will directly compete with. If you plan to set up an accounting firm, you will compete with other accounting firms in your area. If you plan to open a clothing store, you will compete with other clothing retailers in your area.

Again, if you run a clothing store you also compete with online retailers, but there is relatively little you can do about that type of competition other than to work hard to compete in other ways: great service, friendly salespeople, convenient hours, truly understanding your customers, etc.

Once you identify your main competitors, answer these questions about each one. And be objective. It is easy to identify weaknesses in your competition, but less easy (and a lot less fun) to recognize where they may be able to outperform you:

- What are their strengths? Price, service, convenience, extensive inventory are all areas where you may be vulnerable.
- What are their weaknesses? Weaknesses are opportunities you should plan to take advantage of.
- What are their basic objectives? Do they seek to gain market share? Do they attempt to capture premium clients? See your industry through their eyes. What are they trying to achieve?
- What marketing strategies do they use? Look at their advertising, public relations, etc.
- How can you take market share away from their business?
- How will they respond when you enter the market?

While these questions may seem like a lot of work to answer, in reality the process should be fairly easy. You should already have a feel for the competition's strengths and weaknesses... if you know your market and your industry.

To gather information, you can also:

- Check out their websites and marketing materials. Most of the information you need about products, services, prices and company objectives should be readily available. If that information is not available, you may have identified a weakness.
- Visit their locations. Take a look around. Check out sales materials and promotional literature. Have friends stop in or call to ask for information.

- Evaluate their marketing and advertising campaigns. How a company advertises creates a great opportunity to uncover the objectives and strategies of that business. Advertising should help you quickly determine how a company positions itself, who it markets to and what strategies it employs to reach potential customers.

- Browse. Search the Internet for news, public relations and other mentions of your competition. Search blogs and Twitter feeds as well as review and recommendation sites. While most of the information you find will be anecdotal and based on the opinion of just a few people, you may at least get a sense of how some consumers perceive your competition. Plus you may also get advance warning about expansion plans, new markets they intend to enter or changes in management.

Keep in mind competitive analysis does more than help you understand your competition. Competitive analysis can also help you identify changes you should make to your business strategies. Learn from competitor strengths, take advantage of competitor's weaknesses, and apply the same analysis to your own business plan.

You might be surprised by what you can learn about your business by evaluating other businesses.

- Identify Potential Competitors

    It can be tough to predict when and where new competitors may pop up. For starters, regularly search for news on your industry, your products, your services, and your target market. Study trends and keep a track of government policy announcements for your sector.

    But there are other ways to predict when competition may follow you into a market. Other people may see the same opportunity you see. Think about your business and your industry and if the following conditions exist, you may face competition down the road:

    - The industry enjoys relatively high profit margins
    - Entering the market is relatively easy and inexpensive
    - The market is growing – the more rapidly it is growing the greater the risk of competition
    - Supply and demand is off – supply is low and demand is high

◈ Very little competition exists, so there is plenty of "room" for others to enter the market

In general terms, if serving your market seems easy, you can safely assume competitors will enter your market. A good business plan anticipates and accounts for new competitors.

Now distil what you have learned by answering these questions in your business plan:

The Competitive Analysis section for our cycling rental business could start something like this:

Primary Competitors

The in-town bike shops will be strong competitors. They are established businesses with excellent reputations. On the other hand, they offer inferior-quality equipment and their location is significantly less convenient.

Secondary Competitors

We do not plan to sell bicycles for at least the first two years of operation. However, sellers of new equipment do indirectly compete with our business since a customer who buys equipment no longer needs to rent equipment.

Later, when we add new equipment sales to our operation, we will face competition from online retailers. We will compete with new equipment retailers through personalized service and targeted marketing to our existing customer base, especially through online initiatives.

Opportunities

By offering mid- to high-end quality equipment, we provide customers the opportunity to "try out" bikes they may wish to purchase at a later date, providing additional incentive (besides cost savings) to use our service.

Offering drive-up, express rental return services will be seen as a much more attractive option compared to the hassle of renting bikes and transporting them to intended take-off points for rides.

Online initiatives like online renewals and online reservations enhances customer convenience and positions as a cutting-edge supplier in a market largely populated, especially in the cycling segment, by customers who tend to be early technology adapters.

Risks

Renting bikes and cycling equipment may be perceived by some of our target market as a commodity transaction. If we do not differentiate ourselves in terms of quality, convenience and service, we could face additional competition from other entrants to the market.

One of the bike shops in the city is a subsidiary of a larger corporation with significant financial assets. If we, as hoped, carve out a significant market share, the corporation may use those assets to increase service, improve equipment quality or cut prices.

While your business plan is primarily intended to convince you that your business makes sense, keep in mind most investors look closely at your competitive analysis. A common mistake made by entrepreneurs is assuming they will simply "do it better" than any competition. This marginal "me too" approach will not work for you, let alone an investor.

Experienced businesspeople know you will face stiff competition: showing you understand your competition, understand your strengths and weaknesses relative to that competition and that you understand you will have to adapt and change based on that competition, is critical.

And, even if you do not ever plan to seek financing or bring in investors, you absolutely must know your competition.

Past Financials and Future Projections

An investor or potential buyer wants to know that they will get a strong return on their investment. The best and most quantitative way to do this is by looking at the financial performance of your business. Investors get very nervous if they feel the owner does not have a good handle on their business's financial performance. Different investors may have different requirements and a good accountant can help you to prepare and present your key financial data in an optimal way.

Managing current expenses while securing additional funding for new resources can be difficult. However, being prepared is extremely important for small businesses, particularly during hyper-growth. A great way to acquire financing apart from investors is through crowdfunding and loans. Securing these investments prior to gaining traction is crucial for your business to survive because you must be able to meet customer demands. How do you expect to meet them if you do not have the money upfront to deliver whatever it is you are selling?

Present a Professional Financial Picture

Investors like financial order. It is advisable, therefore, to have your financial statements audited or at least reviewed by a professional auditor before being presented to potential investors.

A track record is also useful, so you must try and present financial records for at least three years of business if you have been around or for whatever period you have been operating the business.

The independent validation of your business's numbers and processes by a qualified accounting person will greatly improve prospects of your business earning financial credibility.

Most important, the potential investors in your company and potential lenders will have greater confidence in your business if the financials have been certified by a professional. This may save you a lot of time, cost and potentially increase the available leverage your business can get.

Act Quickly to Cut Excess Costs

Every dollar that your business retains as profit increases the value of the business and its cashflow strength. So, it is very important to quickly eliminate excess costs.

This may seem rather counterintuitive that a business must reduce costs in order to make it prosper, but it is an essential part of showing your potential financiers that your business has the capability to exercise careful financial control.

Retaining cash and maximising cash flow will make your business more attractive to investors and bankers. Ideally, a business should operate for at least a year to prepare it for outside funding.

However, once the decision to seek external investors has been made, you should try as much as possible to eliminate any unnecessary costs if you can.

It is advisable not to take a gradual approach to cut costs but instead, you must cut costs as a day-to-day endeavour. Numbers tell the story. Bottom line results indicate the success or failure of any business.

Financial projections and estimates help entrepreneurs, lenders and investors or lenders objectively evaluate a company's potential for success. If a business seeks outside funding, providing comprehensive financial reports and analysis is critical.

But most importantly, financial projections tell you whether your business has a chance of being viable and if not let you know you have more work to do.

Most business plans include at least five basic reports or projections:

- Balance Sheet: Describes the company cash position including assets, liabilities, shareholdings and earnings retained to fund future operations or to serve as funding for expansion and growth. It indicates the financial health of a business.

- Income Statement: Also called a Profit and Loss statement, this report lists projected revenue and expenses. It shows whether a company will be profitable during a given time period.

- Cash Flow Statement: A projection of cash receipts and expense payments. It shows how and when cash will flow through the business; without cash, payments (including salaries) cannot be made.

- Operating Budget: A detailed breakdown of income and expenses; provides a guide for how the company will operate from a "dollars" point of view.

- Break-Even Analysis: A projection of the revenue required to cover all fixed and variable expenses. Shows when, under specific conditions, a business can expect to become profitable.

It is easy to find examples of all of the above. Even the most basic accounting software packages include templates and samples. You can also find templates in Excel and Google Docs. (A quick search like "google docs profit and loss statement" yields plenty of examples.)

Or you can work with an accountant to create the necessary financial projections and documents. Certainly feel free to do so… but I would first recommend playing around with the reports yourself. While you do not need to be an accountant to run a business, you do need to understand your numbers… and the best way to understand your numbers is usually to actually work with your numbers.

But ultimately the tools you use to develop your numbers are not as important as whether those numbers are as accurate as possible – and whether those numbers help you decide whether to take the next step and put your business plan into action.

Then Financial Analysis can help you answer the most important business question: "Can we make a profit?

Statutory Compliances

Whether you are a giant corporation or a startup, to be successful, it is important to analyse if you are compliant and are following certain laid-down protocols. It is imperative to keep a close eye on the laws in the city or state or country you operate in, failing which you are likely to overlook compliance responsibilities and face damaging penalties and lawsuits that could severely impede the progress of your business entity.

Organisations that have shown a great deal of promise have had founders step down, executives replaced and employees lost due to bypassing important compliance procedures. A business entity that is compliant is automatically trustworthy to its clients and investors.

All businesses, particularly startups, should follow certain compliance protocols.

1. Choosing the right business entity

Choosing the right business vehicle for their venture is a major challenge faced by any entrepreneur. This choice will in the near and long term affect the startup's viability, visibility, sustainability, suitability, and profitability. Your long-term goals, vision and objectives will decide whether the startup will be established as a private limited company, public limited company, partnership firm or a limited liability partnership.

Each of these categories has a different set of compliance procedures and laws. To avoid any backfiring in the form of legal hassles or otherwise, it is better to be aware of all these formalities right at the inception stage.

2. Statutory compliances

The credibility of any business highly depends on its compliance with all the applicable laws. For a Company and LLP, the mandatory compliances with the Registrar of Companies (RoC - India) are the most essential of all. Some of the important provisions include appointment of auditor, conducting board and shareholder's meetings, filing statutory annual returns and maintenance of statutory registers. These criteria should be met and will be verified by the investors.

a) **Appointment of auditors**

The first auditors of a company should be appointed within one month of its incorporation and shall hold office till the conclusion of the first annual general meeting. Thereafter, an auditor who can hold office for a period of consecutive five years shall be appointed.

b) **Conducting board meetings**

At least one meeting should be conducted in every three calendar months. Four such meetings should be held every calendar year. The Chairman of the said meeting signs the minutes of the meeting.

c) **Filing financial statements and annual returns**

Private Limited Companies are required to file its Annual Accounts and Returns disclosing details of its shareholders, directors, etc., to the Registrar of Companies. Such fillings are required to be made once in a year.

d) **Maintaining statutory registers and records**

A Private Limited Company has to maintain various statutory registers and records as required by the Company law such as Register of Shares, Register of Members, Register of Directors, etc. Besides, Incorporation documents of the company, Resolutions of the Meetings of the Board of Directors, Minutes of the Board Meetings and Annual General Meeting, etc., are also required to be preserved by the company.

3. Audit compliances

The purpose of a statutory audit is to determine whether an organisation is providing a fair and accurate representation of its financial position by examining information such as bank balances, book keeping records and financial transactions. Compliances related to audit include appointment of the statutory auditors of the company and finalising annual accounts with the auditors of the company.

4. Payroll compliances

It is obvious that you will have employees working for you when you start an organisation. There will be employees, independent consultants and contractors as well. Such professional relationships are governed by various labour legislations. For instance, in India, a business with an employee strength of over 20 needs to comply with ESI and PF regulations.

5. Taxation

A business has to pay taxes to the Central/State government or local bodies. Thus, every new entrepreneur should have the know-how of the aspects of taxation. Tax laws vary with sector and any recent changes should be within an entrepreneur's radar.

Tax compliance measures vary with the kind of business and the nature of services. A company selling goods would need to comply with the state VAT laws (In India); now GST. Similarly, businesses working as service providers need to obtain service tax registration, make service tax payments and file service tax returns on time. The business should also comply with relevant income tax rules and regulations.

Whether you are a giant corporation or a startup, to be successful, it is important to analyse if you are compliant and are following certain laid-down protocols. It is imperative to keep a close eye on the laws in the city or state you operate in, failing which you are likely to overlook compliance responsibilities and face damaging penalties and lawsuits that could severely impede the progress of your business entity. You will most certainly fail investor due diligence after the months of hard work of finding an interested investor.

Governance

We often use terms that draw parallels to sports when discussing startups - expressions like MVP and key man risk are commonplace in startup spaces, for instance. With this being the case, here's a new sporting term we at Natio Cultus advocate should feature more often in entrepreneurial discourse: the corporate governance playbook.

Corporate governance is often misunderstood. It is not, as most entrepreneurs believe, a practice reserved for large multinationals and publicly listed firms. It is not a science, nor is it something that is complex to implement.

When working with entrepreneurs, we describe their corporate governance playbook as a document that identifies the roles, authority and timing in key business decisions between shareholders, directors and the CEO. It is an important aspect of your enterprise and here's why you should focus on corporate governance at the outset of any venture:

- It manages complex decision-making startups are just as complex as large multinational firms, albeit in a different fashion. Founders are often the CEOs of their venture, they also hold shares, and sit on the Board of Directors. Many angel investors will also require a board seat to oversee their investment. If you have raised funding from venture capital firms, then you will need to manage their interests in the shareholding structure, the composition of your board and the role of the CEO. As your startup grows, the interplay between these three levels requires active management. The responsibilities, authority levels and timing of decision-making need detailing. Your playbook should outline when meetings occur, what decisions require board approval and the structure of your board of directors.

- It saves you time. Anyone that has been involved in a startup knows that decisions need to be made quickly. Your ability to manoeuvre and take swift decisions can make or break your strategy. One of the hardest things to hear from a board member or shareholder is: "Why was I not told about it?" Or: "Let's discuss this at the next board meeting." Clearly laying out the authority matrix of your business and the timing and subjects of your board meetings in advance can shape a corporate culture that not only empowers CEOs, but delineates accountability when the tough decisions need to be made. Sketching your playbook and agreeing on it in advance can save you time in the long run.

- ◆ It promotes investor confidence. As an investor, a corporate governance playbook is one of the first things I ask to see at a startup requesting funding. Seeing a well laid out approach to accountability, responsibility and timing of decisions between shareholders, boards of directors and the CEO gives an investor clarity and confidence on the structure of your venture. Understanding how the board is composed, the process of appointment and how votes are dealt with, clarifies a lot of unknowns before shareholder agreements are negotiated. A clear way to differentiate yourselves from other startups and impress investors is to be proactive and share your playbook with them.

Getting started with your playbook is not a difficult task. Think about the major decisions that your startup may face in the long run and highlight the way in which the three levels will engage to overcome challenges. Corporate governance playbooks are not static documents and they will continue to evolve as your startup grows. Liken yourself to a coach of a sports team and the effort that he puts into making his playbook. I personally often use sailing to draw parallels to corporate governance: if your sailboat is your startup, then your corporate governance playbook clearly lays out the relationship between your stakeholders before race day. When you go out onto the racecourse for your fiscal year, you can concentrate on what CEOs need to focus on, which is, steering the ship

Governance is about more than just management and in today's fast-moving world of digital tech and innovative business models, it has never been more important.

It Is Tough & Complicated

The way a founder chooses to act within their business is a very personal and subjective thing. Take the example of former Google director and now Twitter and Dropbox advisor, Kim Smith. In 2000, she was the founder and CEO of Juice Software and she had one thing to do: price her product. She had blocked off her whole morning to make this decision.

The moment she stepped into the office, co-workers confronted her. One wanted to discuss a health concern, another about his kid excelling at school, another about a disintegrating marriage. She listened to each one in turn and you guessed it, never priced the product. "For a minute I thought, this is where the assholes really have the advantage," said Scott. "But that's not right either. Good managers give a damn."

This example illustrates the dilemma of governing a small or medium-sized enterprise (SME) perfectly. How should founders position themselves within a business? How should they adapt as the business grows? Today's founders are expected to be friends, co-workers, managers, shareholders and directors all at the same time. This is the challenge of entrepreneurial governance.

Split personality?

Nowadays entrepreneurs must perform several roles within their startup:

1. You work in your business

You have day-to-day tasks like any other team member and as a manager must be ready to roll up your sleeves to ensure results are achieved.

2. You work at your business

You are responsible for the business' longevity: you deal with various stakeholders in and around your business and must look ahead as you try to improve it.

3. You are a stakeholder

As an owner you seek short and long-term value through financial results because, after all, you are investing your own time and money in the business.

4. You are a director

You must distance yourself from the business in order to monitor it according to your goals and make objective decisions, but also act as a sparring partner – someone who co-workers can bounce ideas off in an informal way.

In the corporate world, these responsibilities are divided between various roles. Meanwhile, entrepreneurs have to switch between them on a daily basis. As a modern entrepreneur, it is no longer enough to work in your business as a manger. Governance is more than management. It involves maintaining an overview of your business with regards to team members, investors, competitors and market trends. Governance helps to realise the creation of short and long-term value, is a balancing act between change and stability. It is also no longer optional.

The essence of entrepreneurship in the twenty-first century is responsiveness: to people, market trends, competition, developments in technology and the global economy. All successful start-ups are dynamic, but creating this dynamism does not happen overnight and can be hard to maintain as the business grows and processes are set. It takes time to put the right structures in place and develop a culture that balances innovation with stability.

Governance can lay the foundation for smart entrepreneurship. Today all major corporations are built on strong corporate governance. But how do we account for governance in SMEs where roles can shift and business models can change rapidly?

Various Aspects & Tools

Corporate governance concepts are crucial for the long-term success of a business. Listed companies (e.g., those with listed debt or equity instruments) are even required by most regulatory bodies to adopt a code of governance that complies with the minimum requirements of the listing country. This just highlights how important corporate governance is.

While it sounds intimidating, governance per se simply means establishing and maintaining a set of systems or processes to direct and control the business.

Board of directors

The typical governance concepts heavily focus on the role of the Board of Directors. These people are typically referred to as those charged with governance in most professional texts.

The Board of Directors, in their capacity as those charged with governance, represents the interest of the shareholders of the company in the business. This mechanism provides a check-and-balance between the management (i.e. c-suite and below) and the shareholders (as represented by the Board of Directors).

The startup scene

Most startups are initially structured with peers working together to develop a product and do not necessarily involve external parties. Although there are several companies that are externally funded (e.g., through venture capitals or angel investors), these only represent a small portion of the startup population.

Startups that do not have a formal board structure and established practices in good governance are at risk of failing. Several startup post mortem reports show that around nine out of 10 startups fail for various reasons.

Good governance

Before I go further into discussing the bridging mechanism that startup founders can adopt, it would be good if I discuss first what good governance actually means. The UK Corporate Governance Code, as published by the Financial Reporting Council, indicates the following underlying principles of good governance:

- Accountability
- Transparency
- Probity
- Focus on sustainable success

Accountability refers to the board's overall responsibility on the nature and extent of risks taken by the company to achieve its strategic objectives.

Startups that do not have a formal board structure and established practices in good governance are at risk of failing.

Transparency refers to the full disclosure of potential conflicts of interest between the board and the company. It also applies to the decision-making process of the board.

Setting the tone at the top should not be just on the management level; probity and ethics should be the driving force that the Board of Directors should represent.

And lastly, sustainable success provides the big picture of corporate governance. Governance at its best is not about taking excessive risks (even to the extent of fraud) but making sure that the business can continue long-term.

- Bridging the gap

    The lack of a formal board structure presents a unique challenge for startups. I'll talk about governance here in two parts. The first one will be on the governance role of the founders themselves and the second part will be about governance role of external parties.

Internal mechanisms

Governance mechanisms for startups begin with establishing a system to ensure trust and confidence that the founders do their fair share of work. This is the foundation for the owner-founder structure; a breach of trust can mean the collapse of the business itself.

The process of establishing governance mechanisms is usually waived due to strong relationships among the founders. But failing to draw a clear line between work and personal relationships can cause future misunderstandings within the founding group.

Implementing internal governance involves at least a clear delineation of the following:

- Individual roles and responsibilities of founders
- Scope of work
- Payment schemes for founders and employees
- Agreement on crucial business processes (e.g. recruitment, procurement and business development)

Establishing a clear governance policy upfront might sound a bit uptight. But making sure that business relationships are well-managed provides a solid ground for a sustainable business.

External mechanisms

The expansion of the startup community has established a strong network of mentors and founders. These support groups help most new founders and entrepreneurs in navigating the business landscape.

While most of the businesses do not have the support of an incubator to help them learn how to manage their businesses, a lot of founders owe their success to a mentor. Richard Branson is an example. When he was launching Virgin Atlantic, Sir Freddie Laker served as his mentor in gaining experience in the aviation industry.

How to assess external advisors

Here are some traits you need to look for in a mentor or consultant or advisor:

- Provides you the knowledge/expertise that you need for your business
- Gives you advice on long-term strategies and guides you on getting up to speed
- Covers you off on financial and accounting requirements
- Keeps you within the bounds of the legal framework
- Or should I just formalize the board?

Formalizing the board is a good idea when the business is relatively stable and long-term growth prospects are much clearer. When you reach this stage, proceed with learning more about establishing the perfect board for your business.

- Do You Have a Finalized, Comprehensive Agreement with Your Cofounders?

It is a classic story: a couple of friends get together to work on a great idea without having an agreement over ownership or at least one that's been finalized in a clear, comprehensive, legally operative document. Then, when money begins to flow in or even the idea of investment becomes more real, everything changes and conflicts and misunderstandings arise. Some tension and awkwardness over finalizing an agreement with your cofounders is natural and fine, but the time to work through those issues is before you approach angel investors, not after. Make sure you have either a finalized, duly-executed operating agreement if operating as an LLC or a stockholders' agreement if your company has incorporated. These agreements should cover topics such as management rights, what happens if a founder dies or leaves the company early and restrictions on transferring their stock.

Conclusion: Company Readiness

"Potential is a dangerous aphrodisiac, it will thrill, chill and kill your company, before you experience the high"

In each business experience, there have been a handful of growing pains and I've learned that in order to prepare yourself, you need to make sure you are ready on all fronts. Before investors begin flocking to your gates, ensure things at home are taken care of. Take precautionary measures to guarantee your business is presentable on all fronts, has a strong online presence and that standard operations are smooth. It is important to have a strong foundation built before a whirlwind of events takes you by surprise. In doing so, you can make sure you do not miss out on lead generation, overall growth and potential marketing opportunities.

Selling your business is often complex and time-consuming. A great adviser can help you to sell your business at the maximum valuation and keep as much money from the sale as possible, by:

- Discussing your key objectives
- Exploring all the available options
- Helping you to choose the optimal sales strategy
- Working with you on a realistic valuation
- Assembling and presenting key financial information
- Minimising your tax liabilities from the sale
- Assessing (and recommending) potential investors or buyers
- Drafting paperwork
- Support with negotiations

Selling your business or receiving investment have huge implications, so it is best to seek out an advisor that is highly experienced in supporting businesses through investment rounds and/or acquisitions.

Using tools like the Funding Readiness Report developed for the India Fund Fest is a quicker and more objective way to assess your businesses readiness for external funding.

PART III
Investor Readiness

"Our character caps the extent of our success"

Overview: Investors' World

An entrepreneur with an idea and a solid business plan cannot figure out why investors are not flocking to offer startup capital. From their perspective, it seems like the company should be an investor magnet. Unfortunately, they have no idea how to change the situation and attract funding.

Every investor wants to bet on a winning horse. I mean what is the point in losing money on purpose? But that is the risk taken on a gamble. And the same can be said about investing in startups.

One of investors' chief complaints is that entrepreneurs come to them unprepared, pitching business models that do not qualify for investor funding. These angels wish entrepreneurs would not waste time seeking an investment they have no hope of getting, but instead would take time to better educate themselves before asking for their concepts to be considered.

Having gone through the first two parts of this book, you are well prepared as an entrepreneur and as a business. It is now time to get ready to face investors.

In my experience, there are more people looking to invest money in a good venture, than entrepreneurs looking for investors. Part of the gap that entrepreneurs perceive is due to their own ill preparedness. The world of investors is brutal, with their own language, methods of evaluation, calculations and outlook. If you have ever borrowed money from a bank or dealt with the accountants in your company, you will understand what I mean.

Reverse the situation for a bit and humour me. If you had a couple of million dollars of your hard earned money and you could spare it for investment, where would you put it?

- A banks' fixed deposit with negligible risk earning 6–8% interest per annum
- Loan in the private market at 3% per month
- A piece of property that could appreciate over years and possibly provide rental income
- Gold that is time tested and has stable returns if you wait long enough

- Stock market (directly or through a mutual fund) earning anywhere between 20–40% depending on the country and sectors

- Or in a startup that has a 90% chance of failing in the first two years?

Now figure this, have you ever asked for money from your friends and family? Was it easy to ask or get? Were you asked questions? Did you feel belittled? What was the success rate? Remember this is among trusted people and probably small amounts of money. So, how and why do you expect a stranger to give you a load of money for uncertain return and no collateral?

When pitching, it is essential for entrepreneurs to know how investors think about:

- The promise of high returns. Angels are drawn to investments that pay back at least six to ten times their initial capital infusion. Most attractive to them is a highly scalable business model or a new business in an actively growing market segment. Without a clear strategy for generating this level of return, investors will not put up their money.

- Speed of return. Angels expect to achieve their returns in three to five years. This usually means that, at the three to five-year mark, someone either will be looking to acquire the startup or it will be well on the road to going public.

- Where the deal originates. Most investors find their best deals through trusted networks or referral sources. Entrepreneurs need to understand which groups and individuals investors rely on and they need to build relationships with the intermediaries who can get them in front of investors.

- The people behind the idea. What angels look for in a good investment has more to do with the people running the business than with the company's idea, its financials or even its projected return. Investors look for common themes, including past evidence of business or professional success, the willingness to be mentored and the depth of understanding of the industry in which the company will operate. No business plan survives the first contact with customers and investors already anticipate that things will not unfold exactly as expected. They look for leaders who can handle adversity and are quick to adapt.

- How to determine valuation. Valuation is a subjective topic and angel investors debate it all the time. Because there are not any universally accepted formulas for calculating a valuation, entrepreneurs will find varied perspectives.

If you are an entrepreneur looking for startup capital, failing to increase your investor IQ is as big an offense as not talking with your customers before launching your product. Very few business ideas are attractive for investors and competition for startup dollars is fierce. By taking to heart the investor insights, you will learn how to refine your pitch so it stands out.

Types of Investors

Professional/Institutional funding works like gears. A typical startup goes through several rounds of funding and at each round you want to take just enough money to reach the speed where you can shift into the next gear.

Few startups get it quite right. Many are underfunded. A few are overfunded, which is like trying to start driving in third gear.

Funded companies soon realize that all the worst problems they face in their startup are due not to competitors, but investors. Dealing with competitors is easy by comparison. Competitors punch you in the jaw, but investors have you by the balls.

Trouble with investors is one of the biggest threats to a startup, managing them is one of the most important skills founders need to learn. But well before that it is important to understand each class of investors and how they operate.

Then we will trace the life of a hypothetical (very fortunate) startup as it shifts gears through successive rounds.

Friends and Family

A lot of startups get their first funding from friends and family. This is especially true of first time entrepreneurs, early stage startups and service model startups.

If your friends or family happen to be rich, the line blurs between them and angel investors. The advantage of raising money from friends and family is that they are easy to find. You already know them. There are three main disadvantages: you mix together your business and personal life; they will probably not be as well connected as angels or venture firms; and they may not be accredited investors, which could complicate your life later.

The SEC defines an "accredited investor" as someone with over a million dollars in liquid assets or an income of over $200,000 a year. The regulatory burden is much lower if a company's shareholders are all accredited investors. Once you take money from the general public you are more restricted in what you can do. There are similar laws in India by SEBI and most other countries and the thresholds are coming down.

A startup's life will be more complicated, legally, if any of the investors are not accredited. In an IPO, it might not merely add expense, but change the outcome. A lawyer I asked about it said:

When the company goes public, the regulatory authorities will carefully study all prior issuances of stock by the company and demand that it takes immediate action to cure any past violations of securities laws. Those remedial actions can delay, stall or even kill the IPO.

Of course, the odds of any given startup doing an IPO are small. But not as small as they might seem. A lot of startups that end up going public did not seem likely to at first. Much of the value of a startup consists of that tiny probability multiplied by the huge outcome.

It is not because they are not accredited investors that most entrepreneurs do not ask their parents for seed money, though. They just do not know about the concept of an accredited investor and do not stop to think about the value of investors' connections. The reason they do not take money from parents is that they did not want them to lose it.

Angel Investors

Angels are individual rich people. The word was first used for backers of Broadway plays, but now applies to individual investors generally. Angels who have made money in your industry are preferable, for two reasons: they understand your situation and they are a source of contacts and advice.

The contacts and advice can be more important than the money. When del.icio.us took money from investors, they took money from, among others, Tim O'Reilly. The amount he put in was small compared to the VCs who led the round, but Tim is a smart and influential guy and it is good to have him on your side.

You can do whatever you want with money from friends and family. With angels we are now talking about venture funding proper, so it is time to introduce the concept of exit strategy. Younger would-be founders are often surprised that investors expect them either to sell the company or go public. The reason is that investors need to get their capital back. They will only consider companies that have an exit strategy — meaning companies that could get bought or go public.

This is not as selfish as it sounds. The reason is that employees are investors too — of their time — and they want just as much to be able to cash out.

If your competitors offer employees stock options that might make them rich, while you make it clear you plan to stay private, your competitors will get the best people. So the principle of an "exit" is not just something forced on startups by investors, but part of what it means to be a startup.

Another concept we need to introduce now is valuation. When someone buys shares in a company, that implicitly establishes a value for it. If someone pays $20,000 for 10% of a company, the company is in theory worth $200,000. I say "in theory" because in early stage investing, valuations are voodoo. As a company gets more established, its valuation gets closer to an actual market value. But in a newly founded startup, the valuation number is just an artefact of the respective contributions of everyone involved.

Startups often "pay" investors who will help the company in some way by letting them invest at low valuations. If I had a startup and Bill Gates wanted to invest in it, I'd give him the stock for $10, just to be able to brag that he was an investor. Unfortunately, it is impractical (if not illegal) to adjust the valuation of the company up and down for each investor. Startups' valuations are supposed to rise over time. So, if you are going to sell cheap stock to eminent angels, do it early, when it is natural for the company to have a low valuation.

Some angel investors join together in syndicates. Any city where people start startups will have one or more of them. In India you have the Indian Angel network and many private syndicates. However, most angel investors do not belong to these groups. In fact, the more prominent the angel, the less likely they are to belong to a group. Although they may partner with various other Angels to form teams depending on the venture.

Some angel groups charge you money to pitch your idea to them. Needless to say, you should never do this.

One of the dangers of taking investment from individual angels, rather than through an angel group or investment firm, is that they have less reputation to protect. A big-name VC firm will not screw you too outrageously, because other founders would avoid them if word got out. With individual angels you do not have this protection, as many Indian startups find to their dismay. In many startups' lives there comes a point when you are at the investors' mercy — when you are out of money and the only place to get more is your existing investors. When you get into such a situation, your investors could take advantage of it in a way that a name-brand VC probably would not.

Angels have a corresponding advantage, however: they are also not bound by all the rules that VC firms are. And so, they can, for example, allow founders to cash out partially in a funding round, by selling some of their stock directly to the investors. I think this will become more common; the average founder is eager to do it and selling, say, half a million dollars worth of stock will not, as VCs fear, cause most founders to be any less committed to the business.

Deal terms with angels vary a lot. There are no generally accepted standards. Sometimes angels' deal terms are as fearsome as VCs.' Other angels, particularly in the earliest stages, will invest based on a two-page agreement. In markets where many Angels are learning the ropes of startup investing, you may face requests for taking the money as debt with interest; I would advise you walk away from such discussions.

Seed Funding Firms

Seed firms are like angels in that they invest relatively small amounts at early stages, but like VCs in that they are companies that do it as a business, rather than individuals making occasional investments on the side.

Till now, nearly all seed firms have been so-called "incubators." According to the National Association of Business Incubators, there are about 800 incubators in the US. This is an astounding number, because I know the founders of a lot of startups and I cannot think of one that began in an incubator.

What is an incubator? I'm not sure myself. The defining quality seems to be that you work in their space. That is where the name "incubator" comes from. They seem to vary a great deal in other respects. At one extreme is the sort of pork-barrel project where a town gets money from the state government to renovate a vacant building as a "high-tech incubator," as if it were merely lack of the right sort of office space that had, till now, prevented the town from becoming a startup hub. At the other extreme are places like Idealab, which generates ideas for new startups internally and hires people to work for them.

India now has the third-highest number of startup incubators and accelerators in the world after China and the US, says a report by IT industry body National Association of Software and Services Companies (NASSCOM) and Zinnov Consulting.

With 140 incubators and accelerators, India has inched past Israel, whose count stands at 130. However, the gap between the top two is still yawning — China and the US have over 2,400 and 1,500 incubators and accelerators, respectively.

The number of incubators and accelerators in India grew a sharp 40% in 2016, with more than 40 of them seeing the light of day, says the report titled 'Incubators/Accelerators (I/As) Driving the Growth of Indian Start-up Ecosystem–2017.' Of these, 30 academic incubators were established under the government's 'Start-up India Stand-up India' initiative.

Bangalore, Mumbai and Delhi-NCR continue to be the hubs, with more than 40% of all incubators and accelerators concentrated in these areas. However, Tier-II cities are also gaining traction, with the number in such locations rising a steep 66% over last year.

An incubator typically mentors a startup for 6 months to 3 years, providing resources such as dedicated office space, networking with investors and technical training, among other things. In comparison, an accelerator typically hand-holds for 3–12 months, providing sessions on venture capital, road shows, CEO coaching and developer tools. Most incubators in India are run by academic institutions (nearly 51%) while the rest are either corporate (9%), independent (32%) or government-supported (8%).

Some multi-national companies, like payments firm Paypal and pharma giant Pfizer, run their own incubators. IT giant Cisco and e-commerce solutions provider Pitney Bowes run their own accelerators.

The classic Bubble incubators, most of which now seem to be dead, were like VC firms except that they took a much bigger role in the startups they funded. In addition to working in their space, you were supposed to use their office staff, lawyers, accountants and so on.

Incubators tend to exert more control than VCs. And I think it is better if startups operate out of their own premises, however crappy, than the offices of their investors.

Because seed firms are companies rather than individual people, reaching them is easier than reaching angels. Just go to their website and send them an email. The importance of personal introductions varies, but is less than with angels or VCs.

The fact that seed firms are companies also means the investment process is more standardized. (This is generally true with angel groups too.) Seed firms will probably have set deal terms they use for every startup they fund. The fact that the deal terms are standard does not mean they are favourable to you, but if other startups have signed the same agreements and things went well for them, it is a sign the terms are reasonable.

Seed firms differ from angels and VCs in that they invest exclusively in the earliest phases—often when the company is still just an idea. In India the lines can be blurry with seed companies investing upto cash breakeven stage. Angels and even VC firms occasionally do this, but they also invest at later stages.

The problems are different in the early stages. For example, in the first couple of months, a startup may completely redefine their idea. So, seed investors usually care less about the idea than the people. This is true of all venture funding, but especially so in the seed stage.

Like VCs, one of the advantages of seed firms is the advice they offer. But because seed firms operate in an earlier phase, they need to offer different kinds of advice. For example, a seed firm should be able to give advice about how to approach VCs, which VCs obviously do not need to do; whereas VCs should be able to give advice about how to hire an "executive team," which is not an issue in the seed stage.

In the earliest phases, a lot of the problems are technical, so seed firms should be able to help with technical as well as business problems.

Seed firms and angel investors generally want to invest in the initial phases of a startup, then hand them off to VC firms for the next round. Occasionally, startups go from seed funding direct to acquisition and I expect this to become increasingly common.

Google has been aggressively pursuing this route and now Yahoo is too. Both now compete directly with VCs. And this is a smart move. Why wait for further funding rounds to jack up a startup's price? When a startup reaches the point where VCs have enough information to invest in it, the acquirer should have enough information to buy it. More information, in fact, with their technical depth, the acquirers should be better at picking winners than VCs.

Venture Capital Funds

VC firms are like seed firms in that they are actual companies, but they invest other people's money and much larger amounts of it. VC investments average several million dollars. So, they tend to come later in the life of a startup, are harder to get and come with tougher terms.

The word "Venture Capitalist" is sometimes used loosely for any venture investor, but there is a sharp difference between VCs and other investors: VC firms are organized as funds, much like hedge funds or mutual funds. The fund managers, who are called "general partners," get about 2% of the fund annually as a management fee, plus about 20% of the fund's gains.

There is a very sharp dropoff in performance among VC firms, because in the VC business both success and failure are self-perpetuating. When an investment scores spectacularly, as Google did for Kleiner and Sequoia, it generates a lot of good publicity for the VCs. And many founders prefer to take money from successful VC firms, because of the legitimacy it confers. Hence a vicious (for the losers) cycle: VC firms that have been doing badly will only get the deals the bigger fish have rejected, causing them to continue to do badly.

As a result, of the thousand or so VC funds in the US now, only about 50 are likely to make money and it is very hard for a new fund to break into this group. The numbers in India for the 100 odd operating VCs are much worse.

In a sense, the lower-tier VC firms are a bargain for founders. They may not be quite as smart or as well connected as the big-name firms, but they are hungrier for deals. This means you should be able to get better terms from them.

Better how? The most obvious is valuation: they will take less of your company. But as well as money, there's power. I think founders will increasingly be able to stay on as CEO and on terms that will make it fairly hard to fire them later.

The most dramatic change, I predict, is that VCs will allow founders to cash out partially by selling some of their stock direct to the VC firm. VCs have traditionally resisted letting founders get anything before the ultimate "liquidity event." But they are also desperate for deals. And since I know from my own experience that the rule against buying stock from founders is a stupid one, this is a natural place for things to give as venture funding becomes more and more a seller's market.

The disadvantage of taking money from less known firms is that people will assume, correctly or not, that you were turned down by the more exalted ones. But, like where you went to college, the name of your VC stops mattering once you have some performance to measure. So the more confident you are, the less you need a brand-name VC.

Another danger of less known firms is that, like angels, they have less reputation to protect. I suspect it is the lower-tier firms that are responsible for most of the tricks that have given VCs such a bad reputation among hackers.

They are doubly hosed: the general partners themselves are less able and yet they have harder problems to solve, because the top VCs skim off all the best deals, leaving the lower-tier firms exactly the startups that are likely to blow up.

For example, lower-tier firms are much more likely to pretend to want to do a deal with you just to lock you up while they decide if they really want to. The better ones usually will not give a term sheet unless they really want to do a deal. The second or third tier firms have a much higher break rate — it could be as high as 50%.

It is obvious why: the lower-tier firms' biggest fear, when chance throws them a bone, is that one of the big dogs will notice and take it away. The big dogs do not have to worry about that.

Falling victim to this trick could really hurt you. If you were talking to four VCs, told three of them that you accepted a term sheet and then have to call them back to tell them you were just kidding, you are absolutely damaged goods.

Here's a partial solution: when a VC offers you a term sheet, ask how many of their last 10 term sheets turned into deals. This will at least force them to lie outright if they want to mislead you.

Not all the people who work at VC firms are partners. Most firms also have a handful of junior employees called something like associates or analysts. If you get a call from a VC firm, go to their website and check whether the person you talked to is a partner. Odds are it will be a junior person; they scour the web looking for startups their bosses could invest in. The junior people will tend to seem very positive about your company. They are not pretending; they want to believe you are a hot prospect, because it would be a huge coup for them if their firm invested in a company they discovered. Do not be misled by this optimism. It is the partners who decide, and they view things with a colder eye.

Because VCs invest large amounts, the money comes with more restrictions. Most only come into effect if the company gets into trouble. For example, VCs generally write it into the deal that in any sale, they get their investment back first. So, if the company gets sold at a low price, the founders could get nothing. Some VCs now require that in any sale they get 4x their investment back before the common stock holders (that is, you) get anything, but this is an abuse that should be resisted.

Another difference with large investments is that the founders are usually required to accept "vesting"—to surrender their stock and earn it back over the next 4–5 years. VCs do not want to invest millions in a company the founders could just walk away from. Financially, vesting has little effect, but in some situations it could mean founders will have less power. If VCs got de facto control of the company and fired one of the founders, he would lose any unvested stock unless there was specific protection against this. So, vesting would, in that situation, force founders to toe the line.

The most noticeable change when a startup takes serious funding is that the founders will no longer have complete control. Ten years ago VCs used to insist that founders step down as CEO and hand the job over to a business guy they supplied. This is less the rule now, partly because the disasters of the Bubble showed that generic business guys do not make such great CEOs.

But while founders increasingly stay on as CEO, they do have to cede some power, because the board of directors will become more powerful. In the seed stage, the board is generally a formality; if you want to talk to the other board members, you just yell into the next room. This stops with VC-scale money. In a typical VC funding deal, the board of directors might be composed of two VCs, two founders and one outside person acceptable to both. The board will have ultimate power, which means the founders now have to convince instead of commanding.

This is not as bad as it sounds, however. Narayan Murthy is in the same position; he does not have majority control of Infosys; in principle he also has to convince instead of commanding. And yet he seems pretty commanding, doesn't he? As long as things are going smoothly, boards do not interfere much. The danger comes when there's a bump in the road, as happened to Steve Jobs at Apple or recently at Uber.

Like angels, VCs prefer to invest in deals that come to them through people they know. So, while nearly all VC funds have some address you can send your business plan to, VCs privately admit the chance of getting funding by this route is near zero. One recently told me that he did not know a single startup that got funded this way.

I suspect VCs accept business plans "over the transom" more as a way to keep tabs on industry trends than as a source of deals. In fact, I would strongly advise against mailing your business plan randomly to VCs, because they treat this as evidence of laziness. Do the extra work of getting personal introductions.

Investor thinking is, I am not hard to find. I know a lot of people. If you cannot find some way to reach me, how are you going to create a successful company?

If several VCs are interested in you, they will sometimes be willing to split the deal between them. They are more likely to do this if they are close in the VC pecking order. Such deals may be a net win for founders, because you get multiple VCs interested in your success and you can ask each for advice about the other.

Two-firm deals are great. It costs you a little more equity, but being able to play the two firms off each other (as well as ask one if the other is being out of line) is invaluable.

When you do negotiate with VCs, remember that they have done this a lot more than you have. They have invested in dozens of startups, whereas this is probably the first you have founded. But do not let them or the situation intimidate you. The average founder is smarter than the average VC. So just do what you'd do in any complex, unfamiliar situation: proceed deliberately, and question anything that seems odd.

It is, unfortunately, common for VCs to put terms in an agreement whose consequences surprise founders later and also common for VCs to defend things they do by saying that they are standard in the industry. Standard, is nonsense; the whole industry is only a few decades old and rapidly evolving. The concept of "standard" is a useful one when you are operating on a small scale (most angels, seed firms and smaller deal sized investments use identical terms for every deal because for tiny seed-stage investments it is not worth the overhead of negotiating individual deals), but it does not apply at the VC level. On that scale, every negotiation is unique.

A Hypothetical Startup

Most successful startups get money from more than one of the preceding sources. And, confusingly, the names of funding sources also tend to be used as the names of different rounds. The best way to explain how it all works is to follow the case of a hypothetical startup.

Stage 1: Seed Round

Our startup begins when a group of three friends have an idea – either an idea for something they might build or simply the idea "let's start a company." Presumably they already have some source of food and shelter. But if you have food and shelter, you probably also have something you are supposed to be working on: either classwork or a job. So, if you want to work full-time on a startup, your money situation will probably change too.

A lot of startup founders say they started the company without any idea of what they planned to do. This is actually less common than it seems: many have to claim they thought of the idea after quitting because otherwise their former employer would own it.

The three friends decide to take the leap. Since most startups are in competitive businesses, you not only want to work full-time on them, but more than full-time. So, some or all of the friends quit their jobs or leave school. (Some of the founders in a startup can stay in grad school, but at least one has to make the company his full-time job.)

They are going to run the company out of one of their apartments at first and since they do not have any users they do not have to pay much for infrastructure. Their main expenses are setting up the company, which costs a couple of thousand dollars in legal work and registration fees and the living expenses of the founders.

The phrase "seed investment" covers a broad range. To some VC firms it means $500,000, but to most startups it means several months' living expenses. We will suppose our group of friends start with $15,000 from their friend's rich uncle, who they give 5% of the company in return. There is only common stock at this stage. They leave 20% as an options pool for later employees (but they set things up so that they can issue this stock to themselves if they get bought early and most is still unissued) and the three founders each get 25%.

By living really cheaply they think they can make the remaining money last five months. When you have five months' runway left, how soon do you need to start looking for your next round? Answer: immediately. It takes time to find investors and time (always more than you expect) for the deal to close even after they say yes. So, if our group of founders know what they are doing they will start sniffing around for angel investors right away. But of course, their main job is to build version 1 of their software.

The friends might have liked to have more money in this first phase, but being slightly underfunded teaches them an important lesson. For a startup, cheapness is power. The lower your costs, the more options you have — not just at this stage, but at every point till you are profitable. When you have a high "burn rate," you are always under time pressure, which means (a) you do not have time for your ideas to evolve, and (b) you are often forced to take deals you do not like.

Every startup's rule should be: spend little, and work fast.

After ten weeks' work the three friends have built a prototype that gives one a taste of what their product will do. It is not what they originally set out to do—in the process of writing it, they had some new ideas. And it only does a fraction of what the finished product will do, but that fraction includes stuff that no one else has done before.

They have also written at least a skeleton business plan, addressing the five fundamental questions: what they are going to do, why users need it, how large the market is, how they will make money and who the competitors are and why this company is going to beat them. (That last has to be more specific than "they suck" or "we will work really hard.")

If you have to choose between spending time on the demo or the business plan, spend most on the demo. Software is not only more convincing, but a better way to explore ideas.

Stage 2: Angel Round

While writing the prototype, the group has been traversing their network of friends in search of angel investors. They find some just as the prototype is demo-able. When they demo it, one of the angels is willing to invest. Now the group is looking for more money: they want enough to last for a year and maybe to hire a couple of friends. So, they are going to raise $200,000.

The angel agrees to invest at a pre-money valuation of $1 million. The company issues $200,000 worth of new shares to the angel; if there were 1000 shares before the deal, this means 200 additional shares. The angel now owns 200/1200 shares or a sixth of the company and all the previous shareholders' percentage ownership is diluted by a sixth. After the deal, the capitalization table looks like this:

Shareholder	Shares	Percent
angel	200	16.7
uncle	50	4.2
each founder	250	20.8
option pool	200	16.7
Total	1200	100

To keep things simple, I had the angel do a straight cash for stock deal. In reality the angel might be more likely to make the investment in the form of a convertible loan. A convertible loan is a loan that can be converted into stock later; it works out the same as a stock purchase in the end, but gives the angel more protection against being squashed by VCs in future rounds.

Who pays the legal bills for this deal? The startup, remember, only has a couple of thousands left. In practice, this turns out to be a sticky problem that usually gets solved in some improvised way. Maybe the startup can find lawyers who will do it cheaply in the hope of future work if the startup succeeds. Maybe someone has a lawyer friend. Maybe the angel pays for his lawyer to represent both sides. (Make sure if you take the latter route that the lawyer is representing you rather than merely advising you or his only duty is to the investor.)

An angel investing $200K would probably expect a seat on the board of directors. He might also want preferred stock, meaning a special class of stock that has some additional rights over the common stock everyone else has. Typically, these rights include vetoes over major strategic decisions, protection against being diluted in future rounds and the right to get one's investment back first, if the company is sold.

Some investors might expect the founders to accept vesting for a sum this size and others would not. VCs are more likely to require vesting than angels. You should resist accepting vesting, because it makes you harder to push around.

I should add that vesting is also a way for founders to protect themselves against one another. It solves the problem of what to do if one of the founders quits. So, some founders impose it on themselves when they start the company.

The angel deal takes two weeks to close, so we are now three months into the life of the company.

The point after you get the first big chunk of angel money will usually be the happiest phase in a startup's life. You get to work on juicy kinds of work, like designing software. You do not have to spend time on bureaucratic stuff, because you have not hired any bureaucrats yet. Enjoy it while it lasts and get as much done as you can, because you will never again be so productive.

With an apparently inexhaustible sum of money sitting safely in the bank, the founders happily set to work turning their prototype into something they can release. They hire one of their friends — at first just as a consultant, so they can try him out — and then a month later as employee #1. They pay him the smallest salary he can live on, plus 3% of the company in restricted stock, vesting over four years. (So, after this the option pool is down to 13.7%). They also spend a little money on a freelance graphic designer.

How much stock do you give early employees? That varies so much that there is no conventional number. If you get someone really good, really early, it might be wise to give him as much stock as the founders. The one universal rule is that the amount of stock an employee gets decreases polynomially with the age of the company. In other words, you get rich as a power of how early you were. So, if some friends want you to come work for their startup, do not wait several months before deciding.

A month later, at the end of month four, our group of founders have something they can launch. Gradually through word of mouth they start to get users. Seeing the system in use by real users — people they do not know — gives them lots of new ideas. Also, they find they now worry obsessively about the status of their server.

By the end of month six, the system is starting to have a solid core of features and a small but devoted following. People start to write about it and the founders are starting to feel like experts in their field.

We will assume that their startup is one that could put millions more to use. Perhaps they need to spend a lot on marketing or build some kind of expensive infrastructure or hire highly paid salesmen. So, they decide to start talking to VCs. They get introductions to VCs from various sources: their angel investor connects them with a couple; they meet a few at conferences; a couple VCs call them after reading about them.

Step 3: Series A Round

Armed with their now somewhat fleshed-out business plan and able to demo a real working system, the founders visit the VCs they have introductions to. They find the VCs intimidating and inscrutable. They all ask the same question: who else have you pitched to? (VCs are like high school girls: they are acutely aware of their position in the VC pecking order and their interest in a company is a function of the interest other VCs show in it.)

One of the VC firms says they want to invest and offers the founders a term sheet. A term sheet is a summary of what the deal terms will be when and if they do a deal; lawyers will fill in the details later. By accepting the term sheet, the startup agrees to turn away other VCs for some set amount of time while this firm does the "due diligence" required for the deal. Due diligence is the corporate equivalent of a background check: the purpose is to uncover any hidden bombs that might sink the company later, like serious design flaws in the product, pending lawsuits against the company, intellectual property issues, and so on. VCs' legal and financial due diligence is pretty thorough, but the technical due diligence is generally a joke.

The due diligence discloses no ticking bombs, and six weeks later they go ahead with the deal. Here are the terms: a $2 million investment at a pre-money valuation of $4 million, meaning that after the deal closes the VCs will own a third of the company (2/(4 + 2)). The VCs also insist that prior to the deal the option pool be enlarged by an additional hundred shares. So, the total number of new shares issued is 750 and the cap table becomes:

Shareholder	Shares	Percent
VCs	650	33.3
angel	200	10.3
uncle	50	2.6
each founder	250	12.8
employee	36*	1.8 *unvested
option pool	264	13.5
Total	1950	100

This picture is unrealistic in several respects. For example, while the percentages might end up looking like this, it is unlikely that the VCs would keep the existing numbers of shares. In fact, every bit of the startup's paperwork would probably be replaced, as if the company were being founded anew. Also, the money might come in several tranches, the later ones subject to various conditions — though this is apparently more common in deals with lower-tier VCs (whose lot in life is to fund more dubious startups) than with the top firms.

And, of course, any VCs reading this are probably rolling on the floor laughing at how my hypothetical VCs let the angel keep his 10.3 of the company. I admit, this is the romanticized version; in simplifying the picture, I have also made everyone nicer. In the real world, VCs regard angels the way a jealous husband feels about his wife's previous boyfriends. To them the company did not exist before they invested in it.

I do not want to give the impression you have to do an angel round before going to VCs. In this example, I stretched things out to show multiple sources of funding in action. Some startups could go directly from seed funding to a VC round; several of the companies I consulted with, have.

The founders are required to vest their shares over four years and the board is now reconstituted to consist of two VCs, two founders and a fifth person acceptable to both. The angel investor cheerfully surrenders his board seat.

At this point there is nothing new our startup can teach us about funding — or at least, nothing good. The startup will almost certainly hire more people at this point; those millions must be put to work, after all. The company may do additional funding rounds, presumably at higher valuations. They may if they are extraordinarily fortunate do an IPO, which we should remember is also in principle a round of funding, regardless of its de facto purpose. But that, if not beyond the bounds of possibility, but that is another chapter altogether.

Deals Fall Through

Anyone who has been through a startup will find the preceding portrait to be missing something: disasters. If there is one thing all startups have in common, it is that something is always going wrong. And nowhere more than in matters of funding.

For example, our hypothetical startup never spent more than half of one round before securing the next. That's more ideal than typical. Many startups — even successful ones — come close to running out of money at some point. Terrible things happen to startups when they run out of money, because they are designed for growth, not adversity.

But the most unrealistic thing about the series of deals I have described is that they all closed. In the startup world, closing is not what deals do. What deals do is fall through. If you are starting a startup you would do well to remember that. Birds fly; fish swim; deals fall through.

Why? Partly the reason deals seem to fall through so often is that you lie to yourself. You want the deal to close, so you start to believe it will. But even correcting for this, startup deals fall through alarmingly often — far more often than, say, deals to buy real estate. The reason is that it is such a risky environment. People about to fund or acquire a startup are prone to wicked cases of buyer's remorse. They do not really grasp the risk they are taking till the deal is about to close. And then they panic. And not just inexperienced angel investors, but big companies too.

So if you are a startup founder wondering why some angel investor is not returning your phone calls, you can at least take comfort in the thought that the same thing is happening to other deals a hundred times the size.

The example of a startup's history that I've presented is like a skeleton — accurate so far as it goes, but needing to be fleshed out to be a complete picture. To get a complete picture, just add in every possible disaster and a few years in time.

A frightening prospect? In a way. And yet also in a way encouraging. The very uncertainty of startups frightens away almost everyone. People overvalue stability — especially young people, who ironically need it least. And so, in starting a startup, as in any really bold undertaking, merely deciding to do it gets you halfway there. On the day of the race, most of the other runners will not show up.

What about Government Grants

I have omitted one source: government grants. I do not think these are even worth thinking about for the average startup. Governments may mean well when they set up grant programs to encourage startups, but what they give with one hand they take away with the other: the process of applying is inevitably so arduous and the restrictions on what you can do with the money so burdensome, that it would be easier to take a job to get the money.

You should be especially suspicious of grants whose purpose is some kind of social engineering – e.g., to encourage more startups to be started in a particular state. Free money to start a startup in a place where few succeed is hardly free.

Financial Terms You Must Know

There are a lot of ways to get tripped up while building a company. Failing to understand financial jargon should not be one of them.

It is not that investors and venture capitalists are evil or anything. It is just that their interests do not perfectly align with those of entrepreneurs. You want to build a company, keep control and earn a fair share of any windfall. Investors want to profit from your company as much as possible, minimize their financial risk and often, gain the operating control needed to do so. Balancing these interests is a delicate process that requires a clear-eyed understanding of the terms involved during negotiations.

So, in the tsunami of legalese that entrepreneurs face during fundraising discussions, I have uncovered ten terms that I think are essential to understand. A familiarity with the phrases below will help you avoid needlessly giving up equity, control and profits in the event of a successful exit. This is no replacement for a lawyer, but it will help you, hopefully, call BS on less-than-forthcoming investors

Pre-money vs. Post-money Valuation

Let us start very simply: valuation is the monetary value of your company. Internally, company shareholders often agree on a formula to determine valuation in the event of a partner's death or exit. When looking for venture or angel financing, your valuation is, frankly, whatever you can convince investors to agree on.

The difference between pre-money valuation and post-money valuation is also very simple. Pre-money refers to your company's value before receiving funding. Let us say a venture firm agrees to a pre-money valuation of $10 million for your company. If they decide to invest $5 million, that makes your company's post-money valuation $15 million.

Post-money valuation = pre-money valuation + new funding

These terms are important because they determine the equity stake you will give up during the funding round. In the above example, the investor's

$5 million stake means he is left with 33% ownership of the company ($5 million/$15 million).

Let us consider a counterexample. Say the company was valued at $10 million post-money instead, implying a $5 million pre-money valuation. This means that the investor's $5 million counts as half the company's valuation. He comes away with 50% of the company in this scenario, rather than 33%. Given the difference in equity, you can see how important it is to clarify between pre and post-money valuations when discussing investment terms.

Convertible Debt (Convertible Notes)

When a company is young, quantifying its valuation is often an arbitrary, pointless exercise. There may not even be a product in hand, let alone revenue. But companies at this stage may still need to raise money and if investors decide on a pre-money valuation of say, $100,000, another $100,000 suddenly buys control.

Convertible debt (also called convertible notes) is a financing vehicle that allows startups to raise money while delaying valuation discussions until the company is more mature. Though technically convertible notes are meant to convert to equity at a later date, usually a round of funding. (Often notes convert to equity during a Series A round of funding.)

Investors who agree to use convertible notes generally receive warrants or a discount as a reward for putting their money in at the earliest, riskiest stages of the business. In short, this means that their cash converts to equity at a more favourable ratio than investors who come in at the valuation round.

Capped Notes vs. Uncapped Notes

As discussed above, convertible notes delay placing a valuation on a company until a later funding round. But investors often still want a say in the future valuation of the company so their stake does not get diluted down the line. When entrepreneurs and investors agree to a "capped" round, this means that they place a ceiling on the valuation at which investors' notes convert to equity.

So, if a company raises $500,000 in convertible notes at a $5 million cap, those investors will own at least 10% of the company after the Series A round ($500,000/$5M).

An uncapped round means that the investors get no guarantee of how much equity their convertible debt investments will purchase, making these kinds of investments most favourable for the entrepreneur. Let us consider a company that raises $500,000 in an uncapped round. If they end up making so much progress that they convince Series A investors to agree to a $10 million, this means that their convertible note investors are left with just 5% of the company, half of what they would get if they capped the round at $5 million. (For the sake of simplicity, we are ignoring discounts and warrants here.)

Again, you can see how important these distinctions are in terms of retaining ownership of your company.

Preferred Stock

Venture capital firms are issued preferred stock, rather than common stock in a company. Preferred stock comes with certain rights attached, some of which we will discuss below. The terms Series A, Series B, etc. refer to the class of preferred stock issued at each fundraising round.

Liquidation Preferences

Let us be very clear: the primary job of venture capitalists is to make money for their investors. Their investments are no good unless they eventually realize a payday. In venture parlance, these paydays are referred to as "liquidity events," the moments when everyone with an equity stake gets a chance to cash out. These events generally come in the form of acquisitions or an IPO. For less successful companies, a liquidation event could also come in the form of a bankruptcy.

Liquidation preferences determine who gets paid what and when during these events. If the company goes bankrupt, for instance, there often are not enough assets left to pay every creditor and shareholder the money they are due. In this instance, liquidation preferences determine the order in which everybody gets paid. Generally, creditors get paid first, then preferred stockholders, then, if there's anything left, common stockholders.

Liquidation preferences are also relevant during more successful outcomes though. The standard liquidation preference is 1x, meaning that preferred stock owners must get their money back (1 x their money) before common stock holders get anything. More on this below.

Participating Preferred vs. Non-participating Preferred Stock

This is where things start to get a little complicated. You see, there are different types of preferred stock, each giving its holder different rights. For our purposes, the rights of participating and non-participating stockholders are most relevant.

Remember that preferred stock owners often get a 1x liquidation preference, meaning that in the event of a sale or bankruptcy, they get their money back before common stock holders get a chance to recoup anything.

Let us say instead that the company realizes a more successful exit and common stock holders are left with equity worth 4x what preferred stock owners paid per share at the time of their investment. In this case, preferred stock owners can still exercise their liquidation preference to get their money back, but if everyone else is making four times that money, it makes more sense to convert those preferred shares into common stock to enjoy the 4x gains. During successful outcomes, preferred stock owners are essentially forced to convert to common stock.

For non-participating stockholders, this is where it ends. They convert their shares to common stock and enjoy the same 4x returns as everyone else. Simple enough.

Participating preferred stock, however, works differently and allows venture investors to essentially double dip in the company's gains. Participating stockholders get to exercise both their liquidation preference and enjoy a pro-rata (see below for an explanation) share of common stock gains simultaneously. So, if a participating stockholder owns 25% of the company at the time of a liquidation event, they get their money back plus 25% of the remaining proceeds. Let us use an example to illustrate the differences:

Say a company sells for $10 million. Investors originally put in $2.5 million at a $5 million post-money valuation, leaving them with 50% of the company. If they have non-participating preferred shares, they are obligated to convert those shares to common stock, leaving them with $5 million. Simple and fair, right?

Now let's say instead that these investors own participating preferred stock. The outcome changes significantly. In this scenario investors can exercise their 1x liquidation preference, leaving them with $2.5 million. But it does not end there. In addition to getting their money back, they are entitled to a 50% share of the remaining $7.5 million. This means that they get another $3.75 million, leaving them with $6.25 million. In this case, they capture most of the exit's value even while owning just half of the company.

Pro-rata Rights

The term pro-rata gets thrown around a lot during financing discussions, often in different contexts. Pro-rata is Latin for "in proportion." Replacing the Latin with it is English equivalent is generally helpful in deciphering its meaning in legal documents.

Pro-rata rights refer to the right of investors to participate in later funding rounds so they can maintain the amount of equity they own in a company. Let's say that a company raises a $5 million Series A round from an investor at a $20 million post-money valuation, leaving that investor with 25% of the company. In a later round, the company raises $10 million at a $100 million valuation. In order to maintain a 25% stake, the investor needs to throw in at least 25% of the new funding or $2.5 million. Otherwise, their stake in the company will be reduced.

Pro-rata rights obligate the company to leave space in subsequent funding rounds so investors can avoid such dilution.

Be on the lookout for "super pro rata rights" which allow investors to increase their equity stake in subsequent funding rounds.

Option Pool

Option pool is a term used to refer to a chunk of equity reserved for future hires. Sounds harmless, right? Unfortunately, the size of your option pool, as determined during a round of funding, has a direct impact on your company's valuation and hence, your ownership.

This is because the option pool is often included in the pre-money valuation of a company. So, let's say investors agree to invest $2 million at a $10 million pre-money valuation, implying a $12 million post-money valuation. Option pools are expressed as a percentage of post-money valuation, so if the deal includes a 20% option pool, that means the pool is worth $2.4 million. Your $10 million pre-money valuation is now effectively a $7.6 million pre-money valuation. The investor is not taking a larger percentage as a result—they will still own 16.7% of the company in this case — but you will be substantially diluted because the option pool will come directly from management's stake. So, if you owned 100% and think you now own 83.3%, you are wrong. That 20% option pool, reserved for future employees, means you now own 63.3% of company.

In preparing to negotiate the size of an option pool, I suggest creating a hiring plan for the next 12–18 months, then adding up the equity you intend to give new hires. Often, this kind of reasoning will leave entrepreneurs with a smaller option pool than investors suggest.

Board Control

Companies are ultimately responsible to their shareholders and to their board. So, even if you manage to maintain a controlling stake of the company after a financing round, if you suddenly take on three outside board members you have effectively lost control of the company. Slip up and your board can now fire you at will.

The composition of the board post-funding is then an important point of negotiation in any fundraising discussion. I, suggest pushing for neutral board members, agreed upon by both the entrepreneur and investors, as a compromise to investors pushing for board control.

Vesting

This term does not directly relate to raising capital, but it is an important financial term to consider nonetheless and investors will expect to know your employees' vesting schedules. A vesting schedule is imposed on employees who receive equity and determines when they can access that equity. This is useful because it means that if you give 5% of your company to a partner, that partner cannot just quit a couple of months later and keep the equity.

A typical vesting schedule takes four years and involves a one year cliff. The "cliff" means that none of the employee's shares vest for at least one year. After that year, typically 25% of the employee's equity is released, and the rest vests on a monthly or quarterly basis.

Pitch Materials

A good fundraising effort requires great supporting documents. Once you have the basics down, it is pretty easy to prepare all of these documents as needed. Here is a comprehensive list of what you will need to prepare when you are ready to initiate your Fundable Plan.

Elevator Pitch

An elevator pitch is a short, consistent synopsis of your business, usually in just a few sentences. Perhaps, surprisingly, getting your pitch to be short and consistent can be pretty difficult. Although the amount of content you need to create is tiny — just a few sentences — the amount of thought that goes into it is extraordinary.

A good elevator pitch conveys a few things quickly: the problem you solve, the solution you provide and the people you do it for. For example, "We allow anyone to easily rent movies from their home computer" would have been a succinct and effective elevator pitch for Netflix.

You will use your elevator pitch often — in introduction emails, in presentations and yes, actually in elevators during chance meetings. Keep rehearsing it and keep it short. It will inevitably prove very useful.

"If you are constructing a way to present your story, you should be aware that most investors have small attention spans. They may be late to the meeting, they may be reading other stuff on their iPhone. So, you want to organize your information in a way that allows them to process it more efficiently."

Pitch Deck

Your pitch deck is your business plan translated into slides, typically in a PowerPoint document.

While a business plan tends to be a long narrative of the business intended for one person to read on their own (which rarely happens), the pitch deck is what you will use to present your concept directly to a room of investors.

The pitch deck is often requested by investors ahead of your presentation so they can get a quick synopsis of your idea, so be sure to have it prepared and ready before you start contacting investors.

Unlike an executive summary, which is also a summary of your business plan, the pitch deck tends to be more visual, highlighting a few key points very well. It is particularly useful when showing off graphs and visual assets that help communicate the value of your idea.

Executive Summary

The point of your executive summary, as the name implies, is to briefly summarize your business plan into just a few pages. Make no mistake though, it is effectively the sales pitch for your business. Not only are you communicating the mechanics of the business, you are selling the value of your idea.

The executive summary tends to distil each key area of your business plan down to a paragraph or two, so that investors can get the gist of your plan easily.

There are two schools of thought on the executive summary. One suggests that you should write your entire business plan and then summarize it in your executive summary. This makes obvious sense, however it overlooks the fact that many people start companies without writing an entire business plan.

The alternative, then, is to try to summarize all the key points of your business clearly in a few pages, using a standard business plan as your guide.

Whichever path you choose, the executive summary will be helpful to have on hand for those investors that want a slightly more detailed narrative behind your elevator pitch. I advise a two page limit.

Business Plan

It may seem as though entrepreneurs must prepare a business plan before approaching investors, but in reality, few do.

There are a few reasons for this. First, authoring a 50-page manifesto on how your future business will operate is typically the domain of MBAs and academics and entrepreneurs rarely have the time, resources or desire to dive into a project of that scope when they just want to get their business launched.

The second is that it is an incredibly time-consuming process if you really want to dig into every step of a business plan from start to finish.

That said, it is also an invaluable exercise.

The real value of a business plan is not in the actual document itself — it is unlikely anyone will ever read it. The value comes from the planning, brainstorming and research that goes into crafting the plan. The result of this effort makes your assault on your new business idea far more credible.

If you decide to build your entire business plan, you will certainly want to have it handy, but make sure if you are introducing yourself to investors you start with more digestible documents like an executive summary or pitch deck. This is a nice teaser that will prompt a request for a business plan if you have piqued their interest.

Website

Not every business absolutely needs to have a website in order to pitch for capital, but it is highly recommended. Your pitch assets tend to be things you will either print or attach to an email. What the website provides is a reference point that provides supporting information for people who are interested in learning more after hearing your pitch.

You do not have to put your company's financial forecasts or secret sauce on your website. You can save that information for more personal communications.

The website should serve as a virtual brochure for your company. That could include screenshots of your product, a short explanation of what you are setting out to do, a personal blog discussing your thoughts on the industry, etc.

What is important about the website is that it gives people a professional view of your company, along with a taste of who you are and what you are trying to accomplish. Your website is a convenient destination for anyone — both investors and consumers — who want to know more about your company. Plus, it is much easier to direct people to your website than to a document.

Do not forget to pay equal attention to the social media pages that are linked to your website. Ensure they are current and relevant.

Financial Documents

If everything is going well, you are going to be asked for your financial documents. These should cover a few aspects of your business, from your revenue forecasts to your operational expenses to your cash flow.

The complexity of these documents can range from a single slide in your pitch deck showing some baseline guesses on where revenues will come from, to highly complicated Excel docs that involve macros and formulas changing outcomes based on key assumptions and scenarios.

For general purposes you will need to cover at least a few aspects of your financial picture. (refer earlier parts of the book)

Summary

It is possible to start your capital raising without all of these documents in place — but it is just not advisable. The documents require you to do a lot of homework and preparation, which is exactly the kind of exercise you need to go through in order to become more fundable as a company.

One of the most important aspects of any presentation is the materials you use to back up your pitch. They can mean the difference between a presentation that bombs and a presentation that gets you to the next level. From brochures and PowerPoint slides to props and snacks, here are the essential things entrepreneurs should bring to their first investor meeting.

PowerPoint Slides

PowerPoint slides are a powerful way to back up any presentation – as long as you use them as a prop and not as a crutch.

"One of the early mistakes I made as an entrepreneur was that I had too many slides," says Ajay Chopra, a venture capitalist with Trinity Ventures who, as a former entrepreneur, raised $15 million through several rounds of VC funding for his startup. "Now, looking at it from the other side, I realize what a typical venture capitalist day is: one meeting after another. If you have a bunch of slides and you cannot really cover any topic thoroughly, then you leave the VC with more questions in mind than answers."

Chopra offers the following advice for PowerPoint presentations:

- ◆ Limit the number of slides. Do not bring more than 20 slides; 15 is optimal.

- ◆ Limit the information to high-level, key issues. Do not go too deep, or you will confuse the people you are presenting to.

- ◆ Keep the slides uncluttered. "What we are trying to gauge is you and not your PowerPoint skills," says Chopra. Just put enough words up to remind you of your key points.

Product Demos and Props

"If you are doing a product presentation, you definitely need to appeal to the five senses," says Drew Stevens, Ph.D., author of Presentation with Muscle and president of Getting to the Finish Line. "The more you can get the audience involved, the better your presentation is going to be."

If your business is service-oriented rather than product driven, you should still bring something that demonstrates your business's strengths. "You want to bring whatever props will help pique curiosity," says Chopra. "We are always looking for evidence of what the customer thinks."

If you are a restaurant or services business, this could be pictures or a printout of a customer's e-mail or letter. "Those are very interesting props to look at to validate the story [you are trying to sell]," adds Chopra. "Do not bring a book of them, though – just a few. Three or four props will do."

Brochures, Handouts and Marketing Kits

Bring any brochures you have to the first meeting, but limit the number of handouts.

"The objective of the first meeting is to get the second meeting," says Chopra. "If you are lucky enough to get a second meeting, that is when you want to come better prepared with more statistics and perhaps a handout or two."

Chopra also advises that marketing and media kits be saved for future meetings. "We want to hear what your marketing plan is, but that should just be captured on one or two slides in the first meeting."

If your company sells products retail, you will need to put together a media and marketing plan, including who you are marketing to, how you plan to attack the market and the nitty-gritty details of the physical nature of the product, including size, weight and box design. If you are an online business, media kits and brochures are less important because most of the marketing is done online. However, you should still dedicate one to two PowerPoint slides to cover the basic information.

Producing Your Materials

"You want the materials to be indicative of what you are representing," says Stevens. "For example, I do consulting. I do not want anybody to think of me a sole-proprietor – a one-stop-shop business that's only doing $50,000 to $100,000 a year. I want them to think I'm a $100 or $200 million company."

The people you are presenting to may know you are not a million-dollar company, but you should still prepare your materials like you are. Stevens offers the following tips for producing high-quality materials:

Make sure your brochures and other materials are printed on heavy, high-quality stock.

- Have all brochures or booklets bound.
- Use semi-gloss, not glossy paper. Glossy paper is too reflective and can be hard to read.
- Full-colour printing is essential.

Have them professionally printed. If possible, skip the FedEx or Kinko's shops and take it to a professional printer and above all, do not print it yourself. "While desktop publishing is very efficient and effective today, the fact remains that materials are better produced by a professional printer than yourself," Stevens says. "Anybody can tell that you printed it yourself; there is a big, big difference between the two."

What NOT to Bring

Sure, you want to prove that you are prepared, but do not get carried away.

- Do not bring your business plan or summary. "I remember when I was an entrepreneur and I had set up my first meeting with venture capitalists, I would go in with my business plan of 30 to 40 pages and my business summary that was eight or 10 pages. Now I know that was not necessary," says Chopra. He advises that business plans and business summaries be limited to two to three PowerPoint slides.
- Do not bring a lot of paper or content-rich PowerPoint slides. "Anyone can read a spreadsheet," says Stevens. "You are the real expert on what your business is. Let them know what's coming from your heart and from your mind."
- Do not bring food. Unless it is a prop for your product or service, Chopra suggests leaving the food at home. Also, drinks and snacks will be provided at most meetings, but you should avoid eating, if possible. "I would suggest reaching out for snacks only if you are really hungry,

so as not to detract from the message you are delivering. Drinks such as water, coffee, Coke, etc., are OK."

The days of walking into a VC's office, putting up a deck on a screen and then going into your song and dance are largely gone, at least for your first few interactions with a firm. In particular, this is very foreign when you are talking about pitching an angel investor or seed fund, especially if you have done your work to get a good, qualified intro.

Instead, this structure of a deck is super useful in the various interactions that actually happen. For example:

Email

Often, first interactions begin via email. You may be able to open the door through an intro, but often, an investor would love to see a deck. This ask is sometimes made of the referrer or else it is made directly. Usually, this leads to a conundrum. Founders do not love the idea of sending a full deck with all of their hard-learned information to investors with whom they've had very little interaction. But it is also hard to say no to a request like this.

What you are able to do with the short deck is to send along the first 5–7 slides without the appendix. This should give the investor the gist of the status and progress of the company and you as the entrepreneur can tell the investor that you have materials that go really deep into the details in a subsequent meeting.

As part of this, I'd also include a link to the LinkedIn (or Behance, Dribbble, GitHub, etc.) profiles of the team for reference. This just allows for a natural and appropriate level of information sharing via email.

First Meetings

Usually, your first few interactions with a VC are with one or two team members. In that context, what is the most natural thing to do? I promise you it is usually not to go slide by slide through a 15–20 page deck. Even if that is how a VC is wired, I think founders can kind of guide these conversations to seem more like discussions and not a pitch. The meetings could also be a video or audio call, so prepare appropriately.

In almost any scenario, when you meet someone to have a discussion, you start much more casually. You introduce yourself. You talk about how you know the person who referred you. You tell your story about how you decided to start your business and how you met your co-founders. It is more of a narrative that initially does not fit into slide form. From there, it is usually helpful to have some structure, which is why having some slides is usually a good thing.

So, the setup for these meetings is something as follows:

"Let me tell you a bit about who we are and why we started this business. We can keep it conversational, but I have a handful of slides that can help guide the discussion."

You should be able to get through the 5–7 slides pretty quickly. But along the way, an engaged investor will pepper you with questions. This will require some improvisation, but some questions warrant just a verbal response (even if you have a slide) to keep the conversation flowing. But in other instances, you will hit pause and then flip to the FAQ slide and dig deep there.

(Oh and if the investor is not asking questions or is not engaged, just end it and move on. Your time is too valuable and early stage fundraising is not about convincing sceptics, it is about finding true believers.)

If things go well, you leave the investor feeling like:

- There is a simple, coherent and succinct story behind your company.
- You have exuded a mastery of the details of your business and good preparedness.
- The beginnings of a rapport has been built through the flow and authenticity of the conversation.

After the Meeting

After a meeting, many investors will ask for a copy of the deck. This is used for a document of reference and for sharing the story with one's partners for feedback.

As a reference item, this format is again very helpful, because it is very neatly organized by topic. Story matters a lot less for this purpose. And hopefully, this structure reinforces to the investor that this founder really has their act together as a result.

As a sharing deck, the short explainer-plus-kitchen sink deck leaves a good "blink" reaction as it gets passed around from colleague to colleague within the firm. If the recipient is checking it out while on the go, the fist seven slides allow them to get the gist really easily and quickly. They probably will not dig deep into the FAQs in this context, but having them present again communicates that you have your act together.

Other Thoughts

Later in the process: If there are further discussions, usually you stray away from the deck at that point and instead dive into specific questions. But if you are going through the process in a parallel fashion (i.e. with multiple investors progressing along similar stages in your fundraise), and you decide to create material to answer an important question that came up, this material can just be easily slotted into the deck without messing up any sort of flow. So, this short-plus-kitchen sink structure is also very flexible later in the process if you are still using a deck.

Time to create the deck: I submit that this deck format takes a lot less work to create than some other formats. It is actually pretty hard to think about how a story comes together in a coherent fashion and the more you decide what you want to say in your story, the harder it is to weave everything together. This structure allows you to focus hard on a five to seven-page story and from there, you can think about how to best communicate the discreet pieces of your business and strategy that are important to understand.

Do not feel like you need to create every single slide in the templates mentioned above. This list is a superset of what you'd want to include, but it also might leave things out that are critical for your specific business. If you do not have real meat around a question — or just think it is not that important to include — do not force it. I remember in the old days when a lot of founders wrote text-based business plans. I found that most of the content was useless because it was clear that a template was used and thus many sections were filled just because they existed

What Should Your Pitch Contain

Pitching your startup to investors just might be the most nerve-wracking aspect of starting your new business – well, besides the prospect of losing your money and social pride.

I get it. The last thing you want to do when you are sleep-deprived and edgy and suffering startup angst is pitch it over…and over…and over again. It is actually a pretty helpless feeling, asking strangers to decide on the fate of your new venture. If it is your first or second venture, there can be a real learning curve, too. It takes time and feedback to get it right.

See, you really only need ten slides - anything more and you could be overdoing it.

You want to grab their attention and inspire them to ask for more information - you do not need to give away the farm during your pitch.

If you go over every aspect of your startup in painstaking detail, you lose sight of what is truly important. Limiting your pitch to ten slides forces you to really home in on your selling points and convey them concisely.

Great startups do not fund themselves. Raising money from investors for your startup is challenging at any stage and requires a great pitch, even for experienced founders with significant traction in their company.

The good news is that there is a formula for pitching your startup that has helped startup founders raise millions.

I have distilled the investor pitch formula down to the 11 core slides you need in your initial pitch deck. I have also provided specific examples from the deck that Reid Hoffman used to get funding for LinkedIn.

What Investors Look for in Your Pitch Deck

Listed below are the 11 slides every Entrepreneur should look to include in their initial investor pitch deck.

Slide 1: Vision/Elevator Pitch
Slide 2: Traction/Validation
Slide 3: Market Opportunity

Slide 4: The Problem

Slide 5: Product/Service

Slide 6: Revenue Model

Slide 7: Marketing and Growth Strategy

Slide 8: Team

Slide 9: Financials

Slide 10: Competition

Slide 11: Investment 'Ask'

A few important notes about these slides and pitch decks in general:

- It is my opinion that including much more information than this in your initial pitch can be counterproductive. You want to leave some questions unanswered, hit the big points in a clear way and avoid over-sharing.

- I encourage founders to put their key numbers and traction at the very beginning of their deck. This grabs attention and clarifies the market opportunity, especially if the numbers are good. Do not make an investor wait until 5 or 6 slides, just to see what is going on.

- The pitch deck template does not have fancy design, just the content you should include. Design and visuals are a great thing to invest in, as long as they tell your story better by simplifying and clarifying.

- There are other optional slides I suggest in the deck including: Exit Strategy, Product/Demo Shots, and more.

- Use separate documents like an executive summary or dedicated technical documents to cover complex product images and descriptions, patent details, technical explanations and/or detailed financial and marketing items. Let investors choose to dive into those by their choosing, outside the deck.

- Most importantly, use technology. Create teaser videos, use infographics and other tools to make your pitch stand out.

Pitch decks done well are one of the most compelling ways to tell your story and get investor interest, in lieu of face to face meetings. They are also critical to your success in equity crowdfunding.

Here are ways that successful fundraisers use their deck to capture attention and close investors:

Tip 1. Get Intros: Many investors want to "discover" deals, not get pitched a deal by the Founder. Make sure to seek out and ask for direct intros to potential investors - but only do so from people with strong professional reputations.

Quality referrals are one of the best ways to capture the attention of big active investors.

When you ask for intros, give the person making the introduction a very short email 'blurb' of suggested language for them to use. Make sure that blurb includes a single link/call to action. By using a single link to your online profile on a website, you can allow people to pass along your pitch and all your core company info with a single URL. The moment that any potential investor clicks on that link, they experience the pitch and message you have crafted for them online, in a more dynamic and powerful environment than just a PPT attachment.

That message and link could look something like this:

"Hey,

I wanted you to meet Chance, the CEO of Crowdfunder.

He is doing some interesting stuff with equity crowdfunding and the company has some great growth as a leader in the space. I thought you two might want to chat.

His deck and info on the company are here:

http://crowdfunder.com/crowdfunder

Hope you two connect."

This simple message and link showcases your pitch deck, video, as well as your existing investors/advisors/team - all streamlined. What is more, my pitch now has the powerful social proof provided by the people and investors already involved in Crowdfunder who are listed on my Company Profile. Seeing who else is involved or investing can make a real difference for investors taking a first look.

Tip 2. More Story, Less Information: Data and bullets on a deck do not sway investors. What takes your pitch from good to great is the story you tell and how it engages the imagination of an investor.

All great pitches have a basic "meta story" that is emergent from the overall pitch. This meta story can take a few forms, but it generally sounds something like this:

"There is a huge opportunity to do X as a giant business. We have cracked the code and this is how my company is doing it and will dominate this market.

Here is who my team and myself are and why we are the only people to back in this space. It is working and now we need money for X and Y to grow."

Your pitch deck should be more of an experience that communicates this overall narrative/story about you and your startup visually and with words simply by scrolling through the series of slides.

It is also a great idea to start with or include, actual present tense 'user stories' or use cases about your customer experience or customer success that is at the core of your product or service experience. As in, "Jane is looking for investors for her startup. She goes to Crowdfunder and clicks a single button to connect via LinkedIn. This automatically creates a rich and socially connected pitch profile for the company that engages her existing network and is visible to a larger network of active accredited investors on Crowdfunder."

Tip 3. Ask For The Money: Many entrepreneurs fundraising love to drone on about their company and pitch all the features, traction and strategy. But when it is time to define the investment opportunity and ask for an investor to write a cheque, suddenly they are shy and cannot find words.

Be prepared to ask each investor you communicate with to come in to your round directly and even ask them for how much money you want from them and why.

Also, be prepared to succinctly describe the use of funds for the money you are raising and where it will get you.

Think of this as "good hygiene" when fundraising. Make sure you know your numbers, your financing, have a timeline for your round and be clear and direct on your asks.

Tip 4. PDF Your Deck: Do not leave yourself open to the formatting pitfalls of Power Point. Turn your Power Point or Keynote pitch deck into a PDF. This makes sure that investors see the deck the way you designed and intended it.

This also makes sure it displays well if you use it in any online equity crowdfunding efforts.

Tip 5. Continually Update Your Deck: Entrepreneurs who do well at fundraising treat their pitch deck like the most valuable piece of content or advertisement that they will ever write.

Example: A Founder who recently closed $500,000 literally went through 7 iterations of his deck in a few months. Each time his traction grew, he would update those numbers in the deck. Each time he had a big win or development, he would update the deck.

If you are using your deck correctly, you will find that it reflects the rapid learnings and growth you are experiencing as you pitch investors, get feedback and refine your story and approach.

Make sure you spend time both pitching investors in person to learn and get feedback to improve your pitch and take advantage of the new opportunity to get your pitch in front of thousands of investors online using crowdfunding sites.

Time is limited when delivering your pitch to investors and venture capitalists. Both your time slot and the attention span of your audience only allow you 10–20 minutes to deliver your most crucial points, but that is only if you first get their attention. To do this, you will need to simplify your elements of a pitch thoughts and your product.

The 10 Slide Rule

The purpose of a pitch deck is to stimulate interest, not to cover every aspect of your startup and bludgeon your audience into submission. Your objective is to generate enough interest to obtain a second meeting. Thus, the recommended number of slides is ten. This low number forces you to focus on the absolute essentials. You can add a few more but never exceed fifteen. The more slides you need, the less compelling your idea.

The key talking points to include in your pitch presentation and tips on how to properly approach them are:

Cover Information

An effective cover page is informative and memorable, yet concise. You want all necessary information to be visible on the front page if your deck is forwarded. The front page should include your logo, business name, tagline, and contact information. Your tagline should summarize your startup idea in a catchy, but short manner. Ideally, the tag line on your cover page will spark the investor's memory of your product and prompt him/her to use the contact information provided directly below it.

Problem and Opportunity

Your solution is only as important as the problem it addresses. If investors are unable to understand it is a problem that needs solving, you will have a hard time convincing them to fund your concept. The bigger the problem you address, the more urgent your solution becomes. And because your solution is your value proposition, a bigger problem also means a more valuable solution.

Value Proposition

Explain the pain you are alleviating or the pleasure you are providing. Any examples you can provide of your product solving a problem add to your value proposition, whether they are case studies, customer testimonials or any other example you believe demonstrates the benefits of your product.

Underlying Magic

Describe the technology, secret sauce or magic behind your product. The less text and more diagrams, schematic and flowcharts, the better. If you have a prototype, demo or MEP (Minimum Experiential Product) this is the time to transition to it and showcase it.

Business Model

Explain who has your money temporarily in their pocket and how you will get it into yours. After informing investors of the size of your problem, you will need to translate this to market size. How many customers will benefit from your solution? And how much will it cost to acquire these customers? High acquisition costs are a turnoff to investors, so make sure to justify them or include your plans to minimize them. If you do not have customers yet, investors will want to see how you plan to acquire them. If people are already paying then showcase the numbers with growth rates and retention percentages.

Go to Market Strategy

Explain how you are going to reach your customers without breaking the bank for your product, you will need to show how you are going to grow this customer base, moving forward.

You will have a hard time winning over any investor if you are unable to show how you will generate the revenue necessary for them to get a return on their investment. Investors will appreciate seeing different revenue streams with corresponding timelines for each. Include pricing, customer lifetime values and reasons those customers will continue to use your product. Lastly, compare your pricing to that of your competitors and explain any differences in numbers or approach.

Competitive Landscape

Provide a complete view of the competitive landscape. Too much is better than too little on this slide. No matter how unique your product may seem, there are competitors vying for the same space as you. The differences in your product and the competition are most likely bigger in your eyes than those of your potential investors, so make sure to compare your model with competing models without bias. Include other details about competitors such as, if they have been acquired, for how much and by whom.

Founders and Team Members

Provide a complete view of your management team, founders, board of directors, board of advisors, as well as your major investors. Do not worry about having less than a perfect team. If you had a perfect team you would not be pitching. Products and concepts are only as promising as the team members behind them. Investors are backing you just as much, if not more, than your idea. Gain the trust of your audience by letting them get to know the experts behind your product. Any background experience you can provide about yourself or your team relating to your company's industry or the startup industry in general, will help you gain the interest of investors.

Let your audience know if members of your team have a history of working together, as well as any accomplishments stemming from it. Successful exits are great points to highlight to prove to investors you are familiar with acquisition. If you plan on listing your team's advisors, make sure to inform them first.

Financial Projections

Provide a three-year forecast (apart from history of actuals), not only in dollars but with key metrics as well. Metrics such as customer acquisition costs, conversion rates and cost of goods are essential. Do a bottoms up forecast versus a top down one. Forecasting future financials is a challenging task, especially with limited financial history. Your projections will carry more weight if they are based on existing achievements. Provide real numbers in regard to existing partnerships, customers, dates of acquisition and other figures such as cash flows in order to give investors a reason to expect success, moving forward.

Current Status, Accomplishments, Timeline and Use of Funds

Explain the current status of your product, what is the road ahead and how you will use the money raised. Regardless of your intention to raise capital with this pitch, it is important to talk about funding. Let the investors know how much money you have been working with, as well as who has provided it. If you have been working with little to no money, show them how resourceful you have been. If you have received previous funding, explain who gave it to you, how much they gave and the progress you owe to it. Make sure to let investors know if you have been using your own money. Investors are more likely to believe you will spend their money as if it were your own if that is exactly what you have done in the past. Inform investors of how much you intend to raise and what that money will help you accomplish.

Summarize

Grab and keep the attention of investors by summarizing key information before diving in. If you do not get your audience's attention right off the bat, they are even less likely to be paying attention when you are 10 minutes into your presentation. Mention your major accomplishments so far and present anything else you believe would get you interested in your company, if you were the investor in this situation.

Questions

Even after a solid presentation and a strong close, audience members will more than likely have questions. Make sure you are ready to settle their nerves with prepared and informative answers. Performing background research on your audience will help you predict the type of questions they may have. Prepare the following slides and leave them at the end of your presentation.

Press

Include a slide with press for your product after the last slide shown in the presentation. Including this information in your presentation will make it too lengthy, but you will want to have it ready in case an investor asks.

Barriers to entry

Investors may ask about barriers to entry because they want to know how much and how long you will benefit from being first-to-market. They also want to know if there is a good chance that competitors will already be in your space by the time you get to market. Each barrier to entry limits your competition and is an advantage for your product, but highlighting only the biggest ones will be the most efficient use of your time.

Exit strategy

No matter how excited your audience is about investing in your product, many of them are already thinking about how to exit. Make sure you have an exit strategy in place and are ready to discuss it with investors. Listing companies that might be acquiring yours in the future and similar acquisitions that have already occurred will help ease apprehension.

Feel free to add additional slides after your presentation, based on anticipated questions. Because these topics will only be triggered by investor questions, you can have as many as you want without filling up your time slot. However, including too many extra slides may make them hard to navigate, so add them with caution. If a particular investor wants more details on these topics or any other topic in your presentation, let them know they can follow-up with you after the presentation or at a later date.

I am evangelizing the 10/20/30 Rule of PowerPoint. It is quite simple: a pitch should have ten slides, last no more than twenty minutes and contain no font smaller than thirty points. This rule is applicable for any presentation to reach agreement: for example, raising capital, making a sale, forming a partnership, etc.

- Ten slides. Ten is the optimal number of slides in a PowerPoint presentation because a normal human being cannot comprehend more than ten concepts in a meeting — and venture capitalists are very normal. (The only difference between you and venture capitalist is that he is getting paid to gamble with someone else's money) If you must use more than ten slides to explain your business, you probably do not have a business.

- Twenty minutes. You should give your ten slides in twenty minutes. Sure, you have an hour time slot, but you are using a Windows laptop, so it will take forty minutes to make it work with the projector. Even if setup goes perfectly, people will arrive late and have to leave early. In a perfect world, you give your pitch in twenty minutes and you have forty minutes left for discussion.

- Thirty-point font. The majority of the presentations that I see have text in a ten point font. As much text as possible is jammed into the slide and then the presenter reads it. However, as soon as the audience figures out that you are reading the text, it reads ahead of you because it can read faster than you can speak. The result is that you and the audience are out of synch.

How Much Money Do You Need

Raising money for your startup is never fun. It takes time, distracts you from developing your product, is fraught with emotional ups and downs and does not have a guaranteed outcome. Frankly, many founders would rather go jump into an icy lake than take another fundraising meeting where they are not sure what they should say to 'convince' an already hesitant investor to open his purse strings and invest in their company.

So, back to the main question…how much money should I raise?

The flippantly short version of the answer is, "as much as you can"…but in some cases, more is not necessarily better. Although you should raise as much money as your company needs to achieve major proof-points/milestones, overfunding a company can also have its drawbacks.

Let me explain this last point before going further on the 'how much money should I raise' question:

Many founders are obsessed about raising as much money as possible all at once because, well, if you do raise a big war chest, then that is one less problem you need to worry about. However, with a large amount of money comes several potential problems:

1. With more money usually come more investment terms and more due diligence. It is probably a fair statement to say that the more money involved, the more control provisions an investor will want as well as more diligence to make sure that their money is not going to be misused.

2. A high implied post-money valuation. In order to accommodate a large round, investors need to adjust your valuation accordingly. For example, if your business is objectively worth 1 million, but you are raising 2m, unless the investor plans on owning 66% of the company after investment, they need to adjust the valuation upward. Having an artificially higher valuation prematurely can put a lot of strain on a startup if things do not go well and then later need to raise money again, as it increases the likelihood of a subsequent round being a

down-round (when you take a negative hit to your valuation) or rather, other new investors passing on the deal in the future because it is 'too expensive.'

3. A propensity to misuse 'easy money.' You could argue this point from a psychological point of view if you wanted, but suffice it to say, I know many VCs that believe that over-funding a company leads to financial laxity, lack of focus and overspending by the management team. Perhaps, it is lingering fear over the hey-days of the late 90's where parties were rife and everyone got an Aeron chair, but the general fear with overfunding a company is that it will be tempted to expand faster than it can absorb employees into the culture, integrate new systems or expand real-estate needs without substantially disrupting the efficient operations of the company.

4. A last one, which is hard to really quantify and happens only to very few startups, is the media's reaction (positive or negative) to how much money you have raised relative to what you have.

Ok, got it, overfunding can be bad… too much money can be a bad thing, but if you said I should raise as much as I can, where do I start and what is the 'magic' number to ask for then?

Alright, let's look at this question from a different point of view, how an investor evaluates your financial plan, an investor (depending on their areas of focus) may not necessarily know what the exact figures your business will need to grow to its next major milestone, but rather, the investor will rely on your ability to communicate this on your financial plan for the investor to then make a decision on whether you accurately understand your cash needs or not. Tied to this cash need is an implied understanding of your company's milestones.

Let's define what a milestone is before proceeding:

A milestone is a quantifiable achievement, be it in terms of product development, team expansion, or market adoption of your company's value proposition.

Your financial plan will likely be a series of chronologically organized milestones. For example:

Month 6 – Hire UX guy to optimize app Month 8 – Launch mobile app Month 10 – Start charging on the mobile app Month 11 – Hit 10,000 users Month 12 – Launch partnership with key distributor Month 18 – Hire CMO

These are all milestones. Some more important than others and frankly an investor will likely want to talk to you about the importance of each one of them to get a feeling for which ones are the key ones to focus on to determine if your business is going to 'take off.'

The reason for this is simple, the best time to go fundraising, is right before or shortly after the successful completion of a key or series of key milestones. For example, right before a key milestone, you can woo new investors with the promise of how successful you will be at the completion of the milestone and basically you convince them that if they do not get into your company by investing now, they will not have a chance after you have achieved the milestone because many others will also be interested and the competition will be stiff (remember, investors do not want to lose out on potentially hot deals). Shortly after achieving a key milestone is also a good time to try and convince investors because you have effectively accomplished a major thing (like launching a product), which de-risks the investment for them, but they can still get in the company before it 'takes off.' Frankly, the worst time to go fundraising is when your last major milestone has grown stale and the next one is too far away to be de-risked. So, this is why it is key to know your milestones and when they are happening.

Parallel to this milestone timeline is the 'cash timeline.' As in, how much money, in aggregate, you will have spent to get there. So, using my examples from above:

Month 6–60K Month 8–80K Month 10–100K Month 11–110K Month 12–120K Month 18–240K

Ignore whether this is a realistic example for your business for the time being, but I have assumed a 10K cash burn on this example up to the end of year 1 and then starting in Year 2, I have assumed 20K monthly cash burn. If you do not know what your monthly cash burn is, you are in trouble. Monthly Cash Burn is a key figure to know before meeting any investor.

As you can see, an investor could choose any of the milestones above to focus on for your cash needs. The idea is simple, fund your company through the achievement of major milestone(s) (to reduce investment risk and to see if your company has any traction before putting more money in) and then go fundraising for more money, hopefully on a strong note, where you will have met your timelines and expected outcome (be it market traction or successful completion of your product or hiring of the appropriate person).

For example, an Angel investor typically cannot invest millions, so their investments tend to be less than 300K. However, they will want to make sure your business is going somewhere before putting all their money in, so it is likely they will want to come in early to give you enough cash to achieve something plus a little extra to help you fundraise after, but also to see how you achieve the milestone before putting in more. So, perhaps this Angel may opt for funding you through month 10 with your requirement of 100K plus a few more for fundraising. This would get you through your product's launch and give you a couple of months to see how it goes in terms of market traction (all the time you will be speaking to new potential investors) so that you can have something strong to talk about for fundraising purposes.

Alternatively, an institutional investor (one that invests other people's money as well as their own), say a VC fund, may see that your company has some real potential in what it is trying to do, sees that you have a plan that requires 100K to launch before you start trying to monetize, but with their experience of seeing your kind of business having to do a few pivots before getting the launch product 100% right, think that perhaps the best quantity to give you based on your calculations is about 500K for about a year to a year and a half. This should also give you some breathing room to work on achieving your various milestones rather than having to focus on having to be constantly in fundraising mode.

So, now you are probably asking yourself, how is it that some investors have different perceptions of how much money I need and wish to give me? Effectively, how much money does an investor actually think I need vis-a-vis what I ask for?

Your exact calculations may have said that you needed 100K to launch your product, but an experienced investor may have seen various companies like yours and seen that there are usually mistakes done along the way that consume cash without quantifiable progress towards the agreed milestone (you may have learned something, but you may be delayed in your launch because of some screw up). Because of this, investors some times include 'buffers' into the number they offer you in a deal. This buffer could come from the various sensitivity analysis the investor did, such as, what if the company is delayed in launching their product by two months or what if the company cannot find that key employee or what if the company cannot start charging for their product for an extra few months or what if the product needs a pivot or what if people are not willing to pay what the company expected? All these things will affect the cash flow of the company and because of them, the investor may assume some or all will occur, leading to the company needing more money than was planned by the founder. Effectively, your 100K in a perfect execution timeline, may actually be 250K after some minor delays and mistakes and with the extra cash the investor in my example above gave you, you now may have enough cash to go fundraise without having to panic about having to get cash in 'yesterday' or be constantly in fundraising mode.

Keep in mind that this larger amount an investor may be willing to give you will also affect your valuation range too much and it 'inflates' the valuation range your company sits in (as per my earlier point) so an investor will not give you 'excessive' buffer so that it forces the company to be 'overpriced' for them and for the company's future. Inversely, hopefully you can also see where an investor may deem a company to be 'underfunded' if it does not have enough money to get to where it can achieve a meaningful milestone(s) upon which to go fundraising with a strong foot forward for future investors to be attracted.

In conclusion, raise as much as you can but understanding your monthly cash burn and map out your company's important timelines and the cash you will realistically require to achieve them. Then have an engaging conversation with your potential investors as to how much they think you need, based on their experience. As a rule of thumb, try and raise enough money so that you have time to go fundraising after you have accomplished your next key milestone(s). Later in the book I will discuss how much time you should set aside for fundraising, but to make the rule-of-thumb complete, add atleast 6 months to the amount of money you need for your next milestone to include time to go fundraising.

Geographical Influence

A friend of mine emailed in and mentioned that perhaps there was a difference in how investors from different geographies look at this issue of how much they want to invest in a company up front and yes… I would agree with that statement, but the point I am making is merely to provide the reader with a 'framework' by which to approach the question of how much to raise, not so much to answer the multiple varied ways that investors might look at the amount required and subsequent fundraise amount. For example, some investors may choose to just want to back the team and thus will just give them an amount that they think startups typically get for the stage the company is in and others will give an amount of money merely to exclude the investor competition from winning the deal from them!

However, I believe the framework I have mentioned can help a founder assess how much money they may need for a period of upcoming time no matter the risk averseness (or not) of the investors they meet with. Whereas a bolder investor may not really focus on minor milestones, but rather just focus on a larger one such as 'grow the network' and for that the amounts invested is done with far less due diligence and far more quickly, a more risk averse investor will probably be more specific about what you plan on accomplishing with his money.

In the end, the most important thing, is to be keenly aware of your cash needs on a month by month basis, so that if the question comes up, you know how much you plan on spending and by when. You should also focus on raising enough money in your timeline so that you also have time to accomplish your key milestone(s) before going fundraising again and lastly you should include enough buffer in your last fundraise to help you through your next fundraising period post-milestone. If you meet an investor that wants to invest a lot quickly, great, if you meet with various investors that are more risk-averse, at least you will not get caught not understanding your execution plan. If you want another rule of thumb, many Early-Stage VCs will look at the next 12month to 18month worth of cash needs + a buffer to estimate the cash needs of a company. Add to that 6 months of additional cash burn and you have a rough starting point for a 'headline figure' from which to start discussions.

I'll begin with some basic constraints to consider:

When making an investment, investors assess the amount of risk involved, how long it will take the company to reach liquidity and how much effort the investors will have to contribute to help the company succeed and scale. Those inputs then lead to a rough calculation of the amount of ownership that makes the investment worth making versus other opportunities. Generally speaking, the earlier an investment is, the more ownership an investor needs to justify the risk, effort, etc. Quality/experience of the team/entrepreneur, clear market analogues and other factors can reduce that ownership need to some degree.

So, when an investor says they need such-and-such ownership (or they need to put $X amount of capital to work), it is tied to their assessment of the risk and the reward. Generally, experienced investors will be able to triangulate to what is fair for their effort while balancing the need to incentivize founders, management and employees for the risks and the extraordinary efforts required in building a valuable business.

Investor Cash/Risk Limits

The other major factor that dictates how much money an investor is willing to put into a particular opportunity is the amount of capital-at-risk (both initial and total), given the perceived challenges and unknowns in the business. Even when an investor fundamentally believes in an opportunity or an entrepreneur, sometimes the existing risks are too high to warrant committing more than a certain amount of capital at that moment. Also, many firms make soft or hard allocations of capital reserves for future investment rounds in the business at the time of the initial decision. In their minds they are risking or tying-up more capital than you may realize, based on the raise at hand.

The typical investor response when the capital requirement is deemed too high, is to either try to syndicate the investment with other investors (share the risk) or to reduce the duration or complexity of milestones, and thus, the required capital. Entrepreneurs need to be very thoughtful in the latter situation. Reducing or narrowing the scope of the milestones could actually be a good idea for the company. It has the benefit of less dilution if the company successfully achieves the amended milestones, thus providing for a subsequent follow-on raise at a higher valuation. On the flip side, if the achieved milestones are not compelling enough to attract a new lead investor, you might actually be in worse shape. Since the last scenario is not good for the investor either, most experienced VCs are pretty thoughtful about this issue.

The final piece of the puzzle is market pricing and dynamics. Bottom-line: if an investor is willing to give you an above-market valuation that allows you to raise more capital than you need without taking more dilution, it is worthy of serious consideration. But even here, it is not always a slam dunk.

If the markets tumble or you stumble, that super fancy valuation is going to really bite you in the backside when you need more capital to keep the doors open and are desperate. A new investor is not going to pay that same high valuation and all kinds of things like anti-dilution ratchets and down-round recaps become terms you will learn to hate. Again, be very thoughtful about all the possible circumstances that can arise as a result of the financing you accept.

So, it is important to have a realistic plan and a clear view of the meaningful milestones and resources needed to deliver on that plan. If you plan wisely, you will have a pretty specific amount of capital you know you need. The more money you try to raise, the more line-of-sight you will need to have (and prove) in your plan; predicting the future is hard to do if you do not already have a lot of understanding of your market dynamics. Put another way, raising lots of capital and going fast only makes sense when you know the race course. Going fast before then just means you are likely to wreck the car and waste a bunch of money. Also remember, gaining rapid market share in a market that is not well-defined is an oxymoron. So be smart, be specific, be frugal, work the hell out of your plan, and deliver on your milestones.

Getting the Valuation and Investor Play Right

A lot of my time is spent helping early-stage companies get to proof points so that they can raise capital. They might have some seed money and are thinking of raising a Series A based on success of an early release (MVP). Because of this, I have always tried to stay up-to-speed on how early-stage investors look at valuation of companies. What are they really looking for? What do you really need to prove?

We can have an intellectual debate about whether it is the right investment strategy or not to have a minimum threshold. I am only here to tell you that it is the case and better that you know going in. Most VCs want to own between 20–25% minimum of your company. If they co-invest with somebody else that they consider important they might be willing to cut that back to 15%. But most VCs will not want to own 8% of your company. If they do it is likely because they want an option to invest more later.

And by the way, it is OK to ask, "do you guys have a minimum ownership level that you like to hit?" Does not hurt to politely get this out in the open.

Idea-Stage Startups: How to Value Enterprises That Are yet to Take Shape

From the founding team to competition to how quickly a startup can turn profitable, all these factors play an important role in the valuation game.

For idea-stage startups, valuation is more of a creative drill than intricate calculations because they are often pre-revenue in nature and lack historical data. It is hard to put a value on something that does not exist. However, an investor would want to have a fair idea about potential returns.

The only way to value a startup at an idea level is to see how much money it requires to survive for the next 12–18 months until the startup becomes ready to raise the next round. You will have to give the founder enough money to generate good traction. If not, he will not have that sort of traction to convince the next investor.

Another step is to assess the viability and future potential of the idea. The uniqueness of an idea and its competitive intensity, besides the potential of idea for speedy rollout and rapid scalability are select parameters to assign a basic ballpark estimated value to the intellectual property (IP) of the idea and its defendability.

At a seed level, the ballpark figure of stake dilution is 15–30 per cent. So once an entrepreneur says he is willing to dilute 30 per cent for $10K or whatever the amount required until the next round, there emerges a valuation.

Now, people would argue on how one can decide that, since 15–30 per cent would mean that the valuation will double – if I am investing $800K for 15 per cent, it will be $1.6 million. For 30%. However, investors have a bottom range and top range. After that, how they pinpoint a particular number in that range rests solely on how well one negotiates. The better negotiator gets a better deal, I believe it is more of an art than a science.

Valuations also depend on a company's road to profitability. A startup that is projected to be profitable in two years will be valued way more than the one with a five-year profitability plan. Entrepreneurs need to avoid valuation on unrealistic financial assumptions, because they will eventually have to deliver their expectations to investors.

It is hard to come to a logical number. There are three parameters for valuation of an idea-stage startup. Investors think of the possible valuation in the next round and the probability of getting funding. The higher the next-round valuation and possibility of getting funding, the better would be the valuation at the idea level. Second, they look closely at the track record, domain knowledge and opportunity cost of the founders. Finally, it would depend largely on the target stake in the company based on the asked amount.

One way entrepreneurs can put a value on their idea is to look at companies that operate in a similar space. They need to talk to their peers in the ecosystem and also to startups that have received funding from the same investor.

Although not an absolute requirement, many angel investors prefer startups in their locality. It helps them to interact more frequently and directly with the entrepreneurs to get real-time update on their progress. Also, a company in the heart of a startup hub such as Bangalore will be valued higher than a startup in Mysore or Visakhapatnam, just for the fact that competition drives up startup valuation. In a city such as Bangalore, there is a higher degree of competition among investors. Investors agree that negotiating a lower valuation is easy with startups in remote locations.

For some investors the key factor is the team. A lot of average guys come up with brilliant ideas, but investors do not back them because it is not just the idea, the real power lies in execution and that is where you create value. Average people will not be able to foresee the future, they often quit early.

Investors look for entrepreneurs who possess a strong will to survive the hardest times. An idea platform such as Quirky.com backed by GE, which gave 2 per cent equity to the ideators, shut shop. The only chance of getting valued for an idea is when the founding team has a strong patent or experience of building a successful startup.

Angel investors also prefer entrepreneurs to put in their money at the idea stage. There are very few people who back startups at the idea stage because the risk is high. Having an idea is just one per cent; 99 per cent is the execution of the idea. It is all about whether the team has the ability to execute.

Out of 2000 startups, 100 get funded and of this 100, only one will get funded on paper plans; the other 99 startups will have only good traction.

Startup founders should also consider convertible notes, which avoid the valuation dilemma at the initial phase and keep valuations open.

Investor Play

An investor play is an offer to investors that they will find attractive. At the core it is about how much you want to give up for how much money. It is more relevant for late stage startups but is important to understand for every stage. At an early stage, you are more likely to give up 20–30% equity for the initial angel or seed rounds. This could be structured as convertible debt (Convertible Note) or straight equity or a combination. While you need to protect equity, and get as good a valuation as possible, investors need to feel they are getting a good deal. No strict formulas are available but keeping basic principle of deal making is important. For example do not value your startup at the third years projections or take an early stage non revenue generating startup and discount 3–5 years cash flow. Be realistic, be fair and leave enough on the table for an investor. The earlier you seek funding the more you have to leave. I suggest you use an experienced hand to guide you in crafting an attractive investor play.

How to Split Equity Among Founders

One of the most uncomfortable discussions when you start your company is the topic of splitting equity. Early on, your startup was just an idea that you bounced around with some friends. Then, that idea grew on you and you agreed to turn it into a startup. Friends became co-founders. Everyone is working happily toward shipping your first version. No paperwork in the way.

In your mind, you are the CEO. It was clearly your idea. Your friend may be a great coder, but you could have found any developer to implement your product. It is obvious to you that the startup is your baby, and you should own most of it, probably 80% or so. You feel generous that you are about to offer 20% equity for what is just a glorified coding job.

Except you have not had "the talk" yet. You need to sit down with your co-founder(s) and discuss exactly how to split the pie. Beware. "The talk" has caused more startups to fail than you can imagine.

From your co-founder's perspective, he is implementing all of the product, making all the hard design decisions and figuring out all the details that will make the startup a success. All you really did was provide an initial idea — that he improved over many weeks of brainstorming.

How do you imagine he will appreciate your offer of 20% equity? Not so well.

Clearly, if you are too aggressive, you risk losing your co-founders. At the other end of the spectrum, I have met many founders who shy away from having that tough discussion. Instead, they take the easy road and say "we'll split everything equally, 50/50." That is a great way to avoid a painful discussion today, but it will set you up for a failure tomorrow. Most likely you and your co-founder are not the perfect pair. An equal split usually signals a weak CEO who cannot make decisions. When the time comes for any kind of tough call, an equal split multiplies the chance of deadlock among founders. Paralysis is also a far too common startup-killer.

Another terrible way to go about splitting equity is to base it on how much cash each founder is bringing. It may sound rational to Wall Street to set a price per share and let the founders buy as many shares as they can. Except the resulting split has nothing to do with what matters – who is critical to the startup – and instead is linked to who happens to have more cash at their disposal.

Something interesting happens between the time an idea is developed and it becomes extremely profitable. Typically, everyone who had a role in the process – no matter how small or large – begins to jockey for position and to fight for a piece of the company. In other words, everyone wants some equity, regardless of the amount of work they have put in. As a member of the founding team, you should take responsibility for splitting equity in a way that is fair to all contributing parties, while simultaneously positioning your startup for long-term success.

The problem with splitting equity, however, is that there's never a "clean cut." Any time you have more than a couple of people involved, disagreements will erupt over what value people bring to the table, which parties were there from the beginning, etc., etc. But by keeping several guidelines in mind, you can ensure the process is grounded in fairness.

Startup founders also need to think of not only the equity split for the journey that got them till here, but an equitable distribution for the roles, responsibilities, risks, time and money that will be contributed in the future.

Founders face a wide range of decisions when building their startups: market decisions, product decisions, financing decisions and many more. The temptation is to prioritize these choices over decisions about how to structure their own founding teams. That is understandable, but perilous.

Research on equity splits adopted by over 3,700 founders from over 1,300 startups in the U.S. and Canada., has shown that even the best of ideas can falter when the founding team neglects to carefully consider early decisions about the team: the relationships, roles and rewards that will make the founders a winning team.

It is said that a team has succeeded at splitting the equity, if all of the cofounders are equally unhappy. Unfortunately, founder unhappiness tends to get even worse with hindsight; the percentage of founders who say they are unhappy with their equity split increases by 2.5x as their startups mature. Increasing discontent within the founding team is a prime indicator that destructive turnover may be on the horizon.

As memorialized in the movie The Social Network, Mark Zuckerberg's initial equity split with Eduardo Saverin went sour as the company evolved. Mark's attempt to reclaim Eduardo's equity landed him in court — maybe good for winning Academy Awards, but not good for business, let alone personal relationships.

Is there a better way? I think so.

I have been advising startups on this and have come across great hesitancy among founders. Each time, I would sit with all the co-founders and start with my first question: "Who is the CEO?" And then I would ask about everyone's role, how they saw each other's contributions and so on. The questioning would last for a good 30 minutes, after which I could suggest some reasonable ranges. That discussion was a great way to force issues that had been left unspoken for too long. In one case, everyone agreed at the end of the meeting that founder #4 should quit. Even that fourth founder!

Eventually, I got tired of asking the same questions over and over again and I ask founders to use any quick online calculator. While not as precise as a real discussion, it has been used by thousands of startups. A great way to make use of the online calculator is as a discussion starter: tell each co-founder to fill out the questions and share the percentages (but not the detailed answers). Compare and discuss why you think the numbers do not match.

Here are some principles before you get down to the actual task of splitting equity.

- 10% is a minimum to be considered a co-founder. Below that, you are in the range of first employee and should include some salary.
- 4 is the maximum number of real co-founders you should have. If you think you need 6 co-founders, rethink everyone's role and simplify.
- Every co-founder, including you, should have vesting (typically over 4 years), which solves a lot of issues with future co-founder fights.

Here is how you can attack this critical but generally a onetime problem:

1. Take advantage of tools and resources

While there is something to be said for taking a very hands-on approach to splitting equity, do not confuse your desire to play a role in the decisions with a need to manually control the entire process. In other words, take advantage of automated cap-table management tools, which can save time and streamline the process. There are so many sophisticated tools and resources available that you would be foolish to use only an Excel spreadsheet.

2. Place an emphasis on sweat equity

While capital contributions are great (and they can be rewarded by the company issuing convertible debt or preferred stock), what you really want to reward is sweat equity. Equity should almost always be allocated based on who has put in the most work and will continue to do so in the future. If you are unsure of the latter part of the equation, look at the career intentions of the founding partners.

If one person intends to quit his or her current job to work full-time with the new business, that change will entail much more risk than that of the founding partner who is only willing to work part-time until things take off. Equity splits should reward a combination of the highest-valued contribution and the largest undertaking of risk. Sweat equity is governed by laws in almost all countries and you should familiarise yourself with the relevant provisions or use a professional to help.

3. Do not move too quickly

While you certainly do not want to go on too long without determining a concrete equity split, that task is nothing to rush into. Patience is key, and you and your founding team should spend time listening to concerns, asking questions and reviewing all aspects of the split. For companies that end up being very successful, the difference in a percentage point can mean hundreds of thousands of dollars. Do not gloss over the details in an effort to avoid making difficult decisions.

4. Avoid getting caught up in the original idea

While some weight should be given to the co-founder who came up with the idea, that should not be the primary decision factor in who gets what percentage. Actual contributions and sweat equity deserve far more weight than the concept. In many cases, the person with the idea has also put in the most work, but this is not always true. Just keep that in mind. Unless the idea is patented or protected in some way, I normally put a zero value to the idea.

5. Do not let emotions control decisions

Co-founders are often personally connected – either by friendship, family or previous work experience. This usually means you enjoy being around those people or interact with them on a frequent basis (outside of work). This fact can prove particularly cumbersome when it comes to splitting equity, as you do not want to hurt feelings or burn bridges. So, you may have to put in extra effort to avoid letting emotions dictate equity splitting decisions. Bring in an impartial observer or consultant to help get an outsider's perspective.

6. Vest all shares

Finally, it is important to remember that – regardless of how the equity is divided – all shares should be subjected to vesting restrictions. While you may not see this as an issue now, you never know what a co-founder will do in six months or a year. By vesting founder equity, you can ensure that a founder does not leave while he or she still retains a large portion of the company. How you vest is up to you, but typical schedules vest over a period of four to five years, with a large percentage vesting at the conclusion of the first year.

In the end, splitting equity may be the toughest thing you have to do as a member of a founding team. You are going to hurt feelings, make difficult decisions and live with the consequences. However, by keeping these tips in mind, you can rest easy at night knowing you did everything you could to oversee the process as fairly as possible.

Different Approaches to Split Founder Equity

Different teams have different ways of splitting the equity: some do it upfront, others wait to get to know each other; some go through a careful negotiation process, others are quick to shake hands and get on with it. Most important, some divide the equity equally amongst all founders, others come to the conclusion that the fair outcome is actually an uneven split that reflects differences among founders.

Robin Chase, cofounder of Zipcar, a car-sharing company, had heard a horror story from a friend about how the negotiation over founder equity had derailed the friend's startup. Eager to avoid that outcome, Robin proposed to her cofounder a 50/50 split at their very first meeting, just as they were getting to know each other professionally. The cofounders quickly shook hands and accepted the equal split. Robin breathed a sigh of relief, they had avoided the high tensions that often accompany an equity-split negotiation.

At Smartix, Inc., which created a smart-ticketing system for sports venues, the founders adopted a very different model for splitting the equity. The founding team believed that "it is best to delay the equity split because things are still unknown and changing." When they finally split the equity, they took a very deliberate approach, fearing the effects that might emerge if any founder felt that the equity-split process was unfair. In their dialogue, the team delved into each founder's past contributions, outside opportunities, preferences and anticipated future contributions. They decided to split the equity unequally, with the founder-CEO receiving more than twice the stake of the cofounder with the lowest stake.

When founders are splitting the equity early in their company's life, they face the heights of uncertainty — about their business strategy and business model, about their eventual roles within the team, about whether each founder will be fully committed to the startup, and about many more unknowns that will become clearer as they get to know each other. Things are even more uncertain for cofounders who have never worked together. Bypassing a serious dialogue about what each of the founders wants or deserves might be easier in the short-term, but is unlikely to be the right thing for the long-term health of the company.

Dive In or Take Time to Discover?

Robin Chase of Zipcar soon became very disillusioned with her "quick handshake" decision. She had never worked with her cofounder before and had made some bold assumptions about how well they would work together, whose skills would be most valuable and what the level of commitment would be. She threw herself into building the startup, crafting its business plan and going parking lot to parking lot, looking for those precious parking spots that her company so desperately needed. Her cofounder? She did not even quit her day job and contributed from the sidelines, at best. Robin soon came to realize the perils of that quick handshake. Her rushed negotiation had compromised her team's longer-term effectiveness by causing her "a huge amount of angst over the next year and a half."

Research sheds light on what Robin learned the hard way. Looking at the amount of time founding teams spend discussing their equity splits and find statistically significant differences between teams who split quickly – neglecting to have a serious dialogue about personal uncertainties and expected contributions – and those who have a lengthier and more robust dialogue. Robin rushed through that discussion, forfeiting the chance to discover what made her cofounder tick, whether her cofounder was enjoying her existing job, whether she was even willing to join Zipcar full time and so on. In the researched data we find that those teams that negotiate longer are more likely to decide on an unequal split: the harder you look, the more likely you are to discover important differences. More generally, we argue that if cofounders have not learned something surprising about each other from their dialogue, they probably have not engaged in a serious enough discussion yet.

The Perils of Family

The data also indicate that splitting founder equity well between family members is particularly challenging. Cofounders who are relatives usually believe that they already know each other intimately and therefore do not have much to discover about each other. However, we often act very differently at home than we do at the office and also very differently under the extreme stresses that accompany startup life. If you have never cofounded together, it is likely that you will be surprised by how your relative acts as a cofounder, often in negative ways. In short, relatives bypass detailed founder discussions at their peril, yet they are statistically more likely to do so.

Equity splits are a microcosm that beautifully reflect this. In my opinion, I find that founding teams that include relatives spent significantly less time negotiating equity splits. They were also much more likely to split the equity equally. Indeed, research suggests that many founding teams care about displaying outwardly visible equality: not only does everyone get the same equity share, everyone also gets exactly the same salary. This way no one can say afterwards that it was not "fair." This logic frequently trumps the alternative logic that a "fair" split should take into account that different founders contribute different skills, spend different amounts of time on the venture or give up different job opportunities.

Equity Splits Have Longer-Term Impacts

Founders tend to think "our equity split is just between us; it does not affect anyone else." However, that "first deal" between founders could be a first sign of what troubles lie ahead. What do investors make of teams that split the equity equally? My experiences suggest that they are less than thrilled. Even after statistically controlling for a lot of factors, data still suggest the same basic message: companies that have equal splits have more difficulty raising outside finance, especially venture capital. Venture capitalists could obviously tell the founders to come up with a different equity split, but that causes a lot of strife and heightens cofounder turmoil and turnover. Given that venture capitalists invest in less than one out of every hundred companies that come across their desk, they are looking for reasons to say no. An equal split can send worrisome signals about the team's ability to negotiate with others and to deal with difficult issues themselves. Interestingly, my experience suggests that equal splits are more a symptom than the cause of trouble. It is not the equal split per se that turns off the investors, it is that equal splits are a symptom of bigger issues with the company.

Go Organic

Adopt a "more organic" agreement than the static one typically adopted by founders. Vesting, in which each founder has to earn his or her equity stake by remaining involved in the startup or by achieving pre-defined milestones, is one way to achieve the dynamic approach. Yet, for founders' initial equity splits, such agreements are still the exception rather than the rule because there are many barriers to having the difficult conversation about adopting such mechanisms.

Essentially, such agreements are the equivalent of a newly engaged couple grappling with adopting a pre-nuptial agreement. Despite knowing about the high rate of divorce among married couples, we cannot bring ourselves to discuss the adoption of pre-nups with our fiancés. The same goes for the discussion of a "pre-nup" within a founding team. Setting up an agreement up front that outlines negative scenarios that might occur in the future, with corresponding actions to help avoid them, could help founders avoid headaches and increase startups' chances of success

Noam Wasserman, a Harvard Business School professor who has spent 15 years studying high-stakes decisions at more than 6,000 startups, says entrepreneurs too often split equity with what he calls a "quick handshake." Nearly 40 percent of startup teams spend a day or less hammering out an agreement, he says. A large subset of those go the even-steven route. An even split may be the best answer, but if you land there by default rather than after a thorough discussion of expectations and contributions, your team will probably suffer.

Wasserman found that unhappiness within teams almost triples when founders split equity equally by default. He estimates that founders who deserve more equity – because they had the original idea, have more relevant experience or will take a larger role in the company – leave about 25 percent on the table when they agree to an even split, which amounts to an average of about $450,000 in the first round of institutional financing. Here is how to divide equity without sowing division.

Consider Contributions

There is no right way to divide equity. But Wasserman's research shows that founders who had the idea for the company get around 10 to 15 more percentage points of equity than co-founders. Founders who have led other startups generally get 7 to 9 extra points and the one who becomes CEO gets from 14 to 20 extra points.

Ideally, you should allow for unexpected contingencies such as changes in the business model or founders switching roles. If/then planning and vesting schedules are two ways to keep things flexible. "A static split sets you up for disaster," says Wasserman.

Time It Right

Companies that split in their first month with little discussion are more likely to split evenly, says Wasserman. Often, these founders are too optimistic, lack information to make another choice or want to avoid a contentious issue. These companies often take a valuation hit when they go for funding. Investors who believe a simple split does a poor job of appropriately rewarding founders may reduce their investment or insist that the agreement be reworked. A quick, even split "suggests that the founders do not have the business maturity to have a tough dialogue," says Wasserman. But founders who wait too long can create internal tension, and individuals may try to maximize their own value at the expense of the company's interests.

Wasserman says the best time to split varies. In fast-changing industries, founders should establish principles they will use to draft an equity arrangement, but split only when larger uncertainties are resolved. In more stable industries, splitting in the first few months is a good idea. When you negotiate an equity split with co-founders, be clear, logical, and respectful. If you are lucky, the equity split will be just the first of many tough decisions you will make together.

How much is an idea worth? Most importantly, how much is your startup idea worth? Let us think about the subject using one iconic inventor: Thomas Edison.

Edison is known to be the inventor (among a ton of other stuff) of the electric lamp in 1879. Considering the amount of electric lamps that have been sold since then, imagine you could travel back in time to 1800 and invent the electric lamp. How much would your electric lamp idea be worth?

Thousands? Millions? Billions? Trillions? All the money in the world?

Now it is a good time to introduce the startup idea worth formula:

Idea = zero

"Zero? That's not possible," you say. And I retort, "Your idea is 100% worthless. Absolutely nothing, zero, nada, zip."

Here is why:

Do you know the name Humphry Davy? I did not think so. Mr. Davy was the actual inventor of the electric light, in 1809, 70 years before Edison. And he was not alone, after Humphry Davy, 21 other people "invented" the electric lamp before Thomas Edison.

What the hell?

The difference between those 22 inventors and Edison is that the latter had business acumen and invented the first commercially viable and practical electric light bulb.

Ideas are a dime a dozen. Implementation is the only thing that matters.

We do not need to go back in time, modern examples are abundant: Google was not the first search engine, it was just the best in doing that. Microsoft did not invent the graphical OS (and there are lots of arguments that it was not the best graphical OS available either). Apple did not invent the mobile phone. China did not invent manufacturing, etc.

Conclusion: lose the NDAs and secrecy, your idea is worthless without proper execution.

Where are the Investors

When you have a viable business plan for your start-up and you know how much funding assistance you need and what it will be used for, it is time to start looking for investors. This is a scary step to take, but being prepared is always the best route. Remember that you may need to speak to hundreds of investors before you find the right one for your startup. I personally know founders of popular successful startups that had to knock on hundreds of doors before getting funding.

When you are ready to start talking to investors, one of the most challenging parts can be just that: actually talking to investors. Most venture capitalists and angel investors receive dozens of pitches every day and simply do not have time to meet with everyone. To make it more difficult, it is not uncommon for first-time entrepreneurs to need to speak with 50+ investors before closing a round of funding. So, as an entrepreneur, you are going to need to identify dozens of people who could potentially be interested in your company.

In this day of technology and web searches, a lot of information is readily available. It still takes time and a certain astuteness to find relevant information and use it to your advantage.

Here are ten ways to find the right investor for your start-up:

Start-up Launch Platforms

Companies have launched specific platforms that provide information, research and assistance with all aspects of getting a business launched, including ways to connect with investors. Companies like startups.co are providing a convenient channel for locating investors in an efficient way.

Already, Startups.co has 13.9 million members, which makes it the largest start-up community in the world and provides an extraordinary opportunity to get in front of some investors in your space for both funding through fundable and mentoring. Another up-and-coming start-up platform is Gust with $1.8 billion already invested in start-up businesses.

Angel Networks

You can find that angel investor who not only will invest in your start-up, but will also sit on your shoulder, offering mentorship, solid advice, and provide access to their network of contacts. Places to start include Funded.com, Angel Capital Association, and Angel Investment Network, all of which have thousands of angel investors who provide information on the type of investments they are seeking.

To help you find a regional angel investor near you, Angel Capital Association even offers a directory listing by area and platform type. City Chamber of Commerce groups have also started to partner with angel investors to help stimulate new business opportunities for that city, including in areas like New York, Los Angeles and Chicago. India has many as well.

Crowdfunding Sites

Crowdfunding sites provide you with access to many different types of investors – from the general public with an interest to participate in the "next big thing" (Kickstarter, Pererbackers, and Indiegogo) to philanthropists who believe in helping others realize their dream (RocketHub), to accredited investors seeking new ideas to fund such as OurCrowd.

Each crowdfunding site has its own focus and way of incentivizing investors, so study each one carefully to see which one most closely aligns with your strategic goals and vertical.

Incubators and Accelerators

Your start-up is your baby and you want it to grow and flourish, so working with an incubator or accelerator gives you a whole host of investor resources to watch that business grow up and succeed. These investors are primarily interested in taking on a bigger role to help turn your idea into a viable business model as well as provide the funding sources to make it happen.

These incubators and accelerators even offer a physical space to set up your office, making it easy to work with you directly. Since space within the same building is also being used by other start-ups, this is a great place to exchange ideas and grow together.

Start-up accelerators, such as 500 Startups, TechStars, and Ycombinator, offer advice, small seed funding, and exposure to other investors through their own networks.

Small Business Administration

Traditional sources like the Small Business Administration or SME Associations are still a good sources for funding because more programs have been developed in recent years to stimulate the economy. They primarily offer small business loans and grants, but these may be exactly what you need and are available with fair terms without having any interference or expectations that they will get a stake in your business.

Professional Social Networking Sites

Beyond LinkedIn, which is still a place to look for investors, numerous professional social networking sites have been launched that can help connect you with all types of investors across all industry specializations and business segments. Many of these new professional social networking sites even connect you with investors from other countries who want to participate in the global business environment and often bring your product or service to their part of the world.

Some professional social networking sites to consider for investor connections include EFactor, Xing, Plaxo, Startup Nation, Cofoundr, and Meetup.

Private Equity Firms

Considered a traditional path to investor funding, private equity firms give you access to everything from a few thousand to millions in investment, primarily to those start-ups considered to be in the early stage with great growth potential across a wide range of industries.

The objective is to sell their stake a few years after investment to reap a significant profit from investing in your start-up. According to Private Equity Network, private equity firms invested $347 billion in 2015 across nearly 2,100 companies in the U.S.

Online Lending Platforms

With the incredible restrictions now involved with getting bank loans for a start-up, new solutions have emerged through the advent of online lending platforms that serve a similar function. These can be peer-to-peer platforms, non-traditional lending sources or large investors looking to help out small businesses and profiting from the lending terms. Some credible online lending platforms include Prosper, TrustLeaf, OnDeck, Lending Kart and Lending Club.

Personal Marketing Effort

Not only can you spend time finding investors through the channels mentioned here, but you can also help them discover you through a concerted personal marketing effort. This means putting yourself out there where investors are bound to find you, including a website, social networking sites, guest posts on established blogs and personal blog posts, conversations on Quora and traditional media outlets.

Friends and Family

Finding an investor in a friend or family member is not a hard sell because they already believe in you and are passionate about helping you succeed. Just remember if you use this funding avenue, make sure to keep your personal and professional relationships as separate as possible by getting everything in writing and clearly explaining the risk involved in investing in a startup - and make sure they understand they could lose their investment. Do not risk losing friends or family over investments.

Do not be discouraged if you are not flooded with investment offers or you are flat-out rejected - several times, even. Try, try again because it just means you have not found the right investor who aligns with your business needs. Stop now and you may never find your perfect match.

Banks - Private Banking Clients

Private Banking/Wealth management clients of leading banks badger their wealth advisors on good deals in the startup space. Get in touch with the wealth managers and checkout if any of their clients are interested.

The good news is, there are now more resources than ever to help you find the best investors for you —and actually reach them. Here are five tricks I found useful in getting meetings with the right people.

1. Build an angel list profile

AngelList is a great way to both learn about investors and let them learn about you. Creating a profile—including specific info about your company, product and team members — makes it easy for people who are interested in your space to find you.

Once you have filled everything out, share your profile with your friends and professional acquaintances and request references. When people follow your company, it will show up to others they know (and hopefully pique their interest). When we were fundraising, I watched for new investors who chose to follow my personal profile and sent each one a personal note. This ended up leading to several meetings and one investment.

2. Create a strategic list of investors you'd like to meet with

Given the odds of any individual meeting resulting in an investment, it is easy to want to cast as wide a net as possible. But given that more than 500,000 people in the U.S. have made angel investments recently, you can save yourself a lot of time and hassle if you focus your initial efforts on the 30–50 investors who are most likely to be a good fit for your company. (You can always expand the list later.)

I started by going through the education section of AngelList to find people who had invested in other edtech companies that were not directly competitive with us. I then took the list to other entrepreneurs and asked for their thoughts on who I should add or remove from the list, based on their experiences. Fellow entrepreneurs are an invaluable resource for helping you identify potentially interested investors not yet on your radar, as well as for flagging investors known for being difficult to work with or who are not actively investing.

From this process I ended up with a list of about 40 investors who I thought would be most beneficial to meet with. I entered all of them into a spreadsheet and included firm (when applicable), mutual connections, education investments, other relevant investments, location and any notes I wanted to remember (e.g., has two kids in high school).

3. Comb your networks

Because investors receive so many pitches, they often highly favour companies that are introduced by a common contact. (Think about how much stronger an applicant is at your company if he or she is referred by a current employee!)

So, once you have a list of investors you would like to meet with, go through it person-by-person and see if you have any mutual acquaintances. If so, great! But before you ask your contacts for an introduction, get together with them first so you can show them how awesome your company is. Ideally, your common connection should feel like he or she is doing a favour for both you and the investor by making the intro.

When we were fundraising, once someone agreed to make an introduction, I would send a 3-4 sentence pitch on our company so he or she could include it in the initial introduction email. Then I watched closely for the intro so I could follow up as quickly as possible.

4. Thoughtfully craft your own introduction

Of course, there will likely be some investors who you cannot find an introduction to. When this is the case, you simply need to be more thoughtful and selective about who you reach out to, crafting emails that prove you are not just sending out hundreds of cold emails to investors. For example: "I do not usually send cold emails, but between your investment in Company A and your involvement with Project B, I could not help but reach out and introduce myself." When we were fundraising, I had a good response rate from the investors I reached out to cold, but that is because I did not reach out to many and when I did, I had a very specific reason why I thought they would be interested in my company.

5. Give investors a reason to reach out to you

As much as your company wants to find great investors, investors also want to find great companies—meaning the courtship goes both ways. So, make sure you spend some time putting yourself out there. Even if your product is not live, you can still generate attention for your team and your mission via thought leadership.

Now, even with the best fundraising tactics, be prepared to get turned down by investors or not hear back. Do not let that get to you, but also do not be afraid to be diligent about following up in a professional manner. If you do not hear back in a week, send a quick follow up. After that, continue following up if and when you have news to share (e.g., a product launch, key metric that you hit, commitment from a notable investor). This also applies to investors you have met with but have not heard from since.

You are going to hear a lot of "Nos"— but that just makes the first time you hear "Yes!" that much more exciting.

Conclusion: Investor Readiness

"The wise learn from reflection, the smart from infliction and fools believe they learn from their own intellection"

Personal readiness is an exercise in introspection, business readiness an objective analysis at your work from another person's view, but now you step into the unknown world of investors. Unless you are a trained financial professional or have experienced a full funding cycle in the past, you are into unchartered territory. There is no need to feel intimidated and like most things new, a little attention, research and preparation will get you ninety percent ready. The last mile is specialized financial aspects for which, a lawyer, consultant or chartered accountant can be hired.

Here is a recap of getting ready for investors:

- Understand the types of investors, their investment philosophies and factors driving their investment choices
- Familiarize yourself with basic investor speak and terminology
- Lear the various steps of the funding process and hire experts for the technical aspects
- Prepare high quality professional grade pitch collateral
- Use technology for your pitch, like videos
- Keep your pitch brief and stick to maximum of 10–15 slides
- Spend time on a bottom up financial projection and come up with the amount of money you require
- Keep your investment ask suitably small (early stage) and link it to milestones
- Ensure that founders have a written agreement and equity is split in a fair manner not only for the past but also for the future roles, risks and responsibilities
- Get professional help if you want to arrive at a valuation

- Create an attractive investor play, the earlier the stage of funding, the more meat on the bone you have to leave
- Research for matched investors and network obsessively to get intros
- Practice intensively along-with your team and video record it to watch and make improvements

It is exciting to learn something new and step into the real world of investors. However, unlike learning at an institution, real life does not provide too much room for error. Especially since the community of matched investors is likely to be small and relatively better connected than you are. If personal readiness and business readiness require time, focus and an ability to be detached/objective, then investor readiness needs you to have the humility to learn. To be able to put your ego aside and be receptive to a new world of risk, reward, returns and ruthless world of business people, the likes of which you have never experienced. Get ready for the ride of your life.

PART IV
Investor Engagement

"Doubt & Fear shatter more dreams than failure ever can"

Overview: Engaging with Investors

"The challenge is not in becoming an entrepreneur, but in remaining one"

By nature, entrepreneurs are very enthusiastic, optimistic and risk-taking individuals. However, these same positive attributes can sometimes lead them blindly to failure, as many get so captivated by their business model, products or services that they fail to see potential risks or limitations to their potential targeted market.

The key factors that lead to the collapse of modern knowledge-based startups include:

- Inexperience and a weak management team
- Failure to plan
- Failure to evolve
- Inability to raise funds

These factors are interlinked and operate in a manner that generates a vicious cycle, which ultimately leads to the failure of the startup. We will review the challenges associated with the last factor, i.e., fund raising, with an aim to inform potential entrepreneurs and raise their awareness of such challenges and help equip them with key insight to help them plan for success.

Most venture capitalists have certain investment criteria and investment strategy that determine which companies they will include in their portfolio. These criteria may be based on the nature of industry, the company's products and services, geographic location, internal rates of return (IRR), stage of development or amount of capital required. While the average venture capital firm will see thousands of business plans per year, it will only consider a few dozen candidates and may actually close only six deals or less per year.

However, most entrepreneurs blindly target any VC firms, without any consideration to the strategic focus of such firms. This results in unproductive use of time, resources, not to mention the anxiety and stress that comes along with the numerous rejections. Therefore, to improve your chances of funding, you must target the right investors. For, your company's stage of development will determine the kind of venture capital investor you will approach and the structure of the financing you will receive. Accordingly, before starting the search for capital, it is important to:

- Identify which stage of business development and what type of financing you require.
- Take the time to research the venture capital industry to match the characteristics of the proposed investment with the investment strategy and criteria of the VC firm.
- Be prepared before communications or interactions with any potential investors, since you will never get a second chance to make the first impression.

Keep in mind that angel investors or venture capitalists are considering the following criteria when, you are presenting your business plan to or discussing it with them:

- Management and its credibility (leadership, intellectual honesty, vision, motivation, historical success and failures, etc.)
- A validated market need
- Compelling strategy (and preferably with unfair competitive advantage), reasonable deals details (funds deployed thus far, use of funds, valuation, etc.)

The key to your success in the fundraising process will hinge on the aforementioned criteria and how confidently you engage the VCs. You must balance your confidence with a healthy dose of realism so as not to appear as unaware of potential risks to your new venture. While passion and dedication will help you, overselling your idea by dismissing any challenging questions will hurt your efforts. If your VCs are interested in your business plan expect some tough questions from them. If they lose interest in you they will go easy on you and there will not be a second meeting.

Similarly, if you try to hide any information or downplay past business failures, your potential investors will learn about these during the due diligence phase and they will not fund you. Past business failure is not necessarily a deal killer so long as you are able to demonstrate that you have learned from it and you now know how to avoid such failure in the future.

Some entrepreneurs succeed in attracting the VCs to invest in their venture; however, they fail to close the deal during the negotiations.

Many entrepreneurs take on an adversary attitude during the negotiations, because they believe that VCs are out to take advantage of them. If you find an investor willing to invest in you, do not waste this unique opportunity and understand that VCs are also required to protect their interest. Find a competent attorney/consultant/advisor and try to negotiate a winning deal for both parties. If you are in the fortunate position of having more than one VC firm interested in funding you, you will probably get a better valuation than if you were to have only one investor. Use this to develop a better term sheet from both by using the BATNA (Better Alternative To a Non-negotiated Deal) framework. However, do not overplay this to the point where both firms would walk away from you.

Networking as a way to meet and engage investors

If you are thinking about a business opportunity that will require investment, then attend networking events in your area to identify key members of the investor community and meet other entrepreneurs. It is never too early to approach potential investors and it may be easier to create an informal relationship when you are not actively seeking investment for your startup.

Be creative in expanding your network. Attend events, meetings, dinners and speaker series where investors and entrepreneurs meet to make you and your business visible to this community.

- Get an introduction to potential investors

    Once you are ready to raise financing and have developed your target investor list, contact the investors you know directly. For those investors you do not know, get the best quality introduction you can from other sources:

    CEOs and founders of current and past investee companies — they are generally easier to reach directly than an investor, they can be an excellent way to get your business a referral to that investor and they may offer some insight into whether the investor would be a good prospect for your business.

- Other investors who know and have worked with the target firm
- Other industry sector contacts—analysts, executives at large influential organizations and advisors
- Professional firms — law firms, accounting firms and consulting firms

- Neighbours, friends and family
- LinkedIn or other social networking tools — determine if there are any indirect links between you and your target investor and request an introduction

Helping investors help you is a rare, impactful skill for a founder to have. Too few are good at it. Based on my experiences of angel investing, here are the most impactful actions founders can take to capitalize on their investor connections.

Regular Status Checks

The first thing to realize is that it is the investor's job to add value. Startup investors generate returns in three ways: They identify good companies, they add value after investing and they help companies exit. That middle step is crucial.

Every founding team should strive to get the most from their investors. While they generally will not be there with you day-to-day, they can be transformative when it comes to solving specific, discrete problems. You should set aside time every month to do a quick rundown and identify where each investor can bring the most value:

Who this month can:

- Make deals happen.
- Help build my team.
- Help us grow the right way.
- Coach me and give me guidance that is relevant right now.

Deal Maker

Few things build value faster than landing deals. Investors create serious value when they help you close a major customer, introduce a key partner or forge relationships with investors for your next round. Many of your investors will have operational and deal-marking backgrounds, not to mention their huge professional networks. They are natural deal accelerators.

I love it when founders give me a wish list of deals they would like to make within a certain time frame — the ideal customers, strategic partnerships or venture firms they would like to have involved. By making this information completely transparent and a bit aspirational, it lets me lean in where I have connections and keep my eyes peeled for other opportunities. I will always spend time with a wish list like this thinking about how I can get founders in front of the right people.

A great way to get help closing sales is to send regular email updates. There is a lot I can do with an email that gives me the specific names of customer leads for a sales intro or a CEO for a business partnership. As a founder, if you know your investor has a relationship with someone on this list, reach out immediately and ask them directly if they could broker the introduction. Do not hedge.

This is effective more than you might think. One founder I work with sends investors a weekly update of his sales pipeline with progress made and goals against a few key prospects. If you cannot do it weekly, send a monthly email, enumerating all current sales prospects and their status.

Investors can only help if you are transparent all the time, not just in good times.

This sounds like common sense, but a surprising number of founders only want to update investors once they have closed deals. They worry that they will look bad or weak or behind if they share leads that do not convert. This is a bad approach. Your investors have the experience to know that not all leads will end in a deal. And we know there are better and worse months for sales. But we cannot make any conversions happen if we do not know where to direct our efforts.

In Closing Your Next Round

Your existing investors can be one of your best channels for bringing new investors into your next round. They should advocate for you with later-stage funders. Start early working with your investors and sync on your next round goals. Talk through it so they know how to help, who they should be introducing you to (most important) and how to position your growth story. Develop your next round investor wish list with them.

Recently, a founder of one of my consulting assignments called to tell me they were about to go out for their Series A and wanted my help. Over the next month, we talked a couple times a week and traded a lot of material back and forth to make sure the company was putting its best foot forward. I worked with the founders to understand the differences between Series A investors, refine their wish list, build their pitch material and make introductions to their top-tier choices where I could. This expedited term sheet offers.

The Team

Helping you recruit the strongest team is one of the most valuable things your investors can do. They often have large networks to draw from — particularly for senior key hires — but really, you should ask them for help hiring across the board.

Make sure everyone is aware of the positions you are looking to fill. When sending investor email updates, include your open positions. If one of your angels has depth in a particular area, ask them personally for help with a specific role. Dig into their networks ahead of time using LinkedIn and tell them which introductions will move the needle the most.

Be more specific about your hiring. A founder recently sent me a very detailed job spec for a hard-to-hire engineering role. He spelled out in detail the personal and technical qualities of the ideal candidate. His detailed spec was much more useful than the too-frequent request for a "rockstar backend engineer." It dramatically sharpened the focus of who I should refer. It is easy for your investors to cast too wide a net. This leads to wasted effort and running out of bandwidth initiating the wrong conversations. Narrow the field for the best results.

You should leverage your investors beyond sourcing too. For important roles and areas outside your expertise, consider engaging investors by bringing them into the hiring loop.

Several years ago, I considered an executive role at a hot startup and after meeting with the CEO, she had me interview with the Chairman of her Board. It was a smart way for her to double check her thinking. I took the lesson to heart and now regularly offer services as an interviewer. It is always good to balance your perspective with someone else who has a bit of objectivity and distance from the day-to-day, particularly if you have not hired for this seniority or role before. In many cases, involving the right investor will help you keep the bar high and rising.

Growth Push

So, let's say you were smart enough to select some investors based on their industry-specific knowledge. Now that you have them, are you taking advantage of this expertise? Are you reaching out when you are not sure what to do next? If not, you should. Start taking your hard problems to your investors early and there is a good chance they will help you cut through the noise. In particular, I recommend airing your tactical problems. You do not have to reinvent the wheel on common tasks like contract terms or equity grants or debt financing. It is better to spend 5 minutes having them give you the answer than spending hours figuring it out yourself.

Really digging into industry and strategy questions takes a lot of time; good, quality, face-to-face time. I suggest that founders put work sessions on the calendar with the VCs and angels that can guide them through operational and strategic challenges of growth. Perhaps, the best advice: Bring in investors who have a history as entrepreneurs and practitioners themselves.

Once you get this time locked in, it is on you, the founder, to create and communicate the agenda. You know the immediate problems. Beforehand, send a detailed email to your investor about the problem (ideally just one). Include supporting materials as you easily can share (context, articles, market and customer data, etc.).

Company building and operations is one area most founders look for guidance. You need to think through organizational structure. You need to create processes, systems and metrics, often for the first time. You need a way to manage the performance of your growing sales and engineering teams. And you need increasingly specialized functions over time. It is a lot of moving pieces. Investors who have been through this before can help founders get it right the first time.

It Is an Investor's Job to Keep an Eye on the Big Picture. Leverage Their Perspective

Investors usually work with multiple companies at once and have a history working with even more. If anyone is privy to the macro trends that could influence your startup, it is them. They will see things coming down the line. They will see many different approaches to things like competitive positioning, defining target markets and scoping products. You just have to open the door to them regularly communicating this information, which is all about expectation setting. If you want them to email you whenever they have a new thought for you, encourage them to do it. VCs and angels try to balance helping you out and not getting in your way.

Get Coached

A lot of founders talk about mentorship, but very few seek out and make coaching relationships work. I do not care who you are, you will be better at your job with a good coach and mentor. Great leaders like Steve Jobs and Mark Zuckerberg have relied on coaches and advisors throughout their careers — not just when they hit tough spots — so, you can bet that seeking out solid mentors is worth your time.

My advice: Curate a few mentors who you respect and trust with the fate of your company. Your investors are a natural place to look. Most of them will have accumulated valuable experience, judgment and outside perspectives. Even more importantly, they are vested in your success.

Be frank with them about how important coaching is to you and tell them in very specific terms where you would like them to focus. It might be on building leadership and management skills, it might be pushing you on ideas where others do not or it might be candid feedback about how you interact with other people. Having a candid conversation with your would-be coaches about how you want the coaching process to work is a good way to get started.

A lot of people can and should be mentors — former bosses, industry leaders, your successful uncle. But investors play a distinct role in your mentorship network because they are coming at it from a different angle. They have skin in the game. They are likely to take the mentorship seriously and are incentivized to be more honest and provide an unvarnished opinion where others might not.

The Key to Being a Good Mentee Is to Be Vulnerable

Founders often struggle being vulnerable because of the personality traits that make them great founders to begin with. They are under immense pressure as leaders and everyone is counting on them (and paying a ridiculous amount of attention to their every move). No wonder they feel the need to always present a confident facade. I get that, but the best leaders also know how to get in touch with the areas where they do not feel as strong and turn to knowledgeable people they trust for candid help.

The founders I have the best working relationships with stay in constant contact with me. They are the ones who send me emails throughout the week and call me on Sunday evenings to discuss the next big deal, the under-performing hire or whatever else is keeping them up at night. My ability to coach is built on the trust established while getting to know these founders. If I was not in regular contact or did not have a real-time sense of what they were experiencing, there is no way I could be as helpful.

Tactics for Driving Investor Engagement

Set discrete goals with your investors. Here is one of the most impactful conversations a founder can have with an investor: What outcomes will that investor commit to achieving for the company over the next 6 months? This aligns everyone behind goals and gives investors clarity and healthy accountability. It sounds demanding, but it will not be received that way and everyone will be better off. It will also clarify who actually brought the value they promised when it is time to discuss things like pro rata for follow-on rounds.

Get the time commitment. You need investors to give their time — simple as that. If you do not, nothing else here matters. Set time expectations with investors before you even bring them aboard. While you are discussing a potential investment, tell them, "We are looking for investors who can commit X hours a month to helping us grow." Discuss their availability. You might have angels who are retired and making just a few investments or you may have Fortune 50 CEOs who make 20 angel investments a year. The latter, while influential, just is not going to have the same time. Consider this seriously in your decision.

Narrow the field. When you talk to your investors, focus in on your biggest most timely challenges. I have seen this work like a charm when founders need to land key hires, ask for executive-level introductions to companies they are targeting as customers and more. Be sure to publicly thank investors that have been helpful. Everyone likes to know their efforts were productive and appreciated. They will be that much more likely to help the next time.

Do not be afraid of your investors. It is not unusual to feel intimidated by people who give you money. Maybe they are much older and have big accomplishments. But do not be afraid to engage them frequently. They will respect you more if you exhibit the confidence to communicate with them as peers. As one of my favourite CEOs, puts it: "It is easy to fall into the trap of not engaging your investors because you are afraid of getting asked a question you cannot answer."

Flip the fear in your head and ask them that question you cannot answer.

Manas, founder and CEO of one of the finalists of India Fund Fest, Brightsandz, is one of those model founders who pulls all of these tactics together. Before I ever took him as a client, he spearheaded several conversations to explore how I might be able to help. Early on, he shared specific line items where I could add value. His regular updates are engaging and make targeted requests about how to weigh in on everything from real estate to individual sales deals. He makes it easy to know where and how to help. As a result, I think he gets much more out of his advisors than another founder with the exact same backers would if they were not as proactive.

Some founders do all of this extremely well. The point is, all founders should. Investor engagement is close to a full time job and if done well will catapult you and the company to great heights.

How To Pitch

Back when we first pitched our company to investors, we thought we knew a lot more than we did: Our 45-minute presentation was jampacked with data. And our style was confident: We presented so frequently, in fact, that we could have pitched in our sleep. Our only change after approaching investor after investor, we whittled down the length but kept the heart of our message intact.

Yet, while our pitches generated great enthusiasm, no one cut us a check. So, we revised our presentation again. This time, we trimmed it to 15 minutes, but still kept all those compelling facts, figures, growth projections, competitive analysis and insights about our market opportunity. We remained convinced that our pitch was the best ones these investors had ever seen.

Oh, were we mistaken!

At the end of one presentation, an investor raised his hand and gave us, finally, the cold, hard truth. "Guys," he said, "I have no idea what you do. No clue." The murmurs of agreement throughout the room floored us. We had thought we were nailing it, but we had not even come close to landing a deal. Where had we gone wrong?

We quickly realized that we fundamentally misunderstood what constitutes a great pitch. Four days ahead of our subsequent meeting, our confidence shattered, we read Oren Klaff's Pitch Anything. The book explores the neuroscience of how people respond to sales presentations and opportunities. And reading it was the best thing we could have done because it transformed our outlook.

Humans are wired to assess situations as threatening or safe, a calculation Klaff says is made by what he calls our "crocodile brain." This is essentially the gatekeeper to more advanced, analytical thinking, Klaff explains: When a pitch does not inspire our listeners' confidence early on, their crocodile brains warn them off. No matter how positive their conscious response, they will not hand over money if their subconscious self warns them not to.

And hitting investors over their heads with stats about a company's reliability does not work, either. In fact, overwhelming the crocodile brain with charts and data right out of the gate is a surefire way to lose an investment.

Our success rate skyrocketed once we had revamped our pitch strategy based on Klaff's principles and trimmed the pitch even more to a succinct nine minutes. Here is the approach we now take when presenting to investors. Other entrepreneurs can tweak it to their own needs and (hopefully) replicate our success:

1. Be brief

We start our pitches with a 30-second introduction that covers who we are and just a couple of bullet points why we are credible. Beyond that, the focus is on delivering a tight, concise presentation about our product. Investors' eyes glaze over when teams talk too much about themselves. Get to the point quickly.

Use clean, well-designed slides and always be prepared with more in-depth financial projections and analytics in case they ask.

2. Address market forces

After the introductions, describe three key market forces or problems affecting your industry that are colliding. That gives investors context for why your particular product is innovative, necessary and timely.

3. Explain how you solve the problem

Demonstrate how your product or service uniquely solves people's needs. Note gaps in the current market and be specific when discussing opportunities. Investors look for a clear path to high-scale growth and how you will become the clear market leader.

4. Close with bulletproof stats

We conclude our presentations with a rundown of key numbers that stick with investors. We use data to show the market opportunity, new client acquisition rate, user traction, the high-end clients we have signed, our projections and our plan to allocate funds to scale quickly. That is usually enough for investors to opt in. Remember that they are always asking, "Is this safe?" Make them confident that you have the expertise and pathway to success.

5. Read Pitch Anything

Our pitch is structured on the format and flow of Klaff's system and I cannot recommend it enough. Klaff's understanding of the human brain allows startup teams to approach investors scientifically and hit all the right notes.

Entrepreneurs often think they need to create long, elaborate presentations to win investors' trust. But a short, fact-filled pitch that's optimized for how people actually respond to new information is the real key to securing investments.

Why Business Plans Do not Get Funded

Your business plan is very often the first impression potential investors get about your venture. But even if you have a great product, team and customers, it could also be the last impression the investor gets if you make any of these avoidable mistakes.

Investors see thousands of business plans each year, even in this down market. Apart from a referral from a trusted source, the business plan is the only basis they have for deciding whether or not to invite an entrepreneur to their offices for an initial meeting.

With so many opportunities, most investors simply focus on finding reasons to say no. They reason that entrepreneurs who know what they are doing will not make fundamental mistakes. Every mistake counts against you.

Content Mistakes

Failing to relate to a true pain. Pain comes in many flavours: my computer network keeps crashing; my accounts receivable cycle is too long; existing treatments for a medical condition are ineffective; my tax returns are too hard to prepare. Businesses and consumers pay good money to make pain go away.

You are in business to get paid for making pain go away. Pain, in this setting, is synonymous with market opportunity. The greater the pain, the more widespread the pain and the better your product is at alleviating the pain, the greater your market potential.

A well written business plan places the solution firmly in the context of the problem being solved.

Value inflation

Phrases like "unparalleled in the industry;" "unique and limited opportunity;" or "superb returns with limited capital investment" - taken from actual documents - are nothing but assertions and hype.

Investors will judge these factors for themselves. Lay out the facts - the problem, your solution, the market size, how you will sell it and how you will stay ahead of competitors - and lay off the hype.

Trying to Be All Things to All People

Many early-stage companies believe that more is better. They explain how their product can be applied to multiple, very different markets or they devise a complex suite of products to bring to a market.

Most investors prefer to see a more focused strategy, especially for very early stage companies: a single, superior product that solves a troublesome problem in a single, large market that will be sold through a single, proven distribution strategy.

That is not to say that additional products, applications, markets and distribution channels should be discarded - instead, they should be used to enrich and support the highly focused core strategy.

You need to hold the story together with a strong, compelling core thread. Identify that and let the rest be supporting characters.

No Go-To-Market Strategy

Business plans that fail to explain the sales, marketing and distribution strategy are doomed. The key questions that must be answered are: who will buy it, why and most importantly, how will you get it to them?

You must explain how you have already generated customer interest, obtained pre-orders or better yet, made actual sales - and describe how you will leverage this experience through a cost-effective go-to-market strategy.

"We have no competition"

No matter what you may think, you have competitors. Maybe not a direct competitor - in the sense of a company offering an identical solution - but at least a substitute. Fingers are a substitute for a spoon. First class mail is a substitute for e-mail. A coronary bypass is a substitute for an angioplasty.

Competitors, simply stated, consist of everybody pursuing the same customer dollars. To say that you have no competition is one of the fastest ways you can get your plan tossed - investors will conclude that you do not have a full understanding of your market.

The "Competition" section of your business plan is your opportunity to showcase your relative strengths against direct competitors, indirect competitors and substitutes. Besides, having competitors is a good thing. It shows investors that a real market exists.

Too Long

Investors are very busy and do not have the time to read long business plans. They also favour entrepreneurs who demonstrate the ability to convey the most important elements of a complex idea with an economy of words.

An ideal executive summary is no more than 1–3 pages. An ideal business plan is 20–30 pages (and most investors prefer the lower end of this range). remember, the primary purpose of a fund-raising business plan is to motivate the investor to pick up the phone and invite you to an in-person meeting. It is not intended to describe every last detail.

Document the details elsewhere: in your operating plan, R&D plan, marketing plan, white papers, etc.

Too Technical

Business plans - especially those authored by people with scientific backgrounds - are often packed with too many technical details and scientific jargon. Initially, investors are interested in your technology only in terms of how it:

- Solves a really big problem that people will pay for;
- Is significantly better than competing solutions;
- Can be protected through patents or other means; and
- Can be implemented on a reasonable budget.

All of these questions can be answered without a highly technical discussion of how your product works. The details will be reviewed by experts during the due diligence process. Keep the business plan simple.

No Risk Analysis

Investors are in the business of balancing risks versus rewards. Some of the first things they want to know are what are the risks inherent in your business and what has been done to mitigate these risks.

The key risks of entrepreneurial ventures include:

- Market risks: Will people actually buy what you have to sell? Will you need to create a major change in consumer behaviour?

- Technology risks: Can you actually deliver what you say you can? On budget and on time?

- Operational risks: What can go wrong in the day-to-day operations of the company? What can go wrong with manufacturing and customer support?

- Management risks: Can you attract and retain the right team? Can your team actually pull this off? Are you prepared to step aside and let somebody else take over if necessary?

- Legal risks: Is your intellectual property truly protected? Are you infringing on another company's patents? If your solution does not work, can you limit your liability?

This is, of course, just a partial list of risks.

Even though you may feel that the risks are negligible, potential investors will feel otherwise unless you demonstrate that you have given a lot of thought to what can go wrong and have taken prudent steps to mitigate these risks.

Poorly Organized

Your plan should flow in a nice, organized fashion. Each section should build logically on the previous section, without requiring the reader to know something that is presented later in the plan.

Although there is no single "correct" business plan structure, follow the principles in earlier parts of the book to get the structure right.

Lack of Detail

Your financials should be constructed from the bottom-up and then validated from the top-down.

A bottom-up model starts with details such as when you expect to make certain sales or when you expect to hire specific employees. Top-down validation means that you examine your overall market potential and compare that to the bottom-up revenue projections.

Round numbers - like one million in R&D expenses in Year 2 and two million in Year 3 - are a sure sign that you do not have a bottom-up model.

Unrealistic Financials

Only a very small handful of companies achieve $100 million or more in sales only five years after founding.

Projecting much more than that will not be credible and will get your business plan canned faster than almost anything else. On the other hand, a business with only $25 million in revenues after five years will be too small to interest serious investors.

Financial forecasts are a litmus test of your understanding of how venture capitalists think. If you have a realistic basis for projecting $50–100 million in Year 5, you are probably a good candidate for venture financing. Otherwise, you should probably look elsewhere.

Insufficient Financial Projections

Basic financial projections consist of three fundamental elements: Income Statements, Balance Sheets and Cash Flow Statements. All of these must conform to Generally Accepted Accounting Principles or GAAP.

Investors generally expect to see five years of projections. Of course, nobody can see five years into the future. Investors primarily want to see the thought process you employ to create long-term projections.

A good financial model will also include sensitivity analysis, showing how your projected results will change if your assumptions turn out to be incorrect. This allows both you and the investor to identify the assumptions that can have a material effect on your future performance, so that you can focus your energies on validating those assumptions.

They should also include benchmark comparisons to other companies in your industry - things like revenues per employee, gross margin per employee, gross margin as a percentage of revenues and various expense ratios (general and administrative, sales and marketing, research and development and operations as a percentage of total operating expenses).

Conservative Assumptions

Nobody ever believes that assumptions are conservative, even if they truly are. Develop realistic assumptions that you can support, refrain from using the words "conservative" or "aggressive" in your plan and leave it at that.

Offering a Valuation

Many business plans err by stating that their company is worth a certain amount. How do you know? The value of a company is determined by the market - by what others are willing to pay - and unless you are in the business of buying, selling or investing in companies, you probably do not have an acute sense of what the market will bear.

If you name a price, one of two things can happen: (a) your price is too high and investors will toss your plan; or (b) your price is too low and investors will take advantage of you. Both are bad.

The purpose of the business plan is to tell your story in the most compelling manner possible so that investors will want to go to the next step. You can always negotiate the price later. This does not mean that you do not go in with a number as the investment ask and what you are willing to give in return. Just do not act out a valuation without a firm basis.

Stylistic Mistakes

Poor spelling and grammar

If you make silly mistakes in your business plan, what does that say about how you run your business?

Use your spelling and grammar checkers, get other people to edit the plan, do whatever it takes to purge embarrassing errors.

Too repetitive

All too often, a plan covers the same points over and over. A well-written plan should cover key points only twice: once, briefly, in the executive summary and again, in greater detail, in the body of the plan.

Appearance matters

At any point in time, an investor has dozens if not hundreds of plans waiting to be read. Get to the top of the pile by making sure that the cover is attractive, the binding is professional, the pages are well laid out and the fonts are large enough to be easily read.

On the other hand, do not go too far - you do not want to give the impression that you are all style and no substance.

Execution mistakes

Waiting until too late. The capital formation process takes a long time. In general, count on 6 months to a year from the time you start writing the plan until the time the money is in the bank.

Do not put it off. Your management team should be prepared to invest about 500 hours into the plan. If you are too busy building your product, company or customers (which is arguably a better use of your time), consider outsourcing the development of the business plan.

Failing to seek outside review

Make sure that you have at least a few people review your plan before you send it out - preferably people who understand your market, sales and distribution strategies, the VC market, etc. Your plan may look perfect to you and your team, but that is probably because you have been staring at it for months.

Good, objective reviews from outsiders with a fresh perspective can save you from myopia.

Over tweaking

You could spend countless hours tweaking your plan in the pursuit of perfection. A lot of this time would be better spent working on your product, company and customers. At some point, you need to pull the trigger and get the plan out in front of a few investors.

If the reaction is positive and they want to move forward, great. If the reaction is negative (assuming that the investor was a good fit to begin with), then you may have been heading down the wrong path. Get feedback from a couple of investors and if a general consensus emerges, go back and refine your plan.

Conclusion

It is a tough investment climate, but good ideas backed by good teams and good business plans are still getting funded. Give yourself the best possible chance by avoiding these simple mistakes. Today there are specialized tools like the "Funding Readiness Report" developed for the India Fund Fest and businesses in general. Like you go with a credit rating report for loans, it is advisable to go in with a report of your funding readiness prepared by a third party. It carries certain credibility and investors find it a good starting point.

What Not To Say When Pitching

There are "red flags" which every potential investor unconsciously listens for. Often these are mentioned in the investors world as "entrepreneur lies," but I prefer to think of them as innocent over-enthusiasm or over-confidence that can kill your deal.

Here is my summary of a few from my experience with hundreds of elevator pitches, business plans and executive presentations:

- "Our product is truly disruptive technology." If your product really represents a paradigm shift, you probably have not figured out yet what problem it solves. At best we can count on it taking many years to catch on, just like other disruptive technologies before you. No investor wants to wait that long for his return or fund the years of waiting.

- "Gartner says our market will be $50 billion in 2015." It always amazes me how an entrepreneur can define his market opportunity so broadly, then assess his competition so narrowly in the next breath. You will not impress investors by claiming that everyone in India needs one and nobody else has exactly the same features to compete with you.

- "All we have to do is get 1% of the market." This red flag is the flip side of "the market will be $50 billion." There are two problems with this assertion. First, no investor is interested in a company that is only looking to get 1% of a market. Second, that first 1% is the toughest of any market, so you look naïve implying it is easy to get.

- "We do not believe there are any competitors." This is a terrible statement because there are only two logical conclusions. A first conclusion is that there must not be a market. Or worse yet, the entrepreneur is so arrogant that he has not even used Google to figure out he has competition just down the street.

- "Microsoft is too big/slow to be a threat." Usually the reason the big companies are no threat is that the market is too small. Competing with IBM, Microsoft and other large companies is a very difficult task. Entrepreneurs who utter this line are kidding themselves. They may think it is bravado, but investors think it is stupidity.

- "We have the first-mover advantage." That is probably the soft way of saying, we do not have a patent or any "secret sauce" for a competitive advantage. Unfortunately, a startup with no brand name and no intellectual property is a sitting duck for the big slow company, as soon as they see you gaining a bit of traction. Sleeping giants do wake up.

- "Our projections are conservative." A startup's projections should never be conservative. Plus I have never seen a startup achieve even their most conservative projections. We all know that financial projections are a confidence test on how committed you are to the project, so do not try to minimize them.

- "We have a proven management team." If the entrepreneur and team were that proven, they probably would be funding others rather than asking for money. Truly proven in an investor's eye is a team that has both failed and succeeded at least once, with success meaning 10x or more return to investors.

- "A world-class CEO will be joining us after the funding event." It is easy to get your executive friends to express interest in the huge opportunity you describe, but do not assume they will actually take the big leap down from their high-paying job to the meagre salary you can offer. Rest assured the investor will ask for names and place some calls. Hedges here by your candidates will definitely kill the deal.

- "We have strong interest from a major customer." The mention of unsigned contracts normally takes away more credibility than it adds. You can counter this position by bringing the interested party to the meeting for support or at least showing a Letter of Intent (LOI). Otherwise talk about paying customers only.

- Definitely not inane well known facts like, India is a 1.3 billion people country or India has a 200 million strong middle class or India is one of the fastest growing economies in the world etc. They are not fools, you meet one investor a week if you are lucky, they meet dozens like you and have access to all latest data.

I highly recommend that you screen your business plan and your executive presentation carefully for variations on any of these statements and remove them. Your integrity and honesty are you best assets, so do not jeopardize them with common over-statements, even if your intent is virtuous.

Why Investors Delay

Fundraising for startup businesses is typically a slow and painful process. Most entrepreneurs would rather spend time growing their business than making fundraising prospect lists, scheduling pitch meetings and asking for money.

Unless you have a track record of business success or excellent sales ability, the reality of fundraising for many first-time business owners is that it takes contacting at least four to five interested prospects before you can close your first investor. But this poses a challenge since most entrepreneurs need at least 10 investors to put together a meaningful round of funding – and the process of assembling 40 to 50 fundraising prospects is daunting. So, what is an entrepreneur to do?

I have written about the process of identifying private investors and brainstorming a list of relatives, friends and business associates who would be willing to support your venture. I want to focus on how to maximize your close rate with fundraising prospects. Because rather than expanding your prospecting list to 40 or 50 individuals, wouldn't it be better if you could increase your close rate from 25% to 75% so you need relatively fewer prospects to complete your round of funding?

I have picked up a few nuggets of wisdom about how to close a deal from my own fundraising experiences and from observing clients raise money. Here is my advice:

1. Pick a closing date, then do not enforce it. When raising large sums of money from venture capital firms and institutional investors, closing dates are critical. The interest income on $50 million is about $50,000 per week (which is approximately the same amount as the total legal fees on VC rounds), so the cost of a closing delay is substantial. This explains why your lawyer will give you financing documentation for your startup round of funding that has a closing date clause.

   In practice, angel investors and other individuals who will support your business will ignore your closing date and send you the money when they feel like it. Unless you are convinced that your financing round will be oversubscribed by too much demand, your closing date is likely to be a moving target. Nevertheless, investors like to see a closing date because they like to feel that other investors are interested in your business and investing at the same time.

You should ask your lawyer to modify the standard closing date clause to read "The closing date is [some date in the near future] or another date that is mutually agreeable to both parties." This small change will keep the documentation valid for several weeks after the closing date in case your investor takes extra time to give you the funds.

One of the greatest challenges that entrepreneurs face is answering the question posed by your prospects, "How many other investors are committing money at this closing date?" The smart answer is to avoid giving an answer, since trying to close several individuals on the same date is a long shot.

2. Provide investment options. Flexibility is critical when dealing with non-institutional investors. Take-it-or-leave-it terms seldom work because the motivation for each investor will vary. Raising $10,000 from your close friends may involve different terms than say, raising $50,000 from a business associate. If you are raising money in the form of debt, it is better to offer two or three options for participation in the round: different amounts or thresholds, different time horizons and different repayment schedules. If you are raising money in the form of equity, use convertible debt rather than preferred stock for your friends-and-family round and be sure to provide some flexibility on the investment amount. Trying to enforce a minimum investment threshold of $25,000 or $50,000 will only work if you have several wealthy friends who have liquid funds available to invest.

3. Anticipate follow-up meetings. To keep the courtship process with investors moving forward, it is best to end each meeting with a definite plan for the next meeting. Even if you can tell your entire story in one meeting, it is better to spread it to two or three meetings since that might be how long it takes for the investor to get comfortable with you. It is also a good idea to schedule reference calls with your previous investors, partners and/or board members to demonstrate that you have others involved with your venture who can vouch for you or your business. In my experience, it is best to make this introduction at the

end of the courtship to help you close, rather than early in the process to help the investor conduct early due diligence.

4. Ask about doubts. At the second meeting, I find it is useful to end the meeting by asking the straightforward question: "What are your remaining doubts or concerns about making this investment?" The response to this question will usually indicate whether you will be able to address those concerns or not. This information is also useful when prepping your reference partners for subsequent calls.

5. Stop selling. It is easy to get in the habit of selling. So much so, in fact, that the sales culture of fundraising can seep into your interactions with investors even after they have decided to invest and are simply waiting for the paperwork to be completed. Once they have made the decision to invest, step back and let the process happen without continuing to sell it.

6. Do not forget to ask for the cheque. When raising money, it is easy to get tied up in answering the questions posed by the investors, then get tied up in the negotiations and paperwork, then get tied up in making sure the relationship with your investor continues to be sound after the negotiations are complete. During all these interactions, it is also easy to forget that the purpose of the process is to get the money. You may find that you will get the funding more quickly if you ask for it earlier. One way to ask for the cheque is to ask your investor whether he plans to make a wire transfer or send a personal cheque so you can decide if he needs to receive your bank wire transfer details. It might be presumptive to ask this question too early, but it tends to move the dialogue along very quickly. And remember, the deal is not closed 'till the money' is in the bank.

7. Hit or exceed your annual budget, particularly prior to and during the fundraising process. This also is about buyer and lender confidence.

If, during the sale process, your company does not hit the numbers you said it would, they begin to doubt and second guess the entire transaction.

If, on the other hand, you beat the numbers, they become afraid of losing the transaction and work harder to close as quickly as possible.

Inexperienced angels often get cold feet when the time comes to write that big check. In our startup, one of the two angels in the initial round took months to pay us and only did after repeated nagging from our lawyer, who was also, fortunately, his lawyer.

It is obvious why investors delay. Investing in startups is risky! When a company is only two months old, every day you wait gives you 1.7% more data about their trajectory. But the investor is already being compensated for that risk in the low price of the stock, so it is unfair to delay.

Fair or not, investors do it if you let them. Even VCs do it. And funding delays are a big distraction for founders, who ought to be working on their company, not worrying about investors. What is a startup to do? With both investors and acquirers, the only leverage you have is competition. If an investor knows you have other investors lined up, he will be a lot more eager to close – and not just because he will worry about losing the deal, but because if other investors are interested, you must be worth investing in. It is the same with acquisitions. No one wants to buy you till someone else wants to buy you and then everyone wants to buy you.

The key to closing deals is never to stop pursuing alternatives. When an investor says he wants to invest in you or an acquirer says they want to buy you, do not believe it till you get the cheque. Your natural tendency when an investor says yes will be to relax and go back to writing code. Alas, you cannot; you have to keep looking for more investors, if only to get this one to act.

Is It Tougher as a First Time Entrepreneur?

The inaugural "India Fund Fest" (India's Only Serious Fund Fest – www.indiafundfest.com) had 6800 applicants, of which 70% were from non-metros. This prompted me to travel to the top applying non-metros, like Patna, Lucknow, Indore and a dozen other cities. In each city, I met dozens of first time entrepreneurs—credible, legit ones—eager to start their first business, but were struggling to raise the money to do so. It was an eye-opening experience. I have taken for granted the vibrant ecosystem in Bengaluru, NCR and Hyderabad, I was reminded that the rest of the country is different.

While more difficult outside of major tech hubs, it is always possible to raise funding and a recent law change in India and US on the threshold for Angel investing, will soon help even more. Here are some concrete tips for first-time founders.

Do the Thing You Say You Are Going to Do

Investors are turned off by excuses. Your most important task make potential investors feel that you are going to get things done no matter what. Investors back those that prove they can do a lot with a little; those that are a force of nature. The best way to appear formidable is to actually be formidable. Get it done.

Start Small — Trivially Small — and Then Build Up

Want to open a restaurant, but cannot afford it? Start with a pop-up. Cannot afford the pop-up? Make a deal to work in someone else's commercial kitchen, specialize in a few meals and personally deliver it to local offices. When you are first starting, your goal is not to immediately build a huge business—it is to prove that you can add a small ounce of value to people. Eventually, investors will help you get to the next level.

Make Few People Love You. Then 10. Then 100

Do whatever it takes to make three customers love what you are doing and then build up from there. Your goal is to build a community of supporters, step by step. Your eventual investors will likely be sourced from this pool of supporters, their friends or the people they talk too. Word gets out.

Ask for Advice, Not Money

Wealthy people are asked for things a lot. It can get annoying. Think how you would feel if someone you barely knew launched into a pitch about how you should invest, treating you like a bag of money instead of a human. However, most decent humans (i.e., the sort you would like as investors) enjoy helping promising founders that prove they can get things done. Your goal is to build a relationship and to seek out mentors who you respect and who respect you. They will likely invest eventually.

Be Authentic

Avoid being superficial or overly "salesy." One way to build a relationship with potential investors is to be upfront about your challenges and struggles and involve them in your battle to surround them. Convincing someone to invest in you is about building trust — trust in your ability to think through difficult situations and faith that you will do the moral thing.

Consider an Equity Crowdfunding Campaign When the Time Is Right

In 2017, the law changed in USA, meaning businesses can now raise up to $1 million from their friends and neighbours. Similar changes have been implemented in India as well. Unlike Kickstarter, equity crowdfunding allows people invest in stock, loans or a revenue share. If you have followed the first five steps, you will likely convince at least one wealthy investor to invest a significant amount and set the terms. You might also have a following of a few hundred supporters that would gladly invest. Once you are at this point, an equity crowdfunding campaign can help. Set the minimum target at the smallest level to get you to that next step, even if it is just $20,000 and then set more grandiose goals if you raise $50,000, $100,000, $250,000, $500,000 or $1 million.

Leverage the 'Social Proof' from Crowdfunding

One challenge of fundraising: no one likes being the first investor. It can be extremely difficult — and take months — to convince just one person to invest $10,000. Thankfully, there is a flip side: after each new investor, it typically gets easier to find the next one. Investors assume — rightly or wrongly — that there is safety in numbers. If you start an equity crowdfunding campaign, your goal is to accelerate the momentum as fast as possible by leveraging this social proof.

If you have been struggling for capital and do not know where to start, these tips will get you on the right path. If there is one overall piece of wisdom, it is to start small and take things step by step. If you have a goal to climb Mount Everest, the scale of what you are attempting to accomplish can be intimidating. Just take it one rock at a time. It will seem easier.

What Is the Ideal Time to Approach an Investor

You have to be an opportunist. Firstly, there is no right or wrong time to approach an Angel Investor as long as you are successful in attracting the angel investment. That has to be the attitude of an entrepreneur that is serious about attracting external investment. But understand, there will be specific times in your business cycle that will have the maximum chances of raising angel investment and recognising this as an entrepreneur will place you at the top of the crop of potential investments that are available to Angel Investors.

So, at what stage in a business venture will you have the maximum chances of attracting business angel investment and when is the ideal time to start approaching investors?

The best time to approach an angel investor for the purposes of raising external funding is when you can clearly demonstrate that an angel investment into you will help grow your organisation or business. Sounds easy enough, but, angel investing due to its informality in nature can usually take up to 6–12 months from some investors and it is crucial that an entrepreneur meet private capital and private investors approximately 12 months before their business actually needs the angel investment to get it at the next level.

Clarifying on this point further, let us assume that you are investor-ready now and can demonstrate that a much needed investment will help grow your business. You have demonstrated how the money you raise will be invested and have also clearly demonstrated the return on investment that an investor can expect to receive. You have a good gut feeling so it may be fair to assume that you will attract the money after just a couple of meetings with a few Angel Investors. Sadly, this will most likely not happen as receiving money from an Angel investor is generally very informal and is not like buying property where a buyer negotiates, exchanges with solicitors and then completes within 60 days.

Hence, the most successful entrepreneurs that have attracted angel investment will have started approaching investors approximately 6–12 months before they actually needed the money to hit their company account.

Having conversations with angel Investors earlier than when you actually need the investment will also offer you necessary pointers as to what an investor will want to see in your business before choosing to invest in you, which will then give you the crucial time needed to adapt the business to the investor's requirements.

The best Angel Investors and mentors will pop in and out of your business career, offer you help and guidance, pointers in the right direction, be a voice on the end of a phone and gauge how well you are doing and the progress you are making - all in the hope of one day investing in you.

The conversations with an angel investor will usually start off with you presenting a business plan but the business may not be entirely investor-ready and an angel investor may then suggest certain measures to be implemented along with certain changes before he/she moves forward with you. Ironically, even if the investor then chooses not to invest in your business - the chances are that the changes you would have implemented would have made your business stronger, healthier, increased turnover and made you more investable.

The real knowledge, experience, guidance and investment into your business is through the conversations that you will have with business angel investors at the early stages of your business development.

If during these initial meetings you shine or demonstrate a shadow of potential, these private investors will stick with you until the day comes when you need to expand or purchase the premises or hire those extra people and because you had secured that crucial investor contact and had the foresight to establish the relationship with the Angel investor much earlier on - the money would be available to you and only a phone call away.

From this point of view, if you are serious about growing your business, it really is good practice for entrepreneurs to write a full business plan at the beginning of the business life cycle even if you are a small sole trader and not really seeking investment. Most likely you will not get time to write the business plan after you start-up and having a business plan ready will clearly demonstrate that you have been through that process of fund raising. So, the key is that the more conversations you have with private capital earlier on, the more private investors will be in the position to assist you when you need them and these conversations with private investors will clearly indicate at what stage your business will be able to approach them in the future.

As an example to this, some entrepreneurs' trade as sole traders under their personal name yet seek to raise investment when they have not even formed a LLP or a LTD company. So, an investor may have a meeting with an entrepreneur and conclude that (example) X asset must be assigned to Y company, before opening "Z ltd company."

This is not a rejection for investment but an invite to discuss the funding requirement further when your house is in order.

Ironically, I have seen this tactic backfire on Angel Investors many times. After the initial meeting, an angel investor will set out a things to-do list for an entrepreneur to implement and the entrepreneur with renewed enthusiasm will do the research and implement the recommended changes only to find that the investment of the business angel was no longer needed as the company is now far more valuable than it ever was - and all it took was a one-hour meeting and a free lunch.

So, it is important to know timing wise when to start approaching and talking to Angel investors. Forming a company structure that can accommodate an investment in a business's early days is also a wise practice.

It is difficult for any startup to raise capital, but it is a necessary step in the process of turning a concept into a profitable business. The current market is schizophrenic, with venture capitalists and private equity investors eager to pour money into the "next big thing," while simultaneously showing extreme caution and pushing for better terms. After several years of heavy activity and high valuations, VC funding has declined in other parts of the world and may slow down in the United States and India. Plus, the dreaded "down round" has become more common for companies that raised capital when the market was at its frothiest.

Finding investors is not easy, but it is critically important. Whether you are working with a major VC or trying to find an angel, your entrepreneurial success will be determined by your ability to raise money from the right investors.

Fitting a Square Peg into a Round Hole

The best time to raise capital is when you do not need it, especially, if you can do it during a down market. That gives you the opportunity to grow even faster and more efficiently, as there is less competition for both people and assets. This is where being an opportunist is extremely important. Some businesses need capital when the markets are not open or are not necessarily looking for what that business is doing.

In this scenario, you have to fit a square peg into a round hole. But it is these types of challenges that will ultimately define your success. At the end of the day, the most successful entrepreneurs and businesses have the tenacity and aptitude for risk. The ability to figure out the correct "square peg" for a specific "round hole" is an important attribute for all entrepreneurs. The aptitude to do this helps determine when the time is right to raise capital.

Understanding the Current Climate

Venture capital has changed significantly since my first startup in the mid 2000s. In today's current investor climate, it seems like seed money goes where Series A funding used to wind up and Series B rounds now take up what Series C used to. It is a completely different game today and it is only going to keep changing. The pattern will continue, so it is extremely important to cast a wide net and understand the current venture market's temperature before looking for capital.

If you are seeking your first external investor, the best time is often after you have established that you have a minimum viable product to show investors the value of your concept. Every round of fundraising should get your company from onset of accomplishments to the next and this pattern should continue until you are no longer dependent on investment capital.

Building on Past Success

It is fundamental for entrepreneurs to meet private capital and private investors approximately 12 months before their business actually needs the investment to get it at the next level.

The key is to show proof of concept if you are a startup and initial traction and/or profit potential if you are already off the ground. Remember, investors fund the growth of your company, not what you have already accomplished. But your past accomplishments will be the key when investors decide if you are worth the risk. There is no right or wrong time to approach an investor as long as you are successful in attracting the investment.

Firstly, there is no right or wrong time to approach an Angel Investor as long as you are successful in attracting the angel investment. That has to be the attitude of an entrepreneur that is serious about attracting external investment. But understand, there will be specific times in your business cycle that will have the maximum chances of raising angel investment and recognising this as an entrepreneur will place you at the top of the crop of potential investments that are available to Angel Investors.

Stages of Investment Capital requirements

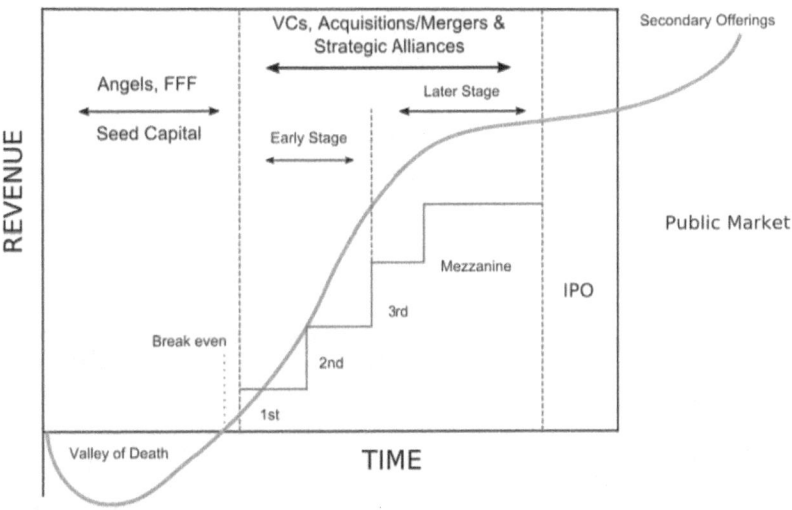

So, at what stage in a business venture will you have the maximum chances of attracting business angel investment and when is the ideal time to start approaching investors?

I cannot tell you how many entrepreneurs first approach investors, either at the wrong time, in the wrong way or in the wrong format. Let's tackle these easy-to-fix pitfalls below.

1. Wrong Time: Make Sure Proof-Of-Concept Is behind You

It is important you have all the required elements in place before approaching investors. This includes completing all the necessary research supporting your business plan . And, if possible, it is preferred to have some type of "proof-of-concept" behind you. This could include a working prototype, closed customer contracts, brand name pipeline, growing traffic to the site, proven team in place, profitably tested customer acquisition metrics, etc. Anything that gets the investor comfortable that the heavy-lifting testing phase of your growth is behind you, there is some initial traction for the product and a solid team is ready to begin execution of the plan. If you do not have these pieces of the puzzle firmly in place, wait before approaching any professional investors.

2. Wrong Way: Look for a Trusted Reference to Make Intro

The proper way to approach an investor is typically through a referral. The investor is much more likely to hear your pitch (among the 1,000 they listen to each year), if it is being sent to them via somebody they already know and trust, that can vouch for you. So, use LinkedIn looking for mutual connections that can open that door for you, if possible. Or, ask your lawyer or accountant for intros. If there are no mutual connections, you have no choice but to cold call the investor, your lowest odds of probability to getting a deal done. But, if that is your only option, it is important you come across as professional, smart, enthusiastic and well-polished in both your information and your delivery.

3. Wrong Format: You Need a Short and Sweet Pitch That Resonates

As for the desired format, I typically find that investors are very busy and are more receptive to getting an introduction via email (which you can access via their website or calling their office). Email gives them a chance to research you and your idea, before committing to a time-consuming phone call or an in person meeting. So, make sure you keep a clean social networking trail on Facebook and Twitter, as they will most certainly be Googling you. And, make sure your LinkedIn profile is complete and compelling with recommendations and endorsements, as it is your online resume.

The contents of that email are the most critical. Remember the short attention span of investors: if they cannot understand your business in 30 seconds of reading, they are moving on to the next one. So, you need a very short and sweetly written covering letter that summarizes your story in a few sentences (not paragraphs!). Something that gets them jazzed up about a large industry problem and your compelling solution.

For example, an email, could have read: "iExplore is the #1 ranked website in the rapidly growing $10BN adventure travel industry with over 1MM visitors per month and a strategic partnership with National Geographic. Our revenues are growing 50% per year and we are raising venture capital which should yield you a 10x return. See attached for more details in our executive summary. Let me know a good time for an introductory call or meeting to discuss further. How do you look on Friday morning?" That is all you really need in a first outreach, including a clickable link to your website so they can easily learn about your product in more detail (so make sure you have a snazzy website, to back up your snazzy pitch).

Notice what that paragraph did, it: (i) described the business and its leading market position; (ii) detailed industry size and growth; (iii) highlighted a brand name strategic partner; (iv) showed the business was driving revenues and how quickly they were scaling; (v) and wet their beak with the opportunity to make a big 10x return, a minimum to get their attention. That was a lot to accomplish in two sentences. The paragraph also closes (as it always should) with a clear call to action, which will be very easy for the investor to hit reply and say "Friday looks fine at 9am."

Now that the cover letter is solid, prepare a 1–2 page executive summary or 10 page power point presentation (with a high level snapshot of the key elements of your business plan, include management bios and five year forecast), that you can attach to the email. That is it. Do not send them any more than this, as they will not read it at this time. They will certainly ask for much more information during the due diligence process, which you will already have prepared with your full business plan sitting in reserve. And, graphics and charts and videos, go a lot further than text to getting your message across as quickly and effectively as you can.

You only have one chance to make a good first impression with a prospective investor. Do not blow it!

Alternate Investment Strategies

Life is full of choices and there are no fixed formulae. For everything that is the norm, there are always outliers to the data set on both extremes. Exceptions abound. So, do options. There are many alternate ways to fund a startup, especially in the early stages. Depending on the amount sought and the reality of your situation, here are some alternate strategies that you could try individually or in combination. To future investors it is a sign of your innovativeness, ability to hustle and a mind open to alternatives.

Ideas do not get funded and neither do business plans. Investors are looking for startups with a proven product/market fit and demonstrated evidence of the founder's ability to run and grow the business.

The bigger challenge, however, is to get that initial funding to develop your product or service model.

But did you know that the source of your seed capital can be sitting right in the corner of your house? The seed capital can be from various places, such as from family & friends or by exhausting your credit card limits.

So, here are some clever funding ideas which can get you started with your business idea.

Keep an Eye on Campaigns by Big Brands

Huggies ran a campaign called Mom Inspired in 2012. They called for applications from all the 'Mompreneurs' who are residing in the United States and are 21 years and older – with an original, innovative and viable new product idea to help make life easier for parents. The prize was $15,000 and advice to help make their business dreams a reality.

Pepsi Co. ran a program called PepsiCo10 program wherein they invited startups to apply with their business ideas. Pepsi evaluated proposals based on an applicant's ability to partner with PepsiCo brands and commercial viability. The winners were then offered an all-expenses paid trip to New York City for an opportunity to meet PepsiCo's marketing leadership team and network with US-based digital influencers.

Latest one in this list is #UberPitch, an initiative by Uber wherein startups get an opportunity to pitch in their innovative business ideas to VC's while having a Uber ride with them. Uber partnered with Google Ventures for this initiative. Now there are at least a dozen such initiatives in India alone.

Win Those Startup Competitions

Jennifer Reich of The Mommy MD Guides created a short video and won a great contest by Office Depot called Survival of the Smartest, for small businesses, which awarded her a very generous amount for her office supplies. With competitions by corporates, industry bodies like CII, NASSCOM and others abounding, there are numerous opportunities to compete, win some capital and meet future investors. It also is a good validation for your idea and business model. Beware of the costs of the competitions in terms of participation fees, travel etc. and select the ones to go to carefully.

Reach out for University Funds

Most of the startups are ideated in college life. Look for funding from that day itself. The University of Waterloo offers a Velocity Fund, which is a non-equity grant program for startups that offers more than $400,000 each year to local startups. Stanford University also invests directly in students' companies. Stanford also gives a $3.6 million grant to StartX, a non-profit startup accelerator for Stanford-affiliated entrepreneurs.

Some universities may partner with the private sector and investment community to offer seed incubator or accelerator programs also such as University of British Columbia's entrepreneurship@UBC Accelerator Program. In India the IIT's and IIM's started the trend and now every university worth its name has a program for startups. Many states have mandated that universities need to have an entrepreneurship cell.

Negotiate an Advance from a Customer

Selling your products before they launch is an often-overlooked and highly effective way to raise the money needed for financing your business. Find a major customer or a potential business, which sees such value in your idea that they are willing to give you an advance on royalty payments to complete your development. Variations on this theme include early licensing or white-labelling agreements. Akansha, a finalist at the India Fund Fest signed a leading IT company as its first customer at a very early stage and that helped it financially as well as in honing its product and having a ready referral.

Get the Office Equipment Financed

This is called vendor financing. Getting finance for tangible assets is a lot easier than a cash advance on future sales or a personal loan. If you need tangible products for inventory, many manufacturers and distributors can be convinced to defer your payment until the goods are sold by you. This really means an extension of the normal 30-day payment terms to a period of months or longer, depending on your credit worthiness and extra fees. This frees up valuable capital that can be used for payroll and other marketing expenses.

Many equipment finance firms offer 100% financing on everything a startup needs, from servers to computers to filing furniture and fixtures. Many tech and tech enabled startups get conditional funds for hosting and equipment from IT majors like Amazon, Google, Intel and Microsoft among others.

Apply the Pay to Work Policy

If you have a great business idea, you can ask people to make a donation in return for a position in your startup. Joanne Lang of About One, evaluated team members according to their willingness to invest – given their circumstances. Founding members who invest and show commitment to the venture were pushed forward in management hierarchy.

Barter Your Services for Office Help

Barter your skills or something you have for something you need. For example, if you feel your product/service is some value to the landlord, you can negotiate a free office space in exchange for a free service.

Carolyn Goodwin of Cake Communications, suggests, "Try finding a partner outside of your industry and not a direct competitor. Offer something of benefit to them such as, co-marketing opportunities, blog writeups, customer referrals in exchange for funding, support or access to resources that you need for your business."

Crowdfunding

Ask people/potential customers to fund your business. In exchange, signup customers at a discount or exclusive support or offers for early birds.

Platforms such as Kickstarter, Indiegogo or Go Get Funding are great resources where you can create your crowdfunding campaign. In 2014, Kickstarter had 22,252 projects raising a total of $529 million and Indiegogo enjoyed a 1,000% increase in funds raised over the past two years.

Ask for Some Local Help

Check with your state, county and municipal economic development offices for funding your startup. The SBA offers Small Business Development Centres, located around the country, that can help connect entrepreneurs with investors. These institutions have an interest in helping businesses succeed to boost local and regional economies. Depending on your location and the type of business you start, these agencies might offer financial resources, including loans and grants.

Peer-to-peer Lending

This is a process whereby a group of people comes together to lend money to each other. It has been around many years, in examples like small business groups or ethnic groups supporting similar efforts. In the startup context, look for a successful entrepreneur peer willing to fund similar new ideas.

Test Your Business Idea on Social Media

Bill Gandy's has been sharing historic photos of Allegheny City, a community on the north side of Pittsburgh on his Facebook page. After the appreciation of his Facebook group he thought of opening a gallery to showcase these photos. Thus, he launched the non-profit Allengeny City Historic Gallery. Bill raised more than $12,000 in funds for the gallery in less than a month.

Create Interesting Content

This story was reported in Reason Digital. During summertime, a 9-year-old Caine set up his arcade shop with a few cardboard boxes he set about building one in his dad's auto-repair shop.

Unfortunately, the shop did not get many customers, until a customer called Nirvan Mullick, stopped by and loved Caine's arcade. He decided to make a film about it and the film became a social media success. After that, people from across the globe visited Caine's arcade and a fund was set up to put him through college. The fund quickly smashed its target of $25,000 and got over $200,000.

Another one, Priska Diaz wanted to fund her invention, a baby bottle called Bare that offers air-free milk, so she created a website showing the concept with pictures of bottle prototypes. The concept earned her an extensive social-media following as potential customers awaited the product's development.

She set up a system for pre-ordering and hosted a presale directly from a website, raising more than $50,000 for her company Bittylab.

Start as a Side-Project

Entrepreneur Alex Genadinik used his revenue from tours he organized on ComeHike.com to launch Problemio.com, which builds mobile apps for planning and starting a business.

Side projects are extremely easy to start because you do not have to depend on them to make a living. You are probably already earning a salary through your day job. So, you do not have to worry about an income source even if you were to fail.

Get Funding as Your Birthday Gift, Literally

In 2008, as Cynthia Kersey, a divorcee who neared 50, wanted to pursue her dream idea of securing a child's right to education. She threw a party for her 50th-birthday and invited everyone she knew. She asked each guest to bring, in lieu of gifts, $100 and announced that she would use the gifts as seed money to open her Los Angeles non-profit, The Unstoppable Foundation.

Cut Down on luxuries

Over 90% of startups are self-funded (bootstrapping). It may take a bit longer to save some money before you start and grow organically. There is no better way to say it, 'Take a sharp cut on your luxuries.' Most business owners who bootstrap their startups, cut down on their expenses to save and invest that amount in the business.

Sell That Additional Stuff

Most people have unused stuff just sitting around the house. This can be a great way to get started with your seed fund. Listing any unused items on Craiglist/OLX or having a garage sale can raise the capital needed to get started.

Brandi Hamrick of You Grow, Girl, says, "When I first started my business and needed cash, I would sell stuff on Ebay. My closet would be clean and I would have more cash to put into my business. Sell last year's handbags and clothes on Ebay and use Craigslist for bulky items such as furniture and appliances. You can even host a neighborhood yard sale."

Have a Big House? Let It Out!

Fay Johnson, founder and editor of deliberate LIFE magazine rented out her apartment to get started on her seed funding. Fay listed her San Francisco apartment on Airbnb and started renting it out for anywhere between five nights and a month at a time. She used the money raised to fund the costs of the first few issues of her magazine.

Second Mortgage

Have a house on loan? Second mortgage can be an option to raise funds. They are also referred to as home equity lines of credit. These loans tap into the locked up equity you may have in your home. To calculate how much you may be able to borrow for a second mortgage take the value of your home and deduct the value of any outstanding mortgage.

Self Employment Assistance

This kind of financing is often overlooked. SEAP (Self Employment Assistance Program) is part of unemployment assistance and can be used by those who are recently unemployed and interested in starting their own business. The Labor Department's Self-Employment Assistance Program is a joint Federal/State effort that helps unemployed go back to work with their own business. You get the support of experienced mentors and an income security of unemployment insurance (UI) benefits. More details here. Similar schemes exist in India like the Mudra scheme, that provide collateral free loans.

Online Lending

U.S. Treasury Secretary Larry Summers said at the '2015 Lend It conference' that he expects online lenders to eventually reach more than 70% of small businesses.

Online lending services such as Lending Kart, OnDeck and Kabbage have become a popular alternative to traditional business loans. Online lenders have the advantage of speed. An application takes only up to an hour to complete and a decision and the accompanying fund scan be issued within days.

Government Funding

There are government funds allocated to support new technologies and important causes, such as education, medicine and social needs. A good place to start looking is Grants.gov, which is a searchable directory of more than 1,000 federal grant programs. Matching grants by government agencies are a popular way, like in Berlin.

Retirement Funds

Investment Retirement Account funds and 401(k)s are an accessible alternative funding source for startups. You cannot use your own self-directed funds for your startup, but many others are willing and able to loan you money from theirs, for the right terms, if they believe in you and your cause.

Debra Cohen of Home Remedies of NY, Inc. took a $5000 loan from her husband's retirement savings plan. She got 5 years to pay it back at a minimal interest rate. This is one option that you should exercise extreme caution in using.

Spread Some Love

Small Business Local Buzz is a website, hosted by Intuit, that gives companies the chance to earn grants from $5,000 up to $25,000. They award 15 small business with $5000 worth of marketing buzz to get the word out. You can participate by entering and sharing your submission with friends and fans, if you encourage them to vote for your entry. It can help you win big buzz! There are community specific grants like those available to the Tibetan community in India or other specific groups in each state.

The Soft Side of Approaching Investors

One of the most popular slides of management workshops is one that shows an iceberg. The point being that what is visible on the surface is only 10% of the whole and that 90% of reality is hidden from an observer. The same holds true for entrepreneurs trying to read into investor behaviour. They are always confounded, on one hand by the encouragement, smiles, platitudes and the reality of not getting a cheque. It is like going on dates where the other person says all the right things and promises to call back, but never does. Worse, no one tells you, why!

A lot of this is to do with the gap between the entrepreneurs' optimism on the business outlook versus the investors realism of expected returns and risks involved. With all the steps outlined earlier you are well placed to improve your odds, but you could do yourself a big disservice if you disregard the softer aspects of approaching investors. How often have you met someone or interviewed a candidate and formed an initial opinion in the first few seconds? Investors do the same. So, it is essential to brush up on your soft skills.

One of the blandest bits of advice that I always hear for pitching to angel investors is to "stand out."

I think I have rolled my eyes at that tip so many times that I am beginning to worry about my vision. Of course, you want to make a memorable impression, but at the end of the day, you want to be remembered for your amazing idea, not for a flashy gimmick.

I have seen hundreds of pitches as an investor, a jury member to various startup contests and more recently at the India Fund Fest. During my time there, I discovered that the best pitches have five elements in common.

1. They Connect with the Heart

Pitching is about understanding what the investors are most interested in and developing a conversation that connects on an emotional level. Tell a story that is relatable, inspirational and addresses the marketplace problem you are solving. Let them see every ounce of the passion that drives you.

Your passion will differentiate you in their minds because it is an admirable character trait that shows promise. It makes a statement that you are going to make your dreams happen with or without their help and that will make them want to be a part of your success story.

2. They Connect with the Head

Telling an inspiring story will not get you far if your idea is still floating in the clouds. It needs to be firmly planted in the ground where it can grow. You have to prove very quickly that you know your stuff or the investors will stop listening.

I once saw a pitch for a waterproof case for iPods. The entrepreneurs utilized fun, attention-grabbing tactics, but what I remember most was their unique value proposition and business model, which involved a good sales distribution strategy that allowed faster time to market. They knew exactly how they wanted to build a company around a product they loved.

Investors want to know why your product solves a problem or is a "must have." Be ready to answer all sorts of questions:

3. They Do not Mimic a Spreadsheet

One of the biggest mistakes I saw in pitches was incorporating too much data and statistics. You want to include the market size and analysis, but do not spend too much time on it. It is more important that you convey a value-oriented, compelling and memorable message, so be precise and simple. Remember the 10 slide rule.

4. They Have a Great Team Dynamics

Investors are looking at you and your management team. They know a bad partnership can ruin a business. Your partners and the team dynamics should help inspire confidence, not raise questions. If investors sense any friction, they will fear your failure. If you have an experienced, seamless team, it is easier to win over investors.

I once saw a pitch from a company that had developed a diagnostic device to detect diseases in women's reproductive organs. This company had an extensive advisory board supporting the product and the CEO had solid experience in taking the company to the next level. The people behind the product made me want to invest.

5. They Leave Investors Wanting More

Angel investors invested more than $28 billion in 2016. To get a slice of that pie, you do not just need a strong conclusion – you need an exit strategy that informs investors how they will get their money back. They could love your idea, but if they do not think they will make money off of it, they will share their wealth elsewhere.

Pitching your idea to investors is daunting. But when you have a great idea, a smart business plan and amazing people backing you up, you can wow investors and get the financial backing you need.

Here are some soft skills and simple tactics I picked up along the way to help your pitch stand out in a crowd:

- ◆ A little humility goes a long way. When pitching to an investor, never underestimate the amount of ego in the room. Applying due diligence and scrutiny is the primary job of the investor. Without it, they would not be successful investors in the first place. Cramming an idea down their throats or intimating that they "just do not get it" when you are challenged or questioned on an aspect of your business plan can be enough to spiral your pitch down the drain. Own the obvious challenges or risks your business faces and let the strengths of your operation generate an organic sense of opportunism in the minds of your potential investors.

- ◆ Make it personal. If you are pitching a B2C product or service, utilize a personal anecdote, story or reference to humanize the experience. If your product solves a problem that most people can relate to, make sure you paint a picture for your potential investors. Ideally, this element of brand storytelling will somehow serve as an underlying catalyst for the creation of your service or product. But be careful to avoid cheesy references or embellishing details too much. If you can get at least one of your potential investors to picture themselves in your narrative, he or she will instantly become more receptive. We advised one investor to utilize this tactic when pitching his company at

Disruptrs by referencing his own experiences reading bedtime stories to his child. Remember, the people sitting before you are more than just a prospective cheque book.

- Use simple data visualization in your deck. Crowding your slides with a barrage of graphs and charts can be overwhelming and difficult to digest. Be selective with your data and keep your pie charts and line graphs readable. Your data should be sequential or chronological when addressing growth and you should utilize creative formatting to call out the numbers you want the investors to be looking at, if nothing else on the slide. Always be prepared to answer questions about ancillary data, particularly financials, after your pitch during the Q&A portion.

- Get your most compelling points across early. The less time you have to pitch your business, the more precious each minute becomes. Ensure that your panel of judges and investors learn the two or three most important things they will need to know at the front of your presentation. Provide them with a proper roadmap at the beginning of your pitch and then place signposts during your presentation for these most compelling aspects of your deck. This will ensure your big wins do not go unnoticed by the judges.

- Conduct a demonstration. If you have a physical product available, including a brief demonstration with a working prototype can be extremely useful, if done right. Sometimes, there is no better substitute than physically getting your working product in the hands of the investors. Also, consider demonstrating your customer experience by producing a video that illuminates your product or service. I was pleased to see both Brightsandz and Blue Water Alkaline use customer experience videos and live product demonstrations to breathe life into their presentations at the India Fund Fest.

- Do your research. Either before or during the event, do your best to read the panel. Align your pitch with the strengths and weaknesses of specific investors if possible. If you know that one of the investors is more likely to see the opportunity in your service or product based on his or her experience, maintain strong eye contact and make sure to feed them the strongest points of your pitch that will resonate. During India Fund Fest fireside chat with investor Shrish Garg, he made it very clear that he is unlikely to invest in someone who clearly has a

Plan B behind their venture. Leveraging key information like this will help to shed light on your dedication and commitment, which can be a game changer during your pitch.

- You will be surprised at how many entrepreneurs get some basics wrong. These could be simple things like dressing right. I advise that you dress conservatively as most investors are likely to be a generation older and anyway it does no harm to be a little formal. Get to the meeting on time along with your team. Take the right team, decide who is handling the questions and who is pitching. Leave out all slang and colloquialisms.

If you are looking for inspiration or more ways to do your homework, look for events that bring together entrepreneurs, experts and venture capitalists in various monthly events. They provide a terrific opportunity to research the tactics and strategy needed to hone your skills and perfect your pitch.

How to Raise Money From Family & Friends

What are the chances of raising $ 100K from a stranger on an unproven business versus raising $ 5,000 each from twenty family and friends? If you cannot find twenty family and friends to invest $ 5,000 each or say ten to invest $ 10,000 each then there is a problem. Among whole host of other realities two things stand out, either your idea is not good enough or people do not trust you. In both cases you should not be in business and are better off trying to make a living or a mark, in some other way.

Unless you are buying a lot of raw material upfront or paying for licences or making some other capital investment upfront; more than likely you need money to fund your cashflow in the following manner

- Upfront money to start the company and get going with initial statutory fees, professional fees and deposits for offices, utilities, etc.
- Money to finance a build phase for a few months
- Running costs till the product is ready and demonstrable
- Initial marketing costs for a pilot or proving in a scaling unit

Thereafter, either clients pay and the company is able to pay its bills or/and an angel/early stage investor steps in. This process takes anywhere between six to ten months although in your mind it has taken place in a few days. Here is what I suggest to fund your company till cash breakeven in a limited scaling unit, before asking for money to scale:

- Go through all the steps of preparation as outlined earlier
- With the bottoms up financial projection up to breakeven, create a month on month cash flow
- Arrive at a total ask till breakeven (with a suitable buffer) and a monthly ask
- Assuming a total ask of $100K out of which you have self funded the first $ 10K to setup the company and kickoff

- For the balance 90K, if you were to divide this over ten friends and family, it would mean an investment of $9K each
- Further dividing this over your cashflow period (say six months), you could ask them to invest $1,500 per month (in advance every month). Or any other installment that your cash flow requires

How much simpler is asking someone to invest $750 - $1,500 per month versus $90K at one go? Especially in an unproven business model. Be sure to consult an accountant as there are laws governing raising money this way and time limits within which shares have to be allotted.

Some other points to note:

- Be fair and allocate 30% of the equity for this at least. You would have given more or as much to an early stage investor with greater loss of control and time spent in the chase
- Have a written agreement that outlines the payment schedule and forfeiture of shares and money paid, if future installments are not paid for any reasons
- You may want a clause that, in the event of a future round of investment within a certain period, either the full quantity of shares is compulsorily transferred back, if a certain investment return is achieved or a partial sell out is guaranteed or a dilution (proportionate or disproportionate) is agreed upon. This is to ensure you have enough equity for future rounds. Think about it, if in 18–24 months you meet your projections and your company is actually valued at $300K for the same 30% equity, you may be better off paying the original investors double ($180K), transferring the same equity to the next investor and keeping the balance ($120K) in the company for the next stage of growth. There are many ifs and buts in this, lots of people have to agree and laws have to be followed. But believe me this is the best way at early stage for a first time entrepreneur and works more often than not.
- One variable is to follow all the steps above but not issue equity, take it in the form of convertible debt

Here is an example with real life dilemmas:

When Mumbai-based entrepreneur Praveen quit his steady job in finance to work on a startup idea, he told his two closest friends during a road trip to Pune City. A few months later, they each wrote Praveen a $15,000 cheque.

Many tech entrepreneurs take investment from friends and family to test the viability of an idea. They raise just enough to fund a developer's salary, office space, monthly rent and a steady supply of Maggi noodle and soup.

It is a time-honoured startup strategy, but it is a risky one. Praveen could make his friends rich, if his startup takes off. But if it craters, that lost $30,000 could haunt their friendship.

For Praveen, the investment buys him enough time to test the market opportunity for his startup, "PRStory." If all goes according to plan, it will earn him a place at a competitive tech accelerator program like TechStars, which he can parlay into additional investment.

"I am solely investing in this idea because of Ramesh," said Prakash, an investment banking managing director. "Anyone I did not know with the same idea, I would not have even looked at the slide deck," he admitted.

Hedge fund manager Ravi Damani knows what he is getting himself into: he has made six "alternative investments" over the years. Five of them were in friends' startup companies. "If PRStory goes bad, I'd consider it to be a bad investment decision on my part," said Damani. "I would not blame Ramesh."

With friends like these, it is difficult to see a downside in taking their money. Typically, it is a darn sight easier than landing a seasoned angel investor. An added benefit for Praveen was using his friends' networks from the finance world. Damani, who has known Praveen since they were 10 years old, brought in a few investment banker friends to invest in PRStorys seed round.

Then there is always the chance that the whole group will get rich and sail off to the Mediterranean in a fleet of matching yachts.

Praveen's case aside, I advise caution in taking money from friends.

"I would not take family and friends money if I had any other choice," said AngelList founder Naval Ravikant in a recent interview. Unlike a professional angel investor like Nandan Nilenkani or Rajan Anandan, your wealthy Uncle cannot be called on for honest, critical feedback about your startup's business model.

Entrepreneurs should ask themselves, "Do you really want to lose your business, friends and family at the same time?" according to Ravikant. Blow your best friend's $25,000 investment on some half-baked idea for a dating app and you may destroy that relationship for good.

Here are some hard and fast rules to consider before taking "friends and family" money:

- Consider those first round problems: The explosion of seed-stage startups has given way to a hotly competitive environment in Silicon Valley and India. Meanwhile, the supply of series A funding has remained steady. The media call it a "Series A Crunch." In the struggle to rise above the noise and make it to the next round, it helps to have a highly respected ally. A professional angel investor can make the requisite connections to most prestigious venture firms.

- Exhaust all other options: Generally speaking, it is better for an entrepreneur to land one professional angel investor than to raise money from a dozen rich uncles. A seasoned angel is typically well connected, cognizant of the risks and can draw on years of experience to guide an inexperienced founder.

- Be upfront about the risks: Praveen and his friends realize that most startups fail. "This needs to be money that if you do not see again, you cannot be mad at me," Praveen explained and described the process as a "big exercise in expectation management." But many entrepreneurs cannot help but sell a grand vision. A friend under the impression that an idea is the next big thing might be tempted to invest money they cannot afford to lose. Most startups fail: Do you want to have to close up shop and inform your best friend that you have blown their kids' college tuition?

- Favour well-connected friends and family: If that wealthy uncle hobnobs with lawyers and attorneys at the local country club, ask for an introduction. Likewise, if a friend has invested in early-stage startups before, that is typically a good sign.

- Keep inexperienced investors at a distance: If a friend wants to be informed about every minute detail — and worse still, if they expect to interject an opinion about the product — you are in trouble. Unless they lack deep domain expertise, offer family and friends a brief update every few months. "Otherwise you can get socially pressured into doing something you do not want to do," warned Ravikant.

- It is a gift, not an investment: Harvard Business School associate professor Noam Wasserman wrote a chapter on this tricky issue in his book, The Founder's Dilemmas: Anticipating and Avoiding the Pitfalls That Can Sink a Startup. He references a serial entrepreneur who views money from family and friends as a gift, meaning that there is no expectation of being paid back.

- As a rule do not take money from retired folk, people's pension funds and generally do not take more than 40% of anyone's annual take home pay.

Why Investors Need a Minimum of 10X Scale

The most intriguing question for early-stage entrepreneurs is most often, "What does a VC look for?" Two of the most common responses from VCs are that they are looking for something that has a large market and that they want to partner with great teams. Many entrepreneurs have told me that they have spent countless number of hours trying to understand why these (particularly #1) matter so much. After all, what should matter is profitability, right?

I too wondered about these questions for years and I was fortunate enough to have interacted with few dozen venture capitalists. In the world of business, when you need to understand how someone thinks, it is a good idea to understand that person's business structure. So, in my interactions with VCs, I tried to understand the dynamics of a venture capital (VC) fund and discovered quite a few actionable insights. Based on that, I would like to share a framework on what a VC thinks, considers when exploring a potential investment (particularly in India), especially in the context of the two common responses from VCs, as described above.

At its core, every VC firm also has investors of its own, typically known as LPs (limited partners). LPs 'lend' money to a VC firm for a long but specified duration (typically 8–10 years). During this time, the VC firm is expected to invest money in promising startups, which are expected to become valuable businesses. Once the investment matures, the VC firm is expected to sell its stake in those companies and return the money back to the LPS.

Naturally, because a limited partner lends money to a VC firm, it expects a healthy return on its investment. So, a VC firm has fiduciary responsibility for this money and has to put in all the effort required to return the money to LPs with appropriate returns. Imagine the future of a fund that fails to return money to its LPs; such a fund will lose the trust of its LPs and the LP is unlikely to lend the VC firm any more money.

During these 8–10 years, the VC firm is expected to return at least 3x the investment. This is hardly an easy task. Devaluation of the Indian Rupee against the USD further increases the difficulty; at the very least, the ability to return this money becomes a matter of survival for a VC firm.

How the fund works across investments:

For our discussion, let's take a fictional VC firm, say "ABC Capital," which raises $30 across its LPs to invest in startups (typically a couple of dozen startups). Let's assume ABC Capital invests this money of $30 equally across 30 startups (i.e. $1 per startup) and takes 20% ownership of each company in lieu of this investment.

As time goes by, not everything goes well in all investments. Some startups fail to raise follow-on rounds, others fail to find a product-market fit and yet others will see founders fight and separate – on average, most of these 30 investments will fail.

If we go by the typical industry benchmark numbers for a portfolio, 65% of investments will go bust; i.e. 20 investments out of 30 will result in nothing. Another 20% will just barely return the principal; i.e. 6 investments out of 30 will return the money invested. Another 10% of startups will succeed and generate 10x returns for ABC Capital; i.e. 3 startups will return $10 each. The remaining 5% of startups, i.e., one out of a portfolio of 30 companies, may become a multi-bagger and return 50x; i.e. return $50.

So, this is how ABC Capital's hypothetical portfolio will look like:

Now comes the interesting part! When ABC Capital invests in these 30 startups, it has no way of knowing which of those 30 companies will result in 50x returns and which ones will not return any money. Had it known this a priori, the folks at ABC Capital would have set up the 50x startup themselves! Overall, our hypothetical portfolio will return 2.9x the money that was invested. As you can see, this barely reaches the acceptable level of return and hence ABC Capital will not qualify as a great VC firm.

So, when ABC Capital makes an investment, it needs to have complete conviction that each of those 30 investments will result in 10x gain and also hope to be lucky enough that one of those 30 investments will result in gigantic returns. This is the only way to create a healthy return for the overall portfolio.

Now let us put this in perspective from the startup's side. A $1 investment in company for 20% ownership will mean that company is valued $4 before a sale or listing or $5 after. To generate 10x for a $1 investment, the startup needs to become a $50 company. Let us extend this example to more realistic numbers. Let us assume a $5M round of seed funding. This will necessitate the startup to become at least a $250M company. So, every single company being invested in should have genuine potential to become a $250M company.

There is no way for a company to achieve those figures unless it operates in a really large market. If we assume that a successful company will capture 20% of the overall market, then the overall market size has to be at least $1.25B. Now you see why the large market size becomes the most important question when investing in any company. If you do not invest in large market then you are fundamentally setting yourself up for failure as the investment will not grow 10x, irrespective of everything else going great for the startup.

Now let us assume you have done a great job at pitching and ABC Capital is convinced that your startup is operating in a really large market. Now what else would ABC Capital need to get convinced about before giving you the cheque?

Reaching that $250M mark will be a time-consuming process spanning across 5–8 years (please remember that recent hyper-valuation rounds where a company reaches a $250M valuation in 6 months is not the norm). Venture capitalists at ABC Capital are not the guys who can manage a startup's day-to-day operations. That is the entrepreneur's job! And this journey of 5–8 years is going to be full of ups and downs. In such a scenario, ABC Capital would like to be satisfied on three more key questions about the entrepreneur.

(A) Does this team have skills or ability to figure things out? Generally, it is very difficult to hire great talent into a startup early on. Founders have to possess the skills and capability to operate startup until it becomes a real business. They have to be able to attract talent around them. If founders fail to execute then, there are very few people in the world who can rescue the startup.

(B) Is this team going to survive through the bad times? You do not want to be left with a company where founders leave when the going gets tough. If a founder loses motivation and moves on, the whole company will become a liability for the investor. Over time, investors will end up owning a majority of the company and hence, will have more to lose.

(C) Is the entrepreneur intellectually honest? This is an obvious attribute to look for whenever you are giving your money to someone. After funding, the cheque signing authority moves to entrepreneur who can use money in many different ways. ABC Capital will not be happy if the entrepreneur keeps showing hockey-stick growth but actually simply keeps buying business.

This framework provides entrepreneurs a few points to think about too. "Is the market really large?" or "Do I have what it takes to execute?" Because if the genuine answers to these questions are negative, then there is very little chance that entrepreneur will make it big. It is probably quite easy to fool someone in ABC Capital on these questions but over time, reality does catch up and at that time entrepreneur is the first one to lose (he or she also has the most to lose). Little wonder then, that VCs always look for great teams to partner with.

Angel investors and early-stage VCs invest in companies at a stage when the assumptions around the business and the entrepreneur's execution capabilities are yet to be proven.

While investors review shortlisted companies very, very diligently based on their perspective of the opportunity, their assessment of the business case and their perception of the entrepreneur's capabilities, quite a few of the companies that they invest in will fail for a variety of reasons. Some of their portfolio companies may do well, but the investors may not get an exit i.e., they may not get a buyer for the equity they hold in some reasonably successful ones.

Not only will the investors not get any returns on these investments in ventures that do not succeed or where they do not get an exit, they will most likely lose their capital as well. Only a few of the companies that they invest in will be successful to the extent that they had assumed they would (or much more than that in rare cases).

And therefore, to cover these losses and to make money on their portfolio as a whole, they need at least a few multi-baggers in their portfolio i.e., companies that will be sold for 10–20 times the capital they had invested in.

Let us understand this with another example...let us take the case of an investor who puts USD 200,000 in 10 startups at the beginning of 2017 and so overall has made an investment of USD 2mn. If this investor is seeking 20% annual return on his capital, then in 5 year's time, this USD 2mn should have appreciated to around USD 5mn by 2022.

Now, of the 10 companies that he/she has invested in...

It is likely that 3–4 companies will fail and shut down or continue to struggle along.

May be 3–4 companies do reasonably well, but not to the extent that follow-on investors are interested. They may be generating profits that keeps the entrepreneurs reasonably happy with the outcome, yet the investor has not yet got any returns because they have not been able to offload the shares they hold in these companies. In other words, their investment is still stuck with no returns.

Over time investments in 1 or 2 of these reasonably well doing companies may fetch 2–3 times the return on investments i.e., the shares bought at USD 200,000 may be sold for USD 600,000. Not a bad outcome on that individual company. But still not enough to cover the losses in the others and provide the required return on investment on the overall portfolio.

So, out of the 10 companies that the investor had invested in, it is now up to the remaining 2–3 companies to return USD 5mn and so unless 1 or 2 of these companies do not return 10–20 times the capital deployed, it does not make sense for the investor to invest in startups. And because you do not know which companies will do well and which will not, when they invest, investors seek companies that they feel have a reasonable chance of returning capital multiple times.

So, what kind of companies can return multiple times the capital invested?

Companies that can scale massively: Smaller companies, even if they are profitable, cannot give the 10–20x returns that investors will need.

Think about it. For a USD 200,000 investment to return USD 2–3mn, the venture will have to be in a position to raise substantial follow-on capital for the next round of investor(s) to offer an exit to the earlier round investors. And next round of large investments will be available only if the company is in a dominant position in a market which still has significant headroom for the company to grow further.

Companies that are in a commanding position in their markets: Why else would someone pay a premium for the company, if it is not in a commanding position and is in an also-ran category?

If you consider the factors above, it is no surprise that investors focus on companies that have the potential to be a dominant player in a very, very large market. Modestly sized businesses, though a healthy outcome for entrepreneurs, may not yield a good return for the investors.

So, if your VC funded venture fails, remember, someone else is covering up for these losses. And if your venture is super successful and provides VCs with healthy returns, you are also covering up for the other loss.

The Paperwork

Almost every startup founder, who raised money, is aware of the pain of completing legal formalities. Most of the first time founders are not familiar with the terms and conditions that are used in funding documents. We, as startup founders wish to focus more on startup growth than understanding internals of funding procedures.

Here, our company, Natio Cultus accelerates the deal-making once you have found an investor for your startup. Currently focused on the facilitation of seed investments, the Cultus team employs every possible tool, tactic and strategy to remove bottlenecks and hurdles in the conduct of these deals. That means working on three angles – qualifying angel investors and founders, orchestrating or syndicating funding rounds and finally, closing deals (locking in commits, managing payments, preparing paperwork).

There are many websites that offer free templates for documents required for startup funding deals. It is advisable to use them only if it is an early stage deal and one that does not have special clauses. Anyone could download the forms from the Internet and use them as-is to complete a deal.

The idea behind it was that most early stage funding rounds are capable of standardization and do not require lengthy negotiations or back-and-forth involving lawyers. And far too many such deals go sour because of the terms. Even when they do not, the bazaar mentality that clouds discussions involving funding results in some level of friction and distrust between the people involved.

When investors extract more than their pound of flesh in an early round (say through excessive liquidation preference) this has an adverse effect on the founder as the startup proceeds to raise funds in successive rounds. This is because, typically, each incoming investor uses the previous round's terms as a baseline and then asks for more.

Idea stage: For example, if you and a friend are beginning to work on an idea that could turn into a startup, you may want to sign a Founder Collaboration Agreement laying out your working relationship, affirming the expectation that the work you do together will belong to a future entity and outlining communication and conflict-resolution steps you will take to get you through any disputes that may come up. If you are putting money into your potential company, you may want to sign a Founders' Agreement (or a Common Stock Purchase Agreement you are already incorporated), describing exactly how much money each founder is putting into the potential company, what ownership stake each is receiving in turn and who owns any intellectual property created. If you have a mentor or advisor, you may want to sign a Founder Advisor Standard Template with them, setting out how they will be helping you and what compensation they will receive. I come across far too many companies that have a founder exit in the first two years. It becomes near impossible to exit a founder amicably in the absence of a Founders Agreement.

Early Stage: When raising a small amount of capital to get things started, usually from friends, family or angels, it is common to use convertible notes, starting with a Convertible Note Term Sheet and a Memorandum of Terms For Sale of Convertible Promissory Notes.

Raising money and splitting equity are serious issues and while it is difficult to spend valuable cash on lawyers, playing DIY-attorney might lead to costly mistakes you will need to solve in the future. Find a startup lawyer that will help you for a reasonable fixed fee or will agree to a cap or alternative payment structures.

Seed stage: Once you begin receiving outside funding, you will likely encounter venture capital term sheets and associated agreements. Term sheets set out the details of any investor funding you receive and they come in a variety of forms, depending on the round of funding they address and the venture capital firm they come from. Many websites provide a number of term sheets and related documents sourced from top incubators and VCs that you can familiarize yourself with and use in your funding deals. Post the term sheet if the due diligence and other negotiations go well, you will sign an elaborate share holding agreement. It is best to engage a lawyer or expert for guiding you through this document.

The Funding Process

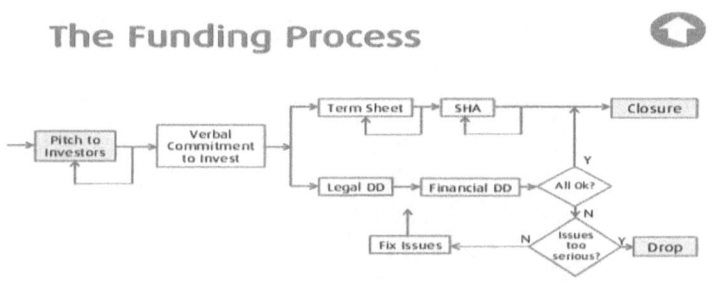

Exit Strategy

How can startups 'exit' and investors make money? It is one of the trickiest questions an entrepreneur has to answer when they seek investment. Not having a strategy may be interpreted as not being serious about giving the investors back their investment with returns. Having one may be perceived as the entrepreneur not being serious about building a business or too opportunistic and short term oriented.

If your startup is your dream, why would you want to think about an exit? It is going to be so successful and so much fun that you do not need to think about what comes after. Wrong. There are two very real and practical reasons why you need to plan an exit:

- ◆ Outside investors want to collect their return. Remember that equity investments are not like loans with interest. The investor sees no return until he cashes out or the company is sold. Even three years is a long time to wait for any pay check.

- ◆ Entrepreneurs love the art of the start. Assuming your startup takes off, you will probably find that the fun is gone by the time you reach 50 employees or a few million in revenue. The job changes from creating a "work of art" to operating a "cookie cutter."

In three to five years, you will be anxious to start a new entity, with new ideas and spinoffs that have built up in your mind and certainty that you can avoid all those potholes you hit the first time around. If your startup was less than a success, you will definitely want to erase it from memory.

While startup financing varies depending on the different stages of a company's life; equally true is the fact that investors pour money into companies with one objective in mind: to get a return on their investment.

Point to be understood by startups looking for funding, as this might affect their relationship with investors. Venture Capitalists, business angels and other types of investors do not look for an exit in the first few years of a startup, but come year 5 to 10 they will probably start getting anxious if some kind of liquidation event is not in sight.

So, you might be asking yourself, what are the exit options and strategies for startups and investors? Here are the most common exit strategies and considerations these days for planning purposes:

Startup Acquisitions

The main exit strategy for startups is to sell the company to a bigger one for a profit. The same goes for investors.

The buyer takes over the startup using cash or stock as a compensation and key executives and employees from the startup often stay at the company for a period of time in order to be able to cash out and vest their stock. Exits provide capital to startup investors, which can then return the money to their limited partners (in the case of Venture Capitalists) or to the investors themselves (in the case of business angels).

Startup acquisitions are much more frequent in the US than in developing markets like India and Southeast Asia. Although it is beginning to catch up.

A different type of acquisition that is very common in Silicon Valley is acquihires (acquisition + hiring). In this case the buyer is not so much interested in the product as it is in the team, the talent. Acquihires often lead to the closure of the products and services that have been acquired and employees end up being transferred to a company usually receive significant hiring bonuses.

Acquihires tend to happen at an earlier stage in comparison to big startup acquisitions, which means that they often provide less capital to business angels and Venture Capitalists.

Let's Float in the Stock Market: IPO as an Exit Strategy

There comes a time for mature and established technology companies where raising more capital from VCs or private equity firms is no longer an option. So, what comes next? An IPO. IPO stands for 'initial public offering' and it basically means that a company starts floating on a stock market, selling a significant number of their shares in the process to institutional and non-institutional investors. These large companies are what VCs dream of, as they often provide large sums of capital to all parts involved (founders, early employees and investors).

This used to be the preferred mode and the quick way to riches. But since the Internet bubble burst in the year 2000, the IPO rate has declined every year until 2010 and is now at about 15%. I do not recommend this approach to startups these days. Shareholders are demanding and liability concerns are high.

Recent IPO boom in the Indian markets has allowed startups like Teamlease, Quickheal etc. to go public, although most of them started 7–10 years ago, a typical cycle to go public.

An interested trend in the startup world when it comes to going public is that more and more companies are taking longer to IPO. This is a consequence of the high amount of capital available in the startup market from Venture Capitalists, private equity firms and other investment institutions.

Startups, you can do initial public offers (IPO) where you sell a part of your business to the public in the form of shares. This strategy offers more benefits in the sense that it enhances access to liquidity for you in the event that investors are seeking returns or refunds earlier than anticipated. Most importantly, it offers you a chance to buy out other companies that are also privately held and trading and have reached a financial roadblock.

Aside from providing an exit strategy by being able to reimburse investors within your own startup, it can be a secondary form of exit for other investors across other companies by taking part in a buy-out. I have been involved in quite a few of these roll-ups where a company that is ready to go public buys up other smaller players as a strategy.

Mergers & Acquisitions

Also commonly known as M&As, these transactions usually imply a merging with a similar and larger company. This normally means merging with a similar company or being bought by a larger company. This is a win-win situation when bordering companies have complementary skills and can save resources by combining. For bigger companies, it is a more efficient and quicker way to grow their revenue than creating new products organically.

Another important and often considered exit is a merger. It is necessary for your startup company to exercise the option to merge with another company should cash flow or liquidity become an issue. All investors want to know whether they can get their money back should the deal go south. By ensuring your startup stays afloat will provide a certain level of security among your investors. I always want to know whether the startups I invest in know that they can sell the company in a merger acquisition.

This type of exit is often chosen by big companies that are looking for complimentary skills in the market and buying a smaller startup is a better way to develop a product than creating it in-house.

M&As are less common than IPOs and straight acquisitions

Sell to a Friendly Individual

This is not an M&A, since it is not combining two entities into one. Yet it is a great way to "cash out" so you can pay investors, pay yourself, take some time off and get ready to have some fun all over again. The ideal buyer is someone who has more skills and interest on the operational side of the business and can scale it.

Private Offerings

Startups, you can conduct a private offering of your shares to individuals or a select group of investors to raise funds. The offerings need not be registered with the SEC or SEBI and are exempt from required reporting arrangements and allows for existing shareholders to be bought out in a new fundraiser round.

Private offerings are less expensive and need less time to conduct since the services of underwriters or brokers are less required. You can choose investors who exhibit similar goals and interests, offering these investors more complex and confidential transactions. If these investors are entrepreneurs themselves, they can help in the company's management.

Online leaders are firms automating this mode of business, such as AngelList, CrowdValley, SeedInvest, Crowdfunder, Fundable, OfferBoard and CircleUp, that use private offerings, taking advantage of the Securities and Exchange Commission's (SEC) Regulation 506D exemption. This regulation allows companies to raise an unlimited sum of money from the public, but on the condition that the investors are accredited (have a net worth of $1 million exclusive of residence or have $200,000 in salary or $300,000 for married couples) and that these investors are sophisticated (have intimate knowledge of the market to be able to navigate the proceedings sufficiently and be able to mitigate any associated risks). They can solicit the public or advertise these offerings under Regulation D, 506c.

Venture Capital/Private Equity

The key to maintaining a level of security among investors is to keep the cash rolling into the startup. Venture Capitalists/PE Firms usually invest large sums of money into businesses and startups that are deemed worthy of note. Currently, there had been a downward trend of investments by venture capitalists due to the length of time it would normally take for investments to mature. Now, however, several venture capital firms, such as Canaan Partners and China-based firm Renren, are investing in crowdfunding platforms globally, which signals a shift not only in the capital structure of several startups but also on the goals and structures of the VC firms. These VC investments provide a steady source of cash to create more investments, expand development and attract other wealthy investors who see the potential for high returns in the future.

Regulation A+/Alternate Stock Exchange

Regulation A+ is a skeleton version of an IPO. Today, this regulation allows you to put your startup company on an exchange after qualifying. You get to benefit from raising money and conforming to particular stipulations laid down by the Securities and Exchange Commission (SEC) without having to publish accounts publicly or file other mandatory paper work that would be required of an IPO.

Ben & Jerry's ice cream is the most famous firm to have used this regulation in the past. They were able to do this by soliciting the public in raising money to finance their ice cream business. Since the passage of the Jumpstart - Business Startups or JOBS Act in 2012 and the subsequent rulings by the SEC making it legal to raise money from large groups of people on the internet. Initially, the money that could be raised was capped at $20 million, but the revised Regulation A law (which is now called Regulation A+) allows higher limits (of up to $50 million). Although you do need to have an experienced lawyer, the cost is unfortunately still an issue. You still have to weigh the pros and cons of raising the funds against the actual costs involved in doing so, since the latter can be quite costly.

Startup, you can utilize Regulation A+ as a way of either introducing capital to the business or increasing it by 'testing the waters' (a phase initially employed for companies to gauge market responses to a new product or service before filing the $50,000+ cost to qualify under this law). Similar provisions exist in UK, Singapore and India for alternate scaled down listing.

Liquidation and Close

Even lifetime entrepreneurs can decide that enough is enough. One often-overlooked exit strategy is simply to shut down, close the business doors and liquidate. There may be a natural catastrophe, like 9/11 or the market you counted on could implode. Make rules up front so you do not end up going down with the ship. In many countries, liquidation is a two to three-year process and highly regulated.

Not Selling a Startup: Milking the Cow

In the same way that not every startup needs to raise money from VCs and business angels (bootstrapping is a viable alternative), not every startup needs to sell itself to a bigger company to provide a return to founders, employees and investors.

Companies that are able to establish a solid business model and scale might choose to stay independent and reinvest the profits in the company. Part of those profits can also be distributed amongst investors as a dividend, providing liquidity to outside partners while avoiding the public markets and the obligations that come with it.

If you are in a stable, secure marketplace, with a business that has a steady revenue stream, pay off investors, find someone you trust to run it for you, while you use the remaining cash to develop your next great idea. You retain ownership and enjoy the annuity. But cash cows seem to need constant feeding to stay healthy.

Cash cows are firms that are able to command a high market share in an industry dominated by low growth. They are able to sustain enough capital to stay afloat for the foreseeable future as they promise years of increased profits. These startups are least likely to exit and will be more able to keep paying dividends to their investors and shareholders.

They will not want to exit, but rather cash in on their products, thus the term 'cash cow.' Instead of an exit strategy, these startups will aim for upping sales. They will keep paying dividends to their investors and other shareholders. However, should any investor feel the need to cash out, then these companies are highly likely to facilitate the request or make an even better offer to refinance these investors; potentially even structuring a management buyout.

The Big Question: When Is the Right Time to Exit?

This is a question that is often asked at conferences and private meetings between investors and startups. When should I sell my company? When is the right time to look for buyers? As an investor, when should I start looking for a return on my investment?

Would you rather sell your company for USD 20 million when you own a lot of the stock or for USD 200 million when you do not own as much?

And the truth is that there is no universal answer for all of the above. Startups want to sell for as much money as possible (so do investors) and buyers want to spend as little as possible, so both parties need to find a balance. Common sense says that for startups to maximize their selling price they should look for an exit when their growth rates are high instead of when they are very profitable.

However, "lower-valued startups take less time to scale and less VC money to fuel, which means founders will likely own higher percentages of their companies when they sell." This implies that these founders might be better off selling for USD20 million when they own a big chunk of the startup instead of waiting for a USD200 million price tag, as by then they might only own a small percentage of the stock.

Each entrepreneur and investor should consider the circumstances of their ventures and make a decision based on that. There is no secret formula, but what is for certain is that entrepreneurs and investors, sooner or later, will look for an exit.

To some, an exit strategy sounds negative. Actually, the best reason for an exit strategy is to plan how to optimize a good situation, rather than get out of a bad one. This allows you to run your startup and focus efforts on things that make it more appealing and compelling to the short list of acquirers or buyers you target.

The type of business you choose should depend on your goals and the way you grow should be aligned with your exit strategy. Do not wait till you are in trouble to think about an exit, rather think of it as a succession plan or a successful transition.

Exit strategies take on different forms, but it is important that your startup should put one in place for your investors. While they are rooting and supporting your business, they are also looking for a return on their investment.

To sum it up, investors will want to know how they will get their money back from your business before they invest. In my real estate investments, I always want to know what my exit strategy will be. Often, I ask myself, do I refinance to buy out investors and retain the property or do I sell the property to recoup my investment? As a startup, you need to have an exit strategy to enable your investors to cash in on their investments as well as to safeguard the value of your startup.

Life After Funding Event

You have barely seen friends and family since you decided to take the plunge into entrepreneurship. Your waking moments have been devoted to building, tweaking, fundraising, networking…whatever you had to do to get your startup off the ground. You have subsisted on so much microwavable mac and cheese that you swear your skin is turning a light yellow. And you cannot remember the last time you had a great night's sleep. You have developed your product and found a market for it. You have even found some seed funding and are raring to take on the world.

No one said startup life would be easy, but it has all been worth it because you did it. You finally received funding. Toss the confetti and bring out the booze, because you have reached the finish line. You have made it.

But not really.

Sorry to burst your bubble. But getting funding is not the be all and end all of your startup journey. Now I am not saying that you should not celebrate. You have worked hard, so now you get to play hard. But after you thank your team by taking them out for drinks and thank your customers for helping you get to the next step, it is time to start hustling again.

Running a startup is kind of like playing video games. Before you received funding you were on level one. You did not have a lot of tools and you might even have died a few times (in the video game sense, of course). But you made it. Now that you are on the second level, you have more health and armour. The journey will still be tough, but at least you will have some desperately-needed resources.

But then you realize you may have walked through the looking glass. The clients are suddenly more demanding, you have to grow your team fast to keep pace and even investors have set up high parameters of delivery. What was merely a challenge when you were starting off with your business idea is now giving you nightmares and you are at a loss of how to build your idea into a business.

Regardless of the funding event (direct angel, Venture capital, merger etc.), once your funding angels have smiled on you and put a pot of cash in your account, what do you do next? Many an entrepreneur has blown away the money. A lot like waiting with elaborate plans for your first bonus and then frittering it away on impulsive spending and wondering if the bonus was a dream.

In a rapidly maturing funding world, investors are getting more demanding and there is no time to take it easy.

Most CEOs and founders already know how this new capital will be used and assuming they have a high degree of confidence that the funding will close, they can get started on putting it to work ahead of time.

Here are some other high-level action items that should be on every to-do list in those crucial first three months; for what to do right away – and just as important, what not to do:

1. Celebrate victories

    Not in an expensive way, but in a team-building way. Share the news with your employees. Explain the potential and also share the credit, ensuring everyone is aligned and pulling 100 percent toward the same goals. This is a great way to reward and recognize the hard work of your team and to excite them at a time when everyone needs to step up.

2. Show gratitude

    Not just to your new investors. Thank any customers or partners who were helpful during due diligence and make sure they are up to date on your expanded plans and potential. The people you leaned on to get to this point most likely will be valuable resources going forward.

3. Do not hire anyone for the first month

    Once money is in the bank, it puts a lot of pressure on you to grow and grow fast. After all, the story you tell investors is one of growth and how money will allow you to grow. But expanding the company does not always mean expanding the team. Growth is not just hiring more people. As a company grows, the one inevitable task every founder will have to take on is to hire more people to build up a team. That is also where most go wrong.

    The CEO should be asking questions – not answering stuff.

While building the TaxiForSure team, Raghu thought the best way was to hire bottom-level executives first.

"But after a year or? two we realized that hiring people in the mid to senior management level was essentially much more effective in growing the company."

IDG's TCM Sundaram concurs. Hiring senior employees who will be able to share a part of your responsibility works much better. The founder also has to learn to let go.

"I would prefer a CEO to not be in a position to answer a question. He should be asking questions and there should be other people able to answer those questions and in charge of departments," he said.

4. When you do hire, start hiring differently.

There can be a big difference in the kind of people you want to hire when you are a small, underfunded company and the kind you want to hire when you are well funded and squarely in the growth phase. When you first get funding, your to-do list is a mile long, making hiring and everything that comes with it an afterthought. So, you end up hiring your second cousin who (shocker!) winds up not being a good fit. Now you have got to fire a family member and will probably have to hear about it for the next 10 Diwalis. Avoid this predicament by making hiring a priority. After all, a startup is only as great as its team.

If you have not already, determine your brand's culture and values. Once you have figured that out, you can seek candidates that align with those values and culture. You will end up hiring people whom you will like working with (and vice versa) and who will stay for the long haul.

Just make sure your culture is inclusive. If your startup screams Boys' Club, then there is an entire group of people who might feel excluded and probably will not even apply.

When you are smaller, you typically want people who are generalists, because you cannot afford to hire specialists. Once you have money in the bank, you should hire specialists who can put their heads down and focus on one aspect of the business.

That is why you should wait before you start hiring. It will take time for your hiring practices to adapt.

If you hire just in the first four weeks, you might not be hiring for the next stage of your company. Use the first four weeks to start socializing, start putting the word out there and then build a new pipeline. We started getting a lot of inbound interest from talented candidates. Give yourself time.

5. Do not hire talented people and assume you will figure out their jobs later.

    It is tempting to hire good people thinking you will figure out later how to deploy them. In a way, that does make sense, because smart people will often create opportunities for you, but you have to realize that just because you now have money in the bank does not mean the scale you operate on has changed.

    For example, you cannot hire an online marketing expert and expect him or her to perform well, if you have not built the infrastructure for his or her role and his or her talents.

    That is another reason to wait at least a month; that gives you time to shift your perspective, think about your organization and figure out how you need to change to take on talented people, so they can truly benefit your company.

    Plus, when you hire talented people and assume they will create work for themselves, that can lead to another issue.

    In addition to looking for people who have the skills to excel in whatever roles you need to fill, also look for qualities that will help strengthen your company as you grow. You do not need an entire office of yes (wo)men. It also helps to have people who are just as passionate as you, so that they are as much invested in the company's success as you are.

    It takes one to know one. Originality attracts quality candidates. Forget asking for the traditional resume and cover letter. They are boring and are hardly the best ways to get to know a candidate. Instead, create an application that captures the spirit and culture of your brand and asks insightful questions. (Hint: Asking people about their greatest weakness is not insightful; it just gives them license to bullshit).

Hire the best people you can find. Many startups are tech-driven, but in truth it comes down to people who really make it happen. Always be in recruiting mode, but particularly when you have fresh capital and buzz to leverage and plans to achieve. Ask board members and investors for staff recommendations — they likely have good connections, have a vested interest in your success and can introduce you to promising candidates.

6. Help the team maintain a true sense of goal and vision.

Raising money is an overwhelming task. A massive amount of activity, prefunding, is focused on achieving that milestone.

Once you do raise capital, there can be a vacuum of direction. It was a very exciting time, everyone was working really hard, the product was doing really well, we landed a number of new customers and then there was this big feeling of validation because the investment community believed in us.

That is exciting – and that can create confusion as to what is next.

For the first four weeks, have team meetings every week, recommunicating the implications of raising money, talking about immediate next steps, discussing how we would use the funds. It is important to enjoy the influx of capital, but it is equally important to bring it back into context and keep the vision straight.

7. Do not forget your investors.

During prefunding, you spend a lot of time talking to investors. Once you close, it is tempting to want to get back to work and focus on customers and building products, etc.

Although you have been talking to them for months, the conversations were more about long-term positioning and midterm execution. You rarely talk about the next three months and the next decision. Essentially you talk numbers, you talk vision, you talk about where you want to go.

Make your investors part of your tactical decision-making process. We scheduled the first official meeting four months after closing. That was too late. In those four months, we lost at least two months of valuable time where they could have helped make decisions and make a positive impact. Call an all-hands, follow-on in one room, within the first four weeks.

8. Hire an accountant.

   Do not mess around with one-off spreadsheets or financial models you have created on your own. It is time to hire an accountant. One, now you have real money and the obligations of managing financials, cash flow, etc. Two, now you have investors who want to know financial performance in various ways.

   One may want a cash-flow analysis, another an income statement, another the tax implications of a new product. For a company that is not finance driven, those analyses may be distracting. Not doing them is not an option and doing them on your own is not efficient. Once you are funded, the value a professional accountant provides is very, very high.

9. Create open dashboards.

   Pick four or five key indicators of business performance and start sharing them with investors and employees. Look at revenue, marketing spending, etc., the key numbers that you have committed for investment, those are numbers that make or break our company.

   In great companies, the common theme for all, is that their customers love their products. That is your goal and open dashboards tell everyone in the company exactly how you are doing.

10. Learn to say no

    My personal experience is that you tend to say yes to everything. But, the most important step towards getting there is to learn the art of saying no. One, you think you are capable of doing it and secondly, you do it because you think otherwise you will lose out – be it the customer, be it the investor, be it an employee. Even if an employee asks for a hike, you think you cannot say no because that person will leave.

    If you are an enterprise startup, there are added challenges. As clients start coming in, there will be myriad requests for customization. It is important to defend your product at that stage. Otherwise, you will have different products for different customers.

11. It is not just the transaction

    The cheque has been cashed, but that is not the end of the line. To grow a business, founders need discipline and some strategic thinking. Startups are all about transaction.

    "You just give me customers... VCs have backed me, so I am all set, startups think. When you do that, a new set of issues start cropping up. They just do not know how to scale and build out to the next level."

    Learning about how to balance growth with focus is an important stepping stone towards graduating to the next league, they said. It is important to prioritize markets, target audience and even product versions.

    One of the biggest mistakes I see entrepreneurs do is to build a product and then they seek out a market. They keep seeking a problem that their solution can solve. The trick is to define yourself first and set goals that you can visit at regular intervals.

    How to scale, how to go about the next round of funding are all things on which people need to prioritize, strategize and then execute.

12. Delegate: Violinist or conductor?

    Sure, your company is your baby. But it is now time to give up on some responsibilities. "Most founders underplay the need to build a team for something that an individual is proficient at," the mentors said. For example, a product manager will think he can do the job and hence not invest in a quality product team. Someone with business knowledge is most likely to go lax on sales because he thinks he can jump in whenever the need be.

    As soon as you start growing, your responsibilities increase significantly and you do not really have enough time to spend on building the product. The longer you hold on to it, the longer it suffers. And most founders do that.

    It is time to let go of those affectations. Time is money, so spend it wisely. Time is the most valuable commodity you have in a startup, so focus your time and energy on high-ROI activities. For example, do not get caught up in sales calls with third-party vendors who are just trying to get a piece of your money (and there will be a lot of those). And do not take every meeting.

What I ask founders is that do you want to be the best violinist in the orchestra or do you want to be the conductor? Somebody can choose to be best violinist and that is fine. But then they have to find a conductor to run the orchestra.

13. Reality-check yourself

    Talking to investors can be scary while scaling up, but it is important to keep growing with the company. Also, investors prefer founders as CEOs, no matter how much pundits advise about the virtue of specialists for the job. Investors prefer founders as CEOs.

    The founder knows the soul of the company. If I look at any company where I think we will have to find another person to be CEO, I would not back it.

    To keep growing, talk to your peers and go for reality checks about what your limitations are. When you face certain challenges, you do not want to always go to the investors because you do not know whether they will help or not. The last thing you want to do is to get them scared. But what do you do? You ask your peer group.

14. Do not undersell yourself

    While overpromising can be a recipe for disaster, it is not smart to have myopic vision either. We will not invest in a team where we can see more potential than the entrepreneur sees. We say, OK, fine, if the entrepreneur's dream is [limited to] that much, I will not like to be a part of the team, says a leading in investor.

15. Be strategic

    One of the toughest asks – and the most important – is to develop your strategic vision for the company at this stage. We find that later stage companies are also in need of a lot of mentoring and help — all the way from getting customers, channels to new geographical markets..

    In other words, while day to day operations will take up the bulk of your time, it is now important for you to define a broader vision. And do not go to your investors for help on daily firefighting.

    "We put money in a team we think can execute, so we cannot handhold them through their journey. If I have to roll up my sleeves and get involved in operations, then I've backed the wrong team," IDG's Sundaram said.

16. Set processes for scale

    Now that you are scaling your business, you need to change your mindset when it comes to the organization of your startup. Certain practices that are okay when you are a small team bouncing from cafe to cafe in search of WiFi, are not as effective when you are working with a team of 50 or 100.

    The larger your team, the more structure that needs to be put in place. Often the main reason startups get poor Glassdoor reviews is because they still act like they are early-stage, even when they have 300 employees. You can have structure and accountability and still be cool. And the lack of chaos helps you keep that amazing team you just hired.

17. Be approachable

    Employees need to feel like they can bring up ideas, no matter how crazy. That is where true innovation comes from – the ability to take risks. Employees cannot take risks if they feel like they cannot talk to the CEO or if they feel like whenever they do something wrong, they are at risk of being fired.

18. Learn from others' experiences

    The 3D printing startup MakerBot secured a great amount of funding and scaled quickly. But as they grew, it was difficult to maintain the same set of values upon which the company was founded.

    For example, as Technically Brooklyn reported, Michael Curry, a MakerBot designer, says he became troubled by how much more slowly the company moved as it grew up. Then its abandonment of the open source principles MakerBot was founded on seem to shake him. Finally, after the acquisition, he seems to feel it has come to be too much, describing the toll a startup can take on a person.

    Unfortunately for MakerBot, these challenges were chronicled in a Netflix documentary for the entire world to see. Your growing pains most likely will not be captured on film, but employees talk, especially disgruntled ones. And it is nearly impossible to attract top-tier talent if you have a negative work environment.

19. Keep it lean and focus on execution

    With funding comes expectations. But with all the excitement that money brings, it can be easy to forget the specific stipulations your investors provided when they funded your startup. That can be a problem if you want to get more funding in the future. Delivering on expectations is what separates the successful startups from the unsuccessful ones.

    The time for making it rain will come later.

    After bootstrapping for what seems like an eternity, it can be tempting to spend any money that you can get your hands on. But remember how hard you worked and all you sacrificed to get this money. Use that to motivate you to be conservative with your finances.

20. Make a plan

    Creating a detailed plan for your expenses will make you look responsible in the eyes of your investors. And having a plan will help you prioritize your expenditures and avoid overspending on things you do not need. If you want to secure more financing in the future and ensure your startup is in it for the long haul, spend wisely.

21. Stay on track

    Meet or beat your near-term goals, be they in sales, development or recruiting. Do not make the new investors question their decision right out of the gate. Be clear with your backers about what the first 100 days will look like and then deliver. This is always important, but particularly right after funding.

    You want to instil confidence in your investors, instead of making them wonder why they saw potential in you in the first place. So, make goals and meet them. Give your investors a plan of what the first three to four months will look like and then go out and make it happen. It is easier said than done, but not impossible. Just remember not to over extend yourself. When it comes to setting goals, ask yourself if they are sustainable. This will prevent you from biting off more than you can chew

22. Integrate

    On-board your new investors and board members thoughtfully. Consider hosting a reception to better connect them to other board members and your management team. This gets the relationship off to a good start and will quicken productive communications between all parties.

23. Communicate

    Do not rely on board meetings alone. Get the most out of your new investors by setting up regular interactions, be they weekly or monthly breakfasts, parties, beers or other gatherings.

24. Move fast

    Be the first to announce your own news. Do not let it leak out via SEC filings, which reporters and bloggers regularly mine for stories. Make sure you get the most out of your announcement and consult with public relations specialists if you do not have any on your team.

25. Reconnect

    You have likely been distracted by the intense fund-raising effort. Make sure you take the time to sync back up with all your key team members and business partners.

26. Leverage

    Consider adding to your 'war chest' with some venture debt. Debt does not make sense in all scenarios, but the easiest time to get a lender to provide capital is when you have just closed a round of equity.

27. Be cheap (on everything but product)

    I am not an HR guy and I have not done extensive studies on intrinsic versus extrinsic motivation, but if your employees need fancy desks, chairs and an office, you are doing it wrong. The work itself should be motivating and interesting enough to keep employees engaged – if it is not, the company is likely not sustainable to begin with.

    Spend a lot on product – the one area where you cannot be cheap. If you are rebuilding your product from the ground up, that is where most of the investment capital will go. If you are rebuilding for scale and have a couple of great folks working on it at the moment, you have to spend money on product – there are no two ways around it. The average engineer at Twitter makes $114K/year and even more at Facebook. To get the best product talent, you need to spend.

28. Do not blindly throw money at advertising

   Unless a marketing initiative is measurable, you should not be spending money on it, period. For example, before you run a pay-per-click ad campaign, have Google Website Optimizer code ready to go, thorough keyword research complete and a clear sales funnel to acquire customers. Rinse and repeat for any type of marketing campaign, including email campaigns (which is all we run at the moment). Remember that every customer acquisition initiative has some sort of cost – paid advertising or not. Bottom line: Unless you can clearly measure customer acquisition cost, you are not ready to run paid marketing campaigns.

Closing Thoughts

"There is a greater likelihood of finding money and fame by chasing your passion, than there is of finding a passion chasing money and fame"

A modern-day curse is the easy access to information. As phones become smarter people seem to get dumber. This goes for entrepreneurs as well. They just do not read enough relevant material. You are different and I applaud you for reading this book and acknowledging that you need to buttress your knowledge and skills.

It is near impossible to be passionate and objective at the same time. Ask any parent and they have the same problem in viewing their children. Having gone through the exercise of preparing yourself, preparing the company, getting investor ready and informed on the various aspects of the investor engagement process, I leave you with a few closing thoughts to carry with you:

- In preparing yourself, research and arm yourself with all relevant information. Be it about the economy, the industry or the competition. Keep updated on who is investing, where are they investing, which cities have the buzz, when new funds are formed and what are the M&A activities taking place.

- When assessing your company, it makes sense to get an outsider's view. Analytical reports such as the "Funding Readiness Report" are a quick and efficient way to identify gaps and areas of strength

- Remember that the right advice and the right timing in the market for your products are more valuable than money

- Treat investors like you would treat a prospective life partner. Just as the latter is not just about sex, the investors are not just money bags

- Long after your business is done and dusted you will remember the journey, so enjoy it while it lasts

- Humility to learn, self-belief and a high emotional intelligence are underrated by most people, but are essential to be a leader

- Crafting a personal brand closest to your personality and protecting it savagely in the modern social media obsessed world is a pre-requisite
- The VC world is a new industry and things are fluid at their end too. There is no formula but the basic principles and knowledge should help you navigate successfully
- No one can get you funded. Only you can
- Set long term goals and not ones defined by fame and/or money. They are like an elusive shadow
- Ability to take various stakeholders along is a key skill. You cannot be a leader without followers
- Last but not the least, if you do not feel blessed and lucky; do not do it

You are a champion for just having chosen a path less travelled, fuelled by a desire to shape your own destiny. Victory and success come in various shapes and forms and you can find fulfilment in various ways. Entrepreneurship is only one of them. All the best!

www.ingramcontent.com/pod-product-compliance
Lightning Source LLC
Chambersburg PA
CBHW031609210526
45464CB00004B/1494